Áedán of the Gaels

Áedán of the Gaels

King of the Scots

Keith Coleman

Pen & Sword
MILITARY

First published in Great Britain in 2022 by
Pen & Sword Military
An imprint of
Pen & Sword Books Ltd
Yorkshire – Philadelphia

Copyright © Keith Coleman 2022

ISBN 978 1 52679 490 1

A CIP catalogue record for this book is
available from the British Library.

Printed and bound in the UK by CPI Group (UK) Ltd,
Croydon, CR0 4YY.

Pen & Sword Books Limited incorporates the imprints of Atlas,
Archaeology, Aviation, Discovery, Family History, Fiction, History,
Maritime, Military, Military Classics, Politics, Select, Transport,
True Crime, Air World, Frontline Publishing, Leo Cooper, Remember
When, Seaforth Publishing, The Praetorian Press, Wharncliffe
Local History, Wharncliffe Transport, Wharncliffe True Crime
and White Owl.

For a complete list of Pen & Sword titles please contact

PEN & SWORD BOOKS LIMITED
47 Church Street, Barnsley, South Yorkshire, S70 2AS, England
E-mail: enquiries@pen-and-sword.co.uk
Website: www.pen-and-sword.co.uk

Or

PEN AND SWORD BOOKS
1950 Lawrence Rd, Havertown, PA 19083, USA
E-mail: Uspen-and-sword@casematepublishers.com
Website: www.penandswordbooks.com

Dedicated to my children, Morgan and Katy.

Contents

Maps

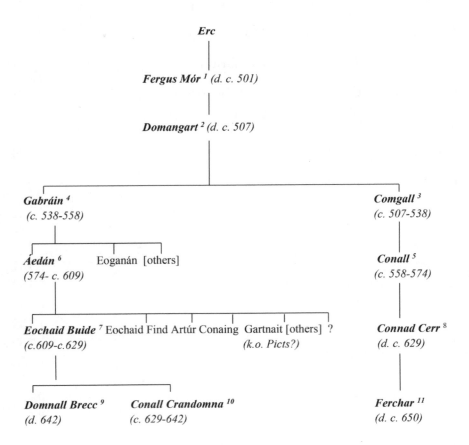

Early Rulers of Dál Riata.

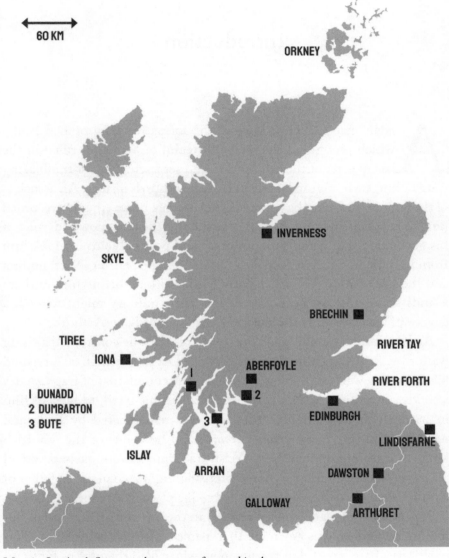

60 KM

ORKNEY

INVERNESS

SKYE

BRECHIN

RIVER TAY

TIREE

IONA

ABERFOYLE

RIVER FORTH

I DUNADD
2 DUMBARTON
3 BUTE

1

2

EDINBURGH

3

LINDISFARNE

ISLAY

ARRAN

DAWSTON

GALLOWAY

ARTHURET

Map 1. Scotland. Some modern names featured in the text.

Introduction

Áedán mac Gabráin, king of the formative state of Dál Riata, which prefigured the medieval realm of Scotland, ruled in the last quarter of the 6th century and set a template for trailblazing warrior kings who figure largely in British and Irish history. An associate of the famous St. Columba (Colum Cille) of Iona, he was the first recorded king to be ordained in the British Isles and was the most powerful ruler of his generation. His astonishing military and political journeys took him from his base in Kintyre/Argyll to Orkney, Angus, Ulster, Northumbria and the Isle of Man. No other Early Medieval king before him in these islands seems to have been able to flex their military might to such a degree (if we leave aside the shadowy character of King Arthur).

Áedán's military ambitions came to a halt when he confronted a rising warlord as strident as himself at the battle of Degsastan in AD 603. Beyond his success in warfare, there is a tantalising accumulation of fragmentary legends concerning Áedán, from stories about his birth, to tales of him in battle with other Irish heroes. He was remembered by Bede and mentioned in the *Anglo-Saxon Chronicle* and he is one of the few Irish kings to feature prominently in Welsh tradition, as a uniquely powerful player in North Britain. Modern writers highlight Áedán as the father of a prince named Arthur, which has led to his place in Arthurian studies.

Any number of warlords rose and fell in the 5th and 6th centuries, but few are remembered as any more than names. The clerical writer Gildas mentions a bare handful of tyrants, men who called themselves kings, in south-west England and Wales. If he had been able to extend his abrasive gaze across the whole of Britain he might have been able to name dozens more such men, jostling to acquire wealth, territory and fame. Few of them achieved it. Several leaders contributed to a legacy and established dynasties which grew to control wider territorial units and kingdoms and had fame imposed upon them retrospectively as founding figures in Ireland, Scotland, England and Wales.

Áedán mac Gabráin was one of these leaders. As king of Dál Riata, he ruled parts of Ireland and what is now Scotland, and was recognised as a founding figure by the rulers of the successor states of Alba and Scotland. Áedán was the sixth known king of the Irish colony which had established itself in Argyll. While there were other Irish colonies up and down the western seaboard of Britain in the 4th and 5th centuries, notably in Cornwall and North and South Wales, Dál Riada uniquely thrived. In Áedán's day the Irish were only one of three or four peoples established in the area which became Scotland. To the east and the north were the Picts, while the Britons occupied almost all of the Lowlands. If there were any English speakers at all, they were confined at this stage to the far south-east of the area. It probably seemed unlikely during Áedán's reign that his people, the Irish (later known as Scots), would grow to be the dominant nation in this patchwork of peoples. The struggle for dominance, made through warfare and strategic political alliances, followed a pattern largely laid down by Áedán mac Gabráin.

There are few definite facts about Áedán. The terse, non hagiographic records focus on his wide ranging aggression, painting an uncompromising figure for many historians. According to one modern historian he was 'a tough opportunist, enemy of all his neighbours and master of most of them'.[1] Another authority admits that his reign 'bristles with problems'.[2] It was Áedán's unique good fortune that his kingdom played host to the cleric Colum Cille (St Columba), whose influence enormously augmented the reputation of the Irish church throughout the British Isles. The saint exerted considerable authority among contemporary rulers of all races, both in Ireland and in Britain, and there is evidence that he used this to assist Dál Riada. Áedán features in the *Life* of this churchman and saint and we can glean some idea about his power and military prowess in this work composed by Adomnán, a later abbot of Iona. But the picture of Áedán given by Adomnán hardly fleshes out the character of the king to the extent we might have wished for. The modern editor of Adomnán's *Life of Columba* admits that Áedán emerges as the first king of Scottish Dál Riata who appears as more than a shadowy figure, though 'we know little more than a poor outline of his career as a political fighter'.[3]

There is no surviving opinion of Áedán from his own lifetime. The Venerable Bede singles out Áedán by name as 'king of the Irish in Britain', in the context of his apparent defeat by king Æthelfrith of Bernicia (part of Northumbria) around the year 603. Irish sources are, as we would expect, more effusive in their descriptions of him. A poem about Áedán's legendary birth associates him with riches and calls him noble and fierce, someone who has seized Alba and 'excelled [in] every vigorous host... [he] who spoiled every plain'.[4] The *Duan Albanach*, the 'Scottish Poem' of the 12th century, was possibly read at the inauguration of Scottish kings. It lists the early rulers of the realm, stretching back to Dál Riata, and of course includes Áedán among the fabled ancestors of the ruling dynasty of Scots. The verses address the 'learned ones of Alba... [the] stately yellow-headed company' and remembers when 'Aodhán of the many dissensions was king'.[5] How accurate this source may be is arguable. The reign lengths given in the poem are generally wide of the mark, although here Áedán is given a reign of twenty-four years, not too far off his actual period of rule, which was probably between the years 574 and around 609. Áedán was preceded as king by his cousin Conall, about whom very little is known. The *Duan Albanach* pointedly states that Conall ruled 'without dissension'. Being a successful warlord in the late 6th century could hardly be achieved without dissent.

Another source drawing perhaps on bardic sources about Irish and Scottish kings is the *Prophecy of Berchán*. It contains a description of a fierce ruler who may be Áedán (and a later hand who glossed the text thought so), though the identification is disputed. According to this source, he was the 'distressed traveller' and 'a red flame who will awaken war'.[6] Not only did Áedán participate in seismic events, he lived through an era where the landscape and the culture of Britain dramatically altered. For much of his lifetime there may have been few signs that the English would become a threat to his people. But, by the time of his death, there was clearly growing ascendancy of Northumbrian power in the north.

The King's Career

Any consideration of the place of Áedán as a 6th century king has to start with an examination of the land which he ruled and the society from which he came. The Ireland of Áedán's time was an island of multiple petty kingdoms. The king of the smallest of these, termed a *tuath*, was subservient to a regional king (*rí ruiri*), with an even more powerful overking (*rí ruirech*) or king of a province (*rí coícid*), sitting at the top of the pyramid of power. In the north of Ireland the king of the province of Ulster, or Ulaid, wielded such authority. Leadership of this province was contested by several neighbouring dynasties.

A king's main responsibility was intrinsically linked with the wellbeing of the land and its people, though he did not make the laws of the land and was not responsible for enforcing them. To rule he had to be free from deformities and he was also hedged around by multiple taboos and codes of behaviour. Individual rulers had limited authority to enact laws and control people within their own territories. At the time when Áedán was born (probably in the early 530s) the Irish royalty to which he belonged was characterised more as highly successful farmers than ambitious, professional war leaders. Power was measured by the acquisition of wealth, the holding of hostages from vassals, gathering cattle, slaves and other booty from cross border raids. The partly imagined glory days of military potentates pictured in the Ulster Cycle of Irish literature was in a dim, prehistoric past. Yet Áedán broke expectations and the pattern by the scale of his aggressive ambition and his geographic reach. Such power as Áedán had, which was probably considerable, came from a ferocious ability to strike out at neighbouring and more distant territories. It would hardly be likely that Áedán acted as a meek ruler within the actual boundaries of Dál Riata, though no information about his domestic rule is ever likely to emerge.

His highly successful career seemed to herald a new kind of ruler, of a sort captured by the 8th century Irish text *Audacht Morainn*, 'The Testament of Morann'. Of the four different types of kings detailed here, Áedán seems to fit the most vigorous and violent profile of *tarbfhlaith*, 'The Bull Sovereign':

> *The bull sovereign – that one strikes, is struck; defends, is defended against; digs up, is dug up; attacks, is attacked; pursues, is pursued. It is because of him that there is perpetual clamour with horns.*[7]

Unfortunately there are no strictly contemporary accounts of Áedán; his importance can be gleaned from the Irish annals which relate his military undertakings. Many of these notices derive from copies of an annal composed on the island monastery of Iona, which was founded by Colum Cille around 563. While there are barely any notices of his Irish predecessors in Dál Riata, the annals record five military encounters in his reign, between the years 580 and 600: an expedition to Orkney, a battle in Manau (either the Isle of Man or in mid Scotland), a fight at Leithreid (unidentified), an unknown battle where several of his sons died (probably in England), and a 'Saxon' battle (likely the Battle of Degsastan). Áedán would have been in his fifties and sixties at the time of these battles, well into old age by contemporary standards.

If the Irish annal entries show a keen interest in the affairs of this fledgling Irish dynasty in Britain, then there is more surprising interest shown by the Welsh *Annales Cambriae*. This source notes the death of Áedán's father, Gabráin, in 558, the same battle of Manau or Euboniam entered under 584, plus an entry recording Áedán's death (placed in the year 607).[8] This Welsh interest is not surprising. Áedán had close contacts with his neighbours, the British kings who inhabited the areas between Hadrian's and the Antonine Walls. There is much evidence, albeit late and fragmentary, which suggests that he had British ancestry and also that at least one of his wives had British origins.

While Áedán was remembered as a powerful ancestral figure by the ruling dynasty of Scotland in the Middle Ages, it is an irony that little information about him has been preserved in Scotland. His descendant Cináed mac Ailpin (Kenneth mac Alpin), who united the Picts and Scots in the mid 9th century, may well have consciously looked back at Áedán as an exemplar of powerful leadership who imposed his will on the neighbouring Picts. The legacy of Áedán was different in Ireland, where he appears in a number of secular works as well as fleeting appearances in the *Lives* of saints. Some of these tales too have vanished over the centuries and we have only the barest outline of the story, or sometimes just the title. In others, such as the 'Tale of Cano', Áedán emerges as a full-blooded and untrustworthy dynast, whose fearful image gives us some clue about how he was perceived by enemies in his own lifetime.

Although we have more details of the career of Áedán mac Gabráin than many of his contemporaries, the record is still extremely scant. Any consideration of his likely character, motivation and achievements must contain a good measure of supposition and guesswork. Whole areas of his life are blank. He lived for four decades before he became a king and there is no hard information about his life during that period. There are clues and traditions that he lived in the land of the Picts, somewhere in central or east Scotland, but the details we have concerning this fall far short of historical evidence.

From the material we possess, the thing about Áedán which impresses most is the powerful reach which he was able to command. This ability to exert authority, albeit fleetingly, over distant areas set a pattern which would be emulated and achieved by kings in the 7th century and later. Most of the powerful kings who unknowingly followed in his footsteps were English. Few were the Scottish and Irish rulers who would be known and feared over such a wide area of either island.

This book contends that the main divisions of Áedán mac Gabráin's life can be sorted into the following periods:

c. 530–574: Birth, upbringing in Dál Riata. Possible establishment of power base in central Scotland/Pictland.

574–581: Consolidation of power in Scotland. Enters into treaty arrangement with powerful Ulster king Báetán mac Cáirell. Attack on Orkney and possible alliance with Pictish king Bridei.

581–590: Attacks Ulster settlement in the Isle of Man. Possible activity in Galloway/north of England. Makes new alliances in the north of Ireland with Cruithin rulers and the Uí Néill dynasty.

590–603: Sponsors his sons' campaigns against the southern Picts and the English of Bernicia.

603–*c.* 609: Possible removal from power and retirement in religious seclusion.

Even the broad outline here is contentious and there are many points in the following pages which can be disputed. Not only are the facts about Áedán few and difficult, the whole history of Scotland at this time is notoriously contentious. Until recently the Picts were seen as an insoluble 'problem' and little was agreed about their ethnic origins, language or power structures. There has been a recent seismic shift in thinking about the Picts which believes their main power base lay in the north, beyond the Grampian Mountains. Whether this new historical thinking will lead to a detrimental underestimation of the southern Picts is an interesting question. It was these people in the south that Áedán had most contact with. Further south, the Britons who spread over the Lowlands have a fragmented history and have also suffered from the neglect of historians well into the 20th century.

The Post Roman Landscape

Following the collapse of Roman rule in the mid 5th century the urban life of what is now lowland England entered into immediate decay. The citizens, Romanized Britons, were unable to effectively organise themselves into political units which could withstand the invasion of Picts, Irish and English from outside the province. The English takeover of southern lands continued piecemeal into the late 6th century, with some degree of natives adopting English speech and culture as well as being driven off the land. On the western side of Britain the 5th century also saw extensive Irish raiding and eventually settlement. The raids, for slaves and other goods, started earlier, and the Irish were partnered (or paralleled) by sea-borne Pictish raiders from the far north, whose opportunist raids made the most of southern weakness. While there is no evidence whatever that the Pictish peoples of Scotland ever tried to colonise any area of the former Roman province, the Irish certainly did so.

The reasons for Irish colonisation, from Cornwall to Argyll, are complex, and do not equate with a concerted exodus conducted at one time. The reaction of the native regions receiving this influx also differed, partly according to the size and intentions of the newcomers. In Cornwall, there may have been available living space provided by a partial movement of the native population to Brittany. There does not seem to be uniform military friction between incoming and native populations. In South Wales, Irish dynasties in Dyfed and Brecon were established and eventually adopted native British ways. The scenario was different in North Wales, at least according to legend. Here the Irish were forcibly ousted from rule by concerted British military effort, albeit the victors were reputedly a warband dynasty imported from North Britain. Dál Riata, in western Scotland, was destined to be different, not least because it left a permanent Irish footprint and transformed the entire northern part of Britain into the nation of Scotland.

Outcasts or Adventurers?

When we think of Áedán's Dál Riata, it means several things. Originally it was a territory in north-east Ireland, a place which was swallowed up by its larger neighbours several centuries after Áedán's time. From this place sprung an unpromising settler community on the unfertile lands of the west, a foothold in Britain for the Irish and no more than that; certainly not an aggressive, expansionist colony which wanted to take over the whole of North Britain. The fact that this settlement did in fact provide the kernel from which the medieval kingdom of Alba, or Scotland, grew was a remarkable achievement, but not one which seemed likely in the first phase of its existence. From the 4th century Gaelic speakers were simply described as *Scotti*, probably meaning 'raiders' or 'pirates', a term which was used to label the north of Britain later in the Middle Ages. If there was almost certainly pressure within Ireland which forced some people to migrate to Britain, there was maybe also some native strain of adventure which prompted a move overseas and influenced Áedán to look far beyond his own borders.

The original homeland of Dál Riata is a perilously narrow strip on the north-west coast of Ireland, measuring approximately 48 by 24 km (30 by 15 miles), running eastward from the River Bush.[9] To the west and south were areas inhabited by the Cruithin territories, an Irish people whose ancestors are reputed to have come into Ireland from North Britain, perhaps in prehistory. Dál Riata occupied the Antrim coast, approximately to the area of modern Larne. Here the territory bordered with another Cruithin province, but it was also very near to the lands ruled by the dynasty of Dál Fiatach, the original rulers of the whole province of Ulaid (Ulster). The chief places in this homeland included Armoy and the fortress of Dunseverick on the coast near the Giant's Causeway. Until recently it was thought that the vanished kingdom was remembered in a district called *The Route* in later centuries, though this identification has been disputed. It has long been wondered how this small, fragile coastal strip could have had a population big enough to sustain a large-scale folk movement into what is now western Scotland. As we will see, there is room to think that there may have been a continuance of the culture which existed in this corner of Britain before the Irish arrived. There is a mystery also in the fact that this small territory was not swamped at an early date by any of its neighbours, all of which were more powerful than Dál Riata.

A bare dozen miles separate the old and new parts of the kingdom of Dál Riata, Ireland and Scotland, across the North Channel at its narrowest point. When we discuss the nature of the formation of the kingdom in Britain the slightness of this gap has to be maintained in mind. The two areas were visible to each other and it is extremely likely that there had been cultural exchange between them reaching far back into the prehistoric period. The new part of the kingdom of Dál Riata was similar in extent to the later Scottish county of Argyll. This name, deriving from Earra-ghaidheal, means 'coastland of the Gael' and is first recorded much later in the medieval period.[10] Áedán's great-grandfather Fergus Mór is claimed as the first Irish king who shifted his seat of power from his native land in north-east Ireland to the western shore of Britain. The 10th century *Annals of Tigernach* contain the following notice which may be a foundation legend, albeit containing a kernel of truth: 'Fergus Mór, Erc's son, with the nation of Dál Riata, held part of Britain; and there he died.'[11]

He is thought to have transferred the kingship in the late 5th century, but there may well have been Irish speakers in this area for generations before. A later tract confirms the foundation myth and states that six of the twelve sons of Fergus shipped out with him and established themselves in the new land. It also states that 150 men went as an expedition with the sons of Erc into the new territory.[12] There was also a separate tale told in medieval Ireland about the migration, but we only have the title of this lost story: *Tochomlod Dáil Riati i nAlbain*, the 'Setting forth of Dál Riata to Britain'.[13] Despite these partial traditions it is hard to credit that a massive folk movement removed a section of the Irish land's population to Scotland in one dramatic episode.

Argyll is a land of archipelagos and islands, easily accessible to the Irish Sea and to Ireland itself. At its heart is the promontory of Kintyre, over 30 miles long, and to the north of this is the district of Knapdale, containing the probable capital of Dál Riata, the hillfort of Dunadd. Argyll is separated from the rest of mainland Scotland by a ridge of mountains, Druim Alban, the 'Spine of Britain'. The aristocratic Irish or Gaelic speakers who ruled this land of water and mountain inhabited drystone enclosures known as *duns*, or sometimes artificial dwellings on lakes, called crannogs. While crannogs were adopted in Ireland in the early historic period, there is evidence that, in Argyll, these man-made islands were first constructed in the Iron Age and continued to be made through the Early Historic Period. This range of dwellings appear different from the most common dwellings of Ireland during the same period. There is also an absence of those remarkable drystone towers named brochs built in the early centuries AD which pepper the landscape of the further north and north-west of Scotland.

Most historians have argued that the Gaelic language and culture was imported wholesale into Scotland from Ireland. But an alternative theory has been proposed whereby the inhabitants of this sea-washed kingdom may have shared a common speech and culture with Ireland.[14] There appears to be little archaeological trace of a population shift from Antrim to Argyll and it has been recognised for centuries that the slim confines of Dál Riata in Ireland could not have provided a large migration without itself being rapidly depopulated. A modified view is that only a Gaelic speaking elite moved across the sea and imposed its rule and culture on the native people of Argyll. A further, intriguing possiblility has been highlighted by historian Alex Woolf, who points out that the territory of Dál Riata in Ireland is surrounded by Cruithin people, the so-called 'Irish Picts', whose roots lie in pre-historic Britain. Were the Dál Riata originally a Cruithin people also, whose roots were later conveniently forgotten?[15] Later dynastic groupings and kindreds often reshaped their own origins to suit their political ambitions.

Whatever theory is followed, it's generally believed that the earlier inhabitants of this region were either British or Pictish. The tribe who lived here were known as the Epidii. They were one of thirty-three tribes detailed in Britain, around the year 140, by Claudius Ptolemy of Alexandria in his *Geographia*. Their territory included a promontory named Epidion (possibly the Mull of Kintyre) and Epidium insula, the island of Mull.[16] It is also possible that this tribal name lies behind the later designation of the Hebrides, Ebudae. This people seem to have spoken a form of P-Celtic, like other peoples in Britain, rather than Q-Celtic or Gaelic. But whether they were proto-Pictish or British is unknown (and there may not have been a distinction in their period). The word Epidii contains the root for 'horse', which makes little sense when you consider how unsuitable this sea-girt and mountainous coastal territory is for horsemanship. Other tribes, both in North Britain and Ireland, were named after animals such as the Grecraige in Ireland, also a 'horse people'.[17] Such names may have a ritual significance that goes beyond a simple descriptive term for tribal lifestyle.[18] It would not be stretching the imagination too much to link the tribal name with the British horse goddess Epona.[19] In this context, it may be significant that Loarn, the eponym behind one of the three *cenéla* of Dál Riata derives from Lovernis, meaning 'fox'.[20]

There is a possibility that the original tribal identity of the area was incorporated into the successor state of Dál Riata. This has been neatly summarised by historian James Fraser as 'equestrian continuity in the ethnic terminology of southern Argyll'. He points out that the later Gaelic terms *réti*, and even later *ríata*, denote a riding horse and also notes the recurrence of the personal name Eochaid, which contains the root for horse, in the kingdom's early magnates.[21] Some later pedigrees of the kings of Dál Riata contain an ancestral figure called Eochaid Riada (otherwise called Cairpre Riata, or Cairpre Rígfota), which also indicates this continuity. The Venerable Bede, writing in the 8th century, states that the Irish 'migrated from Ireland under their chieftain, Reuda'.[22] The latter is sometimes equated with Cairpre Riata, who supposedly lived around ten generations before Fergus Mór.[23] Whether or not it is true that Cairpre Riata led a contingent of Irish many years before Fergus Mór, stories circulating in Ireland in the Middle Ages supported the legend.[24] Several generations after Áedán, the term for the whole territory was known as Corcu Réti, 'descendants of Réti'.[25] The heartland of this realm in Argyll, Kintyre, was later home of a prominent local kindred named MacEachern, an Anglicization of Mac Each-thigearna, 'Son of Horse Lord'.[26] An Irish tale named *Aided Chonrói* notably features a character named Eochu Echbel, 'Horse Lip', who lived in Kintyre.

Another central ancestral figure for the people who came to rule Dál Riata was Conaire Mór, a legendary Irish 'peace king'. The royal line of Scotland proudly claimed to be descended from the 'seed of Conaire' into the 12th century.[27] References to the early kings of Dál Riata contain references to a shadowy character named Nes. The *Annals of Ulster* record the king who ruled around the year 507 as Domangart mac Nisse. He was son of the king supposed to have established the kingship in Britain, Fergus Mór. Elsewhere, Fergus himself is named as son of his father Erc and in the same source as son of his mother Nes, prompting the scholar John Bannerman to wonder whether Nes was an ancestral goddess of his people.[28]

This Irish kingdom in Britain was split into three major *cenéla* or tribes. The Cenél nGabráin, named after Áedán's father, had its heartland in Kintyre and Cowall. Their prominence in the records was due in part to ecclesiastic support and the claim of later medieval kings of Alba, the successor state of Dál Riata, to be descended from them. The Cenél nÓengusa was primarily based in Islay and the Cenél Loairn occupied the northern part of the territory, centred on the district still called Lorne (around Oban). They started to make serious claim to the kingship from the mid-7th century onward. Some genealogies claim that the founders of these two dynasties, Loarn and Angus were brothers of Fergus mac Erc, but are likely false. A fourth tribe, named after Gabráin's brother Comgall, who gave their name to Cowall, were closely associated with Cenél nGabráin. By the close of the 7th century there were at least seven prominent kindreds spread through the territory. These may each have represented a *tuath*, a petty kingdom common in Ireland, whose rulers acknowledged an over king.[29]

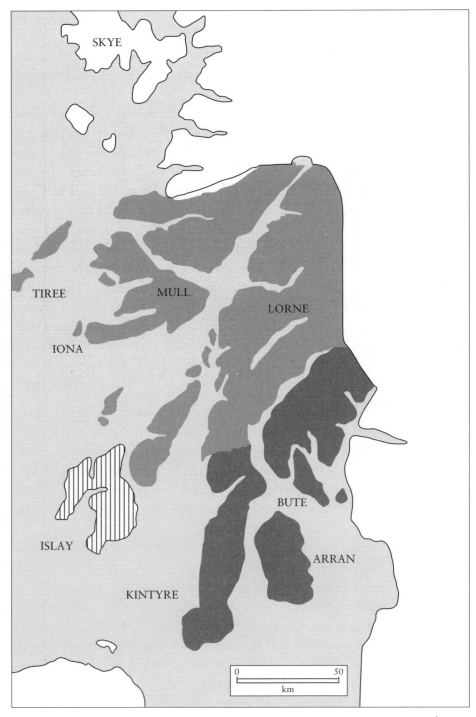

Map 2. Scottish Dál Riata. Conjectural areas controlled by three major kindreds in Áedán's time. Cenél nGabráin area in black. Cenél nLoairn area dark grey. Cenél nÓengussa area striped. (After Bannerman (1974) and Anderson (1973).)

The Machinery of War

Any consideration of Áedán's success has to take account of the resources at his disposal. Every king in the British Isles and Ireland in the Early Medieval period employed a personal retinue. One name for this military band of companions is the Latin term *comitatus*, a group of usually aristocratic members personally attached to a leader. If the organisation of Dál Riata in Britain mirrored small Irish kingdoms in most ways, it was unique in its rulers' partnership with the religious powerhouse of Iona and also in the military strength it was able to muster. Áedán had the ability to send forces successively and possibly simultaneously against enemies in disparate locations.

On occasion Áedán was able to muster armies which were very large. Campaigns against the Picts in the Lowlands of Scotland which were under his overall direction may have been personally mustered by several of his sons who would have led their own military divisions onto the battlefield. Likewise, there is good but fragmentary evidence that Áedán's army which fought against the northern English at the very end of the 6th and beginning of the 7th centuries included high ranking Irish allies who would have each brought their own warbands into combat. I will discuss in another chapter the possibility that Áedán employed semi-outlaw warriors, the *fianna*, who might have included more lowly fighters. The members of the retinue would be bound to their lord by a personal oath of loyalty, pledging to fight to the death on his behalf if necessary. In Welsh, the retinue was *teulu* and a larger warband unit the *gosgordd*.

The word *slógad* was used for large hostings of military forces an Irish king could impose upon his population. But this seems to have been restricted to guarding territory against invasion, repelling an invading army, and thirdly an expedition into another territory to act against a rebellious *túath*, or subordinate bordering region. For this purpose the document known as *Míniugud Senchesa fher nAlba*, which may contain 7th century information, states that the ruling dynasty, Cenél nGabráin, could muster 300 men, Cenél nÓengusa 500 men, and Cenél Loairn 600 men. One editor of the tract points out the error that underestimates the fighting strength of the ruling dynasty. He points out that Irish sources state that a *túath* provided 700 fighting men.[30] Dál Riata would therefore be able to command a force of over 2,000 men from its core territory in Britain.

The exact composition of Áedán's armies is hard to determine. Cenél nÓengusa is known to have been able to demand military support from the external Airgíalla people who originated in Northern Ireland, though whether some of them possibly relocated to the Cenél nÓengusa heartland in Islay is unknown. Irish Dál Riata sustained itself against external pressure for a considerable period. Even after the leadership between the Irish and British halves of the kingdom were apparently sundered in the mid-7th century, the Irish homeland was still able to participate in aggressive military action at the end of that century. Small as it was, the original Irish Dál Riata must have maintained a substantial fighting force and some men from that territory may have fed into the forces which Áedán deployed at various times in his career.

As stated above, a king might also demand military resources from peoples who were subject to him. There may have been populations in Pictland which fell into this category and whose numbers bolstered the ranks on occasion. Adult male hostages resident in Dál Riata as surety for treaty compliance from their home territories might also be expected to bear arms for their host. Individual warriors may also have been drawn to Áedán's court by his fame in order to share whatever booty was gained from his wars and for the opportunity to augment their own reputations. These may well have included well-born Pictish warriors, especially if Áedán maintained his reputed early links with Pictland later in his life. There were exiled Northumbrian princes at the court of Áedán's son and successor Eochaid Buide in the early 7th century and there are reasons to believe that Áedán himself had disaffected dissidents from that region in his court towards the end of his reign.

One of the mentions of Áedán in Welsh literature is a summary of a tale which specifically mentions his warband and says that they 'went to sea for their lord'. Later in the book I speculate that this refers to a raid on the Isle of Man, though this is by no means certain. The fact that they 'went to sea' would be no extraordinary thing for the men obliged to provide military service in Dál Riata, so should hardly merit mention. Does it perhaps imply a longer voyage than was usual rather than the normal regional seafaring around Ulster, the Hebrides and Kintyre? Possibly it hints at an uncomfortably lengthy journey that did not sit well with land-based fighters. Apart from the Isle of Man campaign, Áedán conducted an expedition to Orkney around the year 580 and a battle in Circenn (Angus, eastern Scotland) in the following decade. The former obviously required mobilisation of fighting men by sea and the latter may have required it too.

Míniugud Senchesa fher nAlban gives information about the three *cenéla* of Dál Riata and is probably a later reworking of information gathered in the decades after Áedán's reign. As well as surveying the households and fighting men in the kingdom, it gives us an idea about the naval capacity and importance of communication by sea. The document groups the households in the kingdom in twenties in order to assess sea-going strength. Two seven-benchers were required from every twenty households.[31] An oar would have been manned by two men, so a standard warship would have had at least twenty-eight men on board. Later medieval records in Ireland speak of at least ten classes of ships, but most earlier vessels would have been fairly small, with minimal sails, and were primarily propelled by oars. Many of these vessels would have been standard curachs, timber framed and covered by animal hides, though larger ships would have been constructed entirely of wood and deployed for long-range expeditions. Naval activity appears sporadically in the Irish annals. The native fleet of Dál Riata had an apparent defeat in year 637, suffering at the hands of the Uí Néill, near Kintyre and there was an encounter in 719 between the Cenél nGabráin and Cenél Loairn. In 733 or 734, the Cenél Conaill king Flaithbertach brought the fleet of Dál Riata from Britain to Ireland to engage his enemies.[32] The evidence shows that the fleet at the disposal of Áedán mac Gabráin must have been formidable indeed and quite possibly the largest available to any contemporary ruler in Britain or Ireland.

The Territories in Northern Ireland

Despite the kingdom taking root in what became Scotland, Áedán's kingdom was thoroughly Irish in its culture and political concerns. It has been claimed by one historian that the rulers of Dál Riata were 'closer to being overlords of northern Britain, north of the Forth and Clyde estuaries, than they were to dominating the province of Ulster'.[33] This is true, but following the death of one overlord of that province, Áedán arguably came to a position where he exerted authority over that region in place of rulers from the two peoples who traditionally supplied rulers over Ulster.

In the late 6th century there were several major power blocks in the most northernly province of Ireland which was called Ulster or Ulaid. The traditional rulers of this area were a people who also also called themselves the Ulaid and their dynasty was the Dál Fiatach.[34] The Ulaid inherited a tradition which engendered the Ulster Cycle of legend and literature, featuring the exploits of heroes such as Cú Chulainn, and they proudly termed themselves 'The Children of Ollam are the nobles of Emain…the true Trojan band of Ireland.'[35] However, it was clear that the legendary glory days of their lineage were fading by the late 6th century, though they re-asserted themselves to some extent in later centuries. The assertion of the Dál Fiatach to be the 'true Ulstermen' persisted, but they had been pushed towards the eastern part of the province, in the east of County Down.[36] War with the Connachta before reliable historical reckoning had shattered the Ulaid and destroyed their ancient kingdom centred on the legendary stronghold of Emain Macha (Navan fort).

The Uí Néill dynasty was alleged to have descended from Niall Noígíallach, Niall of the Nine Hostages, and by the early historic era they had reduced the ancient province of Ulster by migrating into the western part of the area. A section of the Uí Néill also came to dominate the Irish midlands. They may originally have risen in Connacht and migrated to the north. The Northern Uí Néill comprised two main distinct septs. The Cenél nEógain had first claimed northern territory in what is present day Donegal and their kings were sometimes styled rulers of their traditional centre at Ailech. The other sept was the Cenél Conaill, who originally settled to the west of the Cenél nEógain. In this period the Cenél Conaill was the dominant part of the Uí Néill, but in later centuries the Cenél nEógain achieved dominance. The displacement the Uí Néill advance caused among the people already mentioned also caused a shift into mid and south Ulster of the group known as the Airgíalla, who were in subject status to the Uí Néill.

The movement of the Northern Uí Néill may have been a large factor in motivating the rulers of Irish Dál Riata into moving across the North Channel into British territory, and this successful operation in turn might have prompted the Dál Fiatach into being more outward looking.[37] The

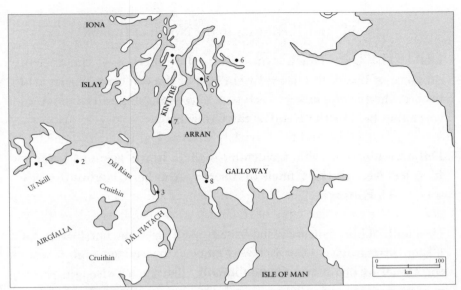

Map 3. North Britain, Ireland and the Irish Sea Zone. 1. Ailech. 2. Limavady/Druim Cett. 3. Islandmagee/Ros na Ríg. 4. Dunadd. 5. Bute. 6. Dumbarton/Alclud. 7. Kilkerran. 8. Loch Ryan/Pen Rhionydd.

neighbours of the Dál Fiatach later formed a kingdom called Dál nAraide. The people who ruled this territory were termed the Cruithin, whose ancestors may have migrated to Ireland from Britain many centuries beforehand. In later times they usurped the claim to be the original Ulaid and they were able to impose their rule as kings of Ulaid periodically, but most of the kings who claimed this regional over-kingship still came from the Dál Fiatach.[38] The Cruithins' other main grouping was Uí Echnach, though the fragmentary nature of their society is shown in their major defeat at the hands of the Northern Uí Néill in 561 at the battle of Móin Daire Lothair, where no less than seven of their kings were killed. The Uí Néill was unable to take advantage of this victory and the outcome may have been more immediately advantageous to the Dál Fiatach. There is no record of military or political participation in major events in Ireland in the 6th century by Dál Riata. Áedán's kindom in Ireland, confined in his day to the coastal strip of north Antrim, was surrounded by the Cruithin.

People and Territories in the North of Ireland

Ulaid. The **Dál Fiatach** dynasty was the inheritor of the ancient province of Ulaid, or Ulster. By the end of the 6th century they had been pushed to the eastern seaboard. Over-kingship of the province was either held by the Ulaid or the Cruithin.

Dál nAriade. The main **Cruithin** kingdom in the north of Ireland. Its rulers were the **Uí Chóelbad** dynasty. Another Cruithin dynasty was the **Uí Echnach**.

Uí Néill. This dynasty established itself in the north-west of Ulster, primarily in what is now Donegal. Its two groupings were the **Cenél nEógain** and **Cenél Conaill**. The Cenél nEógain rulers were sometimes styled **Kings of Ailech** after their stronghold on the Inisowen peninsula.

Airgíalla were a subject people in the south and mid Ulster, allies of the Uí Néill. A part of them also had a military alliance with the Cenél nÓengusa of Dál Riata.

Kings of Tara. Claimants to the ancient stronghold of Tara brought a high degree of status, but did not equate to over-kingship of Ireland. Northern kings who probably achieved (or at least aspired to) this distinction included Áed mac Ainmuirech.

Chapter 1

A Hero's Youth

Bright Gabrán king of Alba of the gold balances had one source of grief which they never concealed namely, that his wonderful wife never gave birth to boys.[1]

If the young Irish kingdom in Britain formed a society like the numerous Irish kingdoms in the homeland, and there is no reason to think it was different, the ruling dynasty would soon have sprouted dynastic offshoots which competed with each other for the kingship. Sometimes this competition would erupt into full-scale violence, and it is notable that the only 6th century evidence we have in Dál Riata for this is a battle named either Delgu or Teloch, which immediately preceded Áedán's ascent to kingship. This may suggest there was opposition to his rule.

By the time Áedán attained power in 574 he was already around 40 years old, a considerable age in contemporary terms, but his subsequent activity in warfare does not suggest that he was hampered by infirmity. There are later medieval traditions of the sons of noble families being placed as fosterlings with non aristocratic families and this may have likely been the case with Áedán. Very young infants were given to care of their *muimme*, foster-mother, and they were later trained by their foster-father, *aite*. In the case of boys, this lasted sometimes until they were seventeen. Even if the tradition is true that Áedán's father Gabráin ruled some part of Pictland, the boy Áedán may have been reared among the Irish in Dál Riata. Irish legend has a recurring theme of children being fostered by the mother's kindred (particularly the mother's brother or mother's factor), but this may have been unlikely if Gabráin's wife was either Pictish or British, as some traditions insist. The time when his father became king in Dál Riata covered a period from before he was ten years old until he was possibly in his mid twenties. Áedán's own incursions into Pictland may have happened in the latter part of Gabráin's reign, or during the leadership of his own cousin Conall (who became king in 558).

The world in which Áedán grew up would be aristocratic and privileged compared to the ordinary population his class ruled over. Even lower than those who tilled the soil were the slaves, captured on raiding parties in all parts of Britain and Ireland. The basic currency in Ireland was based on the worth of a single slave woman. Cattle were highly prized and would be seized on regular raids, becoming an aristocratic sport, plus a rite of passage for adult males and newly installed leaders. Three or four generations after migration, the people of Dál Riata in Britain were still an Irish settler society. They shared the same culture with Ireland and there was no difference in the Gaelic spoken in both nations for many centuries. The new territory they colonised was initially quite small and it would be several generations before Gaelic speakers began to infiltrate into the more northerly Hebridean islands such as Skye and Lewis. Although there are traditions of Irish adventurers penetrating mainland Pictish territory, the stories are vague and hard to substantiate before the 7th century. Yet any foreign nobles who married noble Pictish women could forge lineages which had the opportunity to compete for kingship in Pictland. This was due to the significance of inheritance through the female line in Pictish society, a system not shared by neighbouring Celts or Anglo-Saxons.

There are various traditions which associate both Áedán and his father Gabráin with different parts of Southern Pictland. The fullest accounts associate his immediate family with an area on the upper Forth which was part of the region later known as Menteith. This area is immediately to the east of Dál Riata and north of the Britons who controlled the Clyde and its hinterland. To the east and the north of Mentieth was definitely Pictish territory. It could be that the story of Cenél nGabráin activity in Menteith reflects a history of early Irish incomers from the west.

The Birth Tale

Persistent later tradition attempts to link Áedán with the dynasty of Leinster, and though this appears to have no truth, it was the basis of a birth tale which survives in both prose and verse versions.[2] The stories connect the births of Áedán and Brandub mac Echach, another early king whose name seeped into legends. Brandub was king of the south-east Leinster dynasty called the Uí Cheinnselaig and was a contemporary

of Áedán mac Gabráin, dying around 605. The basis of the tale is that
Gabráin's wife had a daughter and, desiring a son, she was swapped for
one of the twin sons of Brandub's wife, a fact that did not come to light
until many years later.

The poem, written in the late 11th century, tells how Eochu, king of
Uí Chenselaig, and his wife Feidelm journeyed over the sea to Scotland
and were honoured and feasted at the palace of Gabráin of Dál Riata
which was located on the River Forth, which was in foreign territory east
of Dál Riata. Gabráin showered the Leinster royals with gifts and we
are told that he had one sorrow, which was that his wife never gave birth
to sons. The two kings and the queens became close to each other and
the women became pregnant at the same time. When Gabráin went on
an expedition he took Eochu with him and their wives, in residence 'at
Forth', went into labour. The women that night agreed that one of the
twin sons should go to Gabráin's wife and she should take one daughter,
unknown to their husbands. The deceit was prophesied long beforehand.
As a marker to recognise her true son, Eocho's wife placed 'a grain of
gold of the furious foreigners under the top of his shoulder blade'. When
the kings returned, Gabráin called his druid to judge whether the boys
would be supreme rulers, which he pronounced they would be, and they
were baptised. When the druid revealed the truth of the parentage to
Gabráin, the king let it be. Eochu and his wife returned to Leinster. On
her deathbed, Gabráin's wife told Áedán the truth about his parentage. In
reponse, Áedán went to Leinster and met with his real mother Feidelm,
who confirmed the truth and identified the speck of gold beneath his
shoulder blade. She assured him that his fame will abide until doom, and
the poem ends with praise of the two kings.[3]

One short prose version of the story, *Gein Brandub maic Echach ocus
Aedáin maic Gabráin*, states that Eochu was expelled to Scotland by his
brother Fælán.[4] The parallel pregnancies are detailed and this version
states that it was Gabráin's wife who begged Feidelm to save her when
she had two daughters, 'as is not rare'. As incentive for gaining a son,
she gave the Leinster queen a gold diadem, an arm ring, a brooch and
a dress. The motif of the grain of gold is again used, plus the druid's
shrewd identification of the deceit. The boys were brought up as foster-
brothers until the Irish royals returned to their own country. Years later,
'Great was the pride and arrogance of Áedán. He went on a hosting into

Ireland to contest the kingship of Ireland.' He came with an army of Scots and Britons and Saxons to Leinster to claim that territory, based on his claimed descent from Cairpre Rígfota. His true mother met him, though he did not recognise her as such until she revealed herself to him and narrated the circumstances of his birth. The grain of gold, which we are told was the head of the queen's writing stylus, is again located on his back. Brandub and Áedán met and became close friends and Áedán returned peaceably to Scotland without any warfare. A variant at the end of the story says that the suspicious Áedán, when in Leinster, sent for Gabráin's wife to come and confirm the truth of his origin.

Some elements of this legend can be paralleled from elsewhere, such as the grain of gold, but otherwise the tale is original.[5] Although Brandub is associated in legend with a Cruithin hero from Ireland named Mongán (who is also connected with Dál Riata), this story is not linked to Áedán. There may have been an early confusion in Ireland between two women of the same name which gave rise to the legend. Feidelm, the wife of Eochu of Leinster, was of Connaught origin and the other Feidelm was supposedly the mother of Gabráin and therefore the grandmother of Áedán. Áedán's mother is not named in any version of the birth tale, but is called Feidelm in a separate genealogy.[6] The Leinster connection was repeated in a late genealogy, while one source mentions that the birth of Áedán to Eochu's wife was sanctioned by the intercession of saints Cormac and Bridgit.[7] A note attached to the medieval poem called the *Prophecy of Berchán* stating that Áedán belonged to Leinster need not necessarily be early. The historian John Bannerman wondered whether the persistent attempts to link Áedán with Leinster might be based on the early relationship between Iona and the monastery of Tech-Munnu in Leinster.[8] Wider, verifiable early links between Leinster and west and central Scotland are scanty. The female saint Kentigerna, who was reputedly daughter of a Leinster king, was associated with both Lennox and Strathfillan, neighbouring regions of Menteith.

Later history connected with the royal house in Scotland may provide better clues to explain this Leinster connection. King Máel Coluim mac Cináeda (Malcolm II, 1005–1035), was slain at Glamis in Angus. An elaborately carved symbol stone in the village has been considered to contain symbols which allude to the king's murder, and particularly his lineage and the tale of the two royal brothers, Áedán and Brandub, though the link is not convincing.[9] The stone is in fact Pictish and was erected a considerable time before Máel Coluim's reign. Máel Coluim, however, is called 'son of a Leinster woman' by the probably contemporary *Prophecy of Berchán*.[10] The formulation of the birth tale of Áedán may have been a conscious device used by authorities in Leinster who hoped to curry favour with Máel Coluim, who was one of the most renowned leaders throughout the Gaelic world.[11] It demonstrates that the currency of Áedán's fame was still valuable in the Irish world over four centuries after his death.

King of the Forth

The association of Gabráin and Áedán with the River Forth appears to be supported by another piece of evidence which places Áedán in the same region. The connection appears in a *Life* of the Irish saint Berach of Cluain Chairpthe, and though it can't be regarded as a historical document, it deserves some attention.[12] According to this source the saint had a dispute with a poet and druid named Diarmait regarding some land which St Patrick had foretold he should own. The king of Connacht refused to pronounce against the powerful druid, fearful of his threat of satire, so the saint and the poet resorted to Scotland to seek judgement from Áedán son of Gabráin. When they arrived, 'It happened that a great feast was being held at that time by Áedán and the chief men of Alba; and a great number of youths were engaged in sports on the lawn of the fort.' Diarmait, dressed in finery, incited the youths to repel the poorly dressed Berach and 'attack him with dung and cudgels and stones'. The saint transfixed the violent youths, then both he and Diarmait went to the entrance of the fort. There the cleric transformed two mounds of snow into great blazes. The saintly miracles were reported to Áedán, who asked his four druids to find out who accomplished them. His druids 'went on to their hurdles of rowan and new beer was brought to them'. When the druids identified the saint he was brought into the fortress:

and Áedán gave Berach his whole desire, and prostrated himself before him. And Berach cured the youths. And Áedán offered the fort to Berach; that is Eperpuill, a monastery of Berach's in Alba. And the king offered to Berach and to his convent after him his own royal suit, and that of every king after him, and dues from all Alba. And the youths offered their own service to Berach, and that of their offspring and seed till doom, and their districts and territories.[13]

Áedán palmed off the responsibility of settling the land dispute to two other Irish kings after the saint returned to his native land. In Ulster, Berach was given another fort by the Cruithin king Áed Dub (who had historical links with Áedán and Dál Riata). Inevitably, he won his territorial dispute eventually and claimed the land. Whatever the historical merits of this tale, it seems that Eperpuill can readily be identified with the town of Aberfoyle on the upper Forth (formerly in Perthshire).[14] The Latin *Life* of the saint also contains the tale but (unlike the Irish version) does not specify this location. Early in the 20th century the minister of Aberfoyle, the Rev. W. Moncrieff-Taylor, was able to inform Charles Plummer that there were no active local commemorations of Berach on his feast day, 15 February. But the field near the village in which the April and October fairs were held was named Féill Barachan (or Bercháin), which did remember the saint. He further noted the mound north-west of the manse named Tom-na-Glun, the 'Hill of Kneeling', which seemed like the site of an ancient fort.[15] Other ancient sites of interest in the area may include the homestead settlement at Fairy Hill, near Doon Hill, south of the village.[16] The later church sits south of the present village of Aberfoyle and the River Forth, though whether this marks its ancient site is unknown.

Beyond the location in Menteith, the legend is interesting in its detail. A commonplace in saints' *Lives* is the transfer of secular strongholds to holy men as a result of miraculous happenings. In some cases religious re-occupation certainly seems to have happened at such sites. Stretching the imagination, we might believe that the story capures some memory of the *fianna*, young warrior band, of Áedán mac Gabráin somehow captured, albeit in distorted recollection, in hagiographic amber. We can't be absolutely certain which saint is associated with Aberfoyle as there were similarly named clerics who may have been confused in later writings. The late *Life* refers to Berach, son of Amairgin, whose home was modern Kilbarry, County Roscommon. There is a saint of the same name behind the dedication of Kilberry in Argyll. One genealogy makes a cleric named Berach a descendant of Erc, father of the first king of Dál

Riata in Britain.[17] This may in part explain the unexpected presence of the saint at Aberfoyle and also the Argyll dedication. Berach is not widely represented in early church dedications in Scotland. Similarly named clerics include a monk of Iona in Colum Cille's time. There was also Berchán mac Beoaid Bairrfind (otherwise called Mobí) who had a feast day in October, which ties in with the local fair, while Berach of Cluain Chairpthe was commemorated in February.

Áedán may have been inserted into Berach's *Life* on the back of his existing fame in Irish legend. If it was not for the corroboration of the birth legends, the association of Áedán and his father with the upper Forth region would seem tenuous. It has been pointed out that the birth poem also associates other areas of Scotland with Áedán, the islands of Arran and Islay, neither of which is known from any other source to have a special link with him.[18] Yet there are hints that some branches of this kindred infiltrated areas of Pictland further to the east, Fife and Gowrie. Districts further south in central Scotland, meanwhile, may have been partly settled by the Cenél nComgaill, a collateral branch of the main dynasty. It is possible that they first made the association of the famous king Áedán with the area of the Forth to bolster their own territorial claims there. A little more may be gleaned by looking at this region on the upper Forth itself. Geographically straddling the highland line, the later earldom of Menteith is located between the area of Lennox to the west and Stirling to the east. Lennox, around Loch Lomond, was firmly British territory. The area around Stirling comprised some of the land in the territory known as Manau. This fertile and strategically important area was contested by many peoples in early times, but in the post-Roman period may have been partly Pictish and partly British. The same in fact might be true of Menteith, whose early inhabitants spoke Welsh/British rather than Gaelic, though we can't identify their ethnicity.[19] In one verse of the birth tale, and in another source, Gabráin is called 'king of Monadh'. Monadh means 'hilly district' and in later Gaelic sources referred generally to the Grampians and other upland areas.[20] The name Menteith clearly references the River Teith, but the first part may be the element *mon*, so in early times the region could have been called Monadh. A supposed daughter of Áedán is also given this territorial designation.

Leader of Fianna?

If we suspend doubt and credit the story of St Berach with containing a grain of truth about early Scotland, what might this tell us about Áedán's youth? Following the death of his father Gabráin, his cousin Conall acceded to power in Dál Riata. Áedán may have been obliged to leave the kingdom as a possible rival to the throne. He would have likely been in his late twenties and it would be a long sixteen years before he came to power in his own right. A neighbouring territory in the east may have been a convenient place for him to take refuge, especially if he had lived some part of his early adulthood there and carved out a following for himself in Menteith or some other area. Exile among the Britons on the Clyde is another possibility. It was not uncommon for out of favour princes to accept lordly exile along with a loyal band of associates. The dynamics of Irish dynasties would not have guaranteed that a prince such as Áedán would achieve rulership in his homeland.

If Áedán had been active outside Dál Riata at an even earlier period of his life, he may have been involved in youthful military activity of a distinct type which was prevalent in the medieval period. In Irish society young warriors who were denied opportunities in their own ancestral territories (or who were too young to be landowners) often banded together in groups called *fianna*. These groups existed for centuries in Ireland and Scotland and provided a mechanism for landless adolescents and young men to grow into trained warrior elites. While they did have status and were recognised, these groups were on the margins of civilisation and were sometimes portrayed as roaming, degenerate gangs preying on more ordered society. The *fian* band features heavily in Irish legendary literature, but it was a real threat which was condemned by ecclesiastics. The gangs were accused of acts of *díberg*, 'brigandage', associated with violence and heathen behaviour. This kind of warrior fraternity was restricted to border zones or areas of wilderness, marked as dangerous outsiders, even though they were employed at times as mercenaries by kings.[21]

It might be straying too far into speculation to see the young warriors at Áedán's court at Aberfeldy as a record of this type of following. But we can still see the possibility that Áedán, in his youth, was a *rígfhénnid*, a 'chief' or 'royal' *fénnid*. Volunteers from all sectors of society may have joined some bands. An early historical notice of such a leader is Máel Umai

Garg, the 'fierce', who was Áedán's military ally against the Bernician English around the year 600 and notably a royal prince. If Áedán himself had followers such as these during his own formative years, some may have stayed with him into maturity in his personal retinue. A lifestyle of nomadic brigandry was an option for those of adult years who were excluded by various reasons from participating in social structures in their native areas. This scenario might explain why there was violence when he returned from the east in 574 and gained leadership in Dál Riata. A warband with pagan overtones and, moreover, with Pictish associations, may not have been welcomed by all sections of the Irish in Kintyre. It may also have caused alarm among churchmen and particularly the eminent abbot Colum Cille of Iona who is recorded as having reservations about Áedán's elevation to kingship.

We should also consider the ethnic composition of warbands generally in this period. It was long believed that the struggle for power among the fragmented states of post-Roman Britain was clearly aligned with ethnic divisions. But the reality seems more complicated. While there is evidence of inter-ethnic aggression, such as the Northumbrian Æthelfrith driving out British landowners at the turn of the 7th century, groupings may have been more fluid in earlier generations. Later racial animosity between Britons and English, is evidenced by the attitude of Bede and also that of some British clerics against the English. An analysis of the *Gododdin* poem has shown warriors drawn to the British court at Edinburgh from different parts of Britain, attracted by fame and the allure of booty. A member of the war party which went to battle at Catraeth, probably in the mid-6th century, had a conspicuous English name. Several other warriors were foreigners from a region 'beyond Bannog', hills which marked the British boundary east of Dumbarton. In other words, they were probably Picts.[22] It seems that any retinue Áedán retained, or any warband he might muster, if he lived in Pictland, would have contained native Picts as well as Irishmen. There is evidence for royal English exiles among the Irish in the 7th century, some of them in Dál Riata. The Irish were removed from the animosity which developed between British and English in the 7th century, even to the extent that Iona welcomed the rule of Northumbrian kings as overlords. Áedán's court may have been pragmatic and innovative in the practice of welcoming contacts from other races, based on his own experience of living in foreign lands.

The Children of Brachan

Áedán and his father may be linked to another family which places them either in a definite area of Southern Pictland (Eastern Perthshire and Angus) or in a Pictish/British area to the east of Menteith, probably Manau. Gabráin and Áedán are included in a very complex genealogical web of material linked to the ruler named Brachan from Brecheiniog (Brecon) in South Wales. There may have been more than one Brachan, which complicates matters further. In origin, Brachan's family was Irish, but not connected in any way with Dál Riata. Any link between Áedán and a ruler named Brachan based in South Wales is unlikely for a number of reasons. The legendary Brachan suspiciously features in a large number of genealogies throughout Britain via the huge number of offspring he is credited with: twenty-four daughters, according to one source. The document known as *De Situ Breicheiniog* (dating from around 1200) contains a genealogy which states that Lluan, daughter of Brachan, was the mother of 'Haidani bradouac'.[23] A later document which drew on similar traditions is the *Cognacio Brychan*, possibly based on a 13th century source. This gives the confusing information about Brachan's daughter, Lluan, mother of 'Aidan *grutauc*' and mother of 'Gafran (*vradavc*)'.[24] *Vradavc*, signifying 'traitor', was a disparaging term applied to Áedán elsewhere in Welsh literature. Unless we want to get into a genealogical tangle, the best assumption is that the second 'mother' should read 'wife', which is the opinion of modern editors. The name of father and son also crop up in other Welsh sources, such as *Ach Kynauc Sant*, which gives the family connections of Brachan's grandson, St Cadog.[25] It could be argued that the names Áedán and Gabráin refer to other individuals closer to south Wales, but this is far fetched. This genealogy contradicts *Bonedd Gwŷr y Gogledd*, which states that Áedán was related to the British ruling line of Dumbarton. Whether or not the latter information ultimately came from Strathclyde, the document seems to have been written in North Wales. So we are left with a situation where there were two competing genealogical traditions circulating in North and South Wales. It is a measure of Áedán's reputation among the Welsh that there was such wide interest in him. Some historians have tried to validate the Brachan tradition by looking for a northern Brachan in the land of the Northern Britons or Pictland.

The search for a northern alternative to Brecheiniog and Brachan led the scholar W.J. Watson to link this mythical leader to Brechin in Angus. This place-name does derive from someone who had a name like Brachan, though this alone means little. Brechin first appears in the records in the late 10th century when king Cináed mac Maíl Coluim 'consigned the great city of Brechin to the Lord'.[26] There was a long established Christian community here and it has one of only two Irish-type round towers in Scotland. In Pictish times it would have been within the province known as Circenn. This province comprised the later counties of Angus and the Mearns, probably with its core around the great fertile valley of Strathmore, much of which is in Angus. To the west of Angus is a region bordered by the Tay and now contained in Perthshire. Its regional name, Gowrie, may derive from the name of Áedán's father Gabráin. Watson conjectured that Gabráin may have ruled here after marrying the daughter of the man who gave his name to Brechin.[27] The place-names are conveniently close together to warrant consideration of this theory. It would also neatly provide a possible reason for Áedán's subsequent battle in Circenn, which took place late in his career, near the close of the 6th century, if he was trying to reclaim part of his patrimony. Also, while most of the legends of early Irish incursions into Pictland are unprovable at best, there is a tradition which seeks to show that the Munster tribe known as the Eoganáchta infiltrated Circenn. An existing Irish presence in the region may have encouraged fresh Irish eyes to seek territorial gains here.

The naming of areas after early leaders of Dál Riata may support this district name deriving from Gabráin. Within Dál Riata itself, there is Loarn and the district bordering the Dumbarton Britons is Cowal, named after Comgall mac Domangart (Áedán's uncle), and a possible later reference to the men of Gowrie, styling them *Gabránaig*.[28] Angus of course is also named after a Gaelic individual or else the Cenél nÓengusa people of Dál Riata. Against this identification of a Brecheiniog in Pictland, there are several counts. First is that Gowrie may simply take its name from the Gaelic word for 'goat', *gobhar*. The mechanism by which a tradition about an Irishman named Brachan in Pictland became attached to another Brachan in South Wales cannot be easily envisaged. And, if the northern Brachan was supposed to be a Briton, why was he settled in the middle of Pictland? However, it could be argued that there are traces of a northern land of Brachan elsewhere in Welsh tradition. Several of the children of Brachan are supposedly connected with Manau, which is likely the area in central Scotland.[29] In one source Brachan himself is said to have been buried in Manau. A homeland for Brachan in central Scotland, in the marches between Pictland and British domains, would align with the traditions of Áedán in a neighbouring district on the upper Forth, but we are still a long way from knowing whether the land and persona of Brachan were associated with a particular area of Scotland. Modern attempts to weave a northern Brachan into a historical narrative have not been successful.[30]

One poem ascribed to Taliesin in the 14th century *Book of Taliesin*, *Cadau Gwallawc*, describes the wars of the 6th century British ruler Gwallawg ap Llenawg.[31] His area of activity includes action, 'In Gafran, [and] all around Brecheinawg'. The early provenance of the poem is in doubt. There is another Welsh notice of a different place in the north which is named after a Gabráin, and very likely Áedán's father. This is Pentir Gafran, the 'headland of Gabráin' which seems to have been synonymous at an early date with southern Kintyre. Later Welsh tradition lost the exact placement of this territory and used it as a vague term for somewhere even further north, in Caithness.[32] The fact that there is this second place probably named after Gabráin would not invalidate Gowrie's claim to be named after him also, but Kintyre appears to be a more believable setting for his homeland and area of rule. Apart from the fragmentary traditions of Gabráin in Welsh sources there is also an apparently stray mention of Gabráin's father Domangart also. In the medieval tale *Culhwch ac Olwen* one of the myriad of forgotten heroes whose names are invoked in the tale is *Dunart brenhin y Gogled*, 'Dunart (Dyfnarth) King of the North,' who seems to be Domangart of Dál Riata.[33] The Ulster hero Máel Umai may also feature in this tale.

The evidence which links the Cenél nGabráin to the adjacent regions of Menteith and Manau is admittedly thin. Menteith would certainly have been used as one of the main routes for people in Dál Riata travelling east towards the central midlands of Scotland and might have been attractive strategically for an expansive leadership group. The *Prophecy of Berchán* may provide shadowy information about Áedán's activities in the east. This medieval poem detailing Irish and Scottish kings is a composite work which contains a wealth of unique information partly derived from bardic sources. The poem's editor, Benjamin Hudson, believes the passage in question relates to a later king, but there are other opinions which firmly link the information to Áedán mac Gabráin. A further problem in analysing the text is that we do not know which period it is referring to: a time before he became king, or in the last years of the 590s when he was actively pursuing warfare against the Picts. The section of the poem which purportedly deals with Áedán begins with the following admonition: 'Woe to the Picts to whom he will come eastwards... he was not content, with a king setting up in the east, Irish subject to the Picts.'[34] The following stanza states that the Picts will be under this king's authority in the east for a short while. Does this point to a period before Áedán actually gained control of Dál Riata in 574?

The poem then states: 'He is the first man who will rise in the east after his oppression by the Picts; the distressed traveller will be a red flame who will awaken war.' After some poetic allusions and a reference to this king traversing Strathearn in Perthshire, it is stated that he will fight against the Picts for thirteen years, then alludes to his death.[35] Even if we grant that the verse refers to Áedán, the information may not accurately record events. It may signify only that later medieval sources had traditions of Áedán fighting the Picts before he took control as king of Dál Riata in 574. We can return to Berchán later when we consider the wars which Áedán's family fought against the Picts in the 590s.

Possible North British Descent and Connection With Saints

While the two Irish versions of the birth tale of Áedán are basically the same, there are several legends which ascribe him British parentage, and none of them individually appears any more believable than the stories which state he was sprung from Leinster stock. Áedán appears in late 13th century *Bonedd Gwŷr y Gogledd*, the 'Descent of the Men of the North'.[36] This purports to give the descent of several main lineages in the old British North (southern Scotland and northern England). Apart from one apparently anomalous line which concerns the rulers of Cornwall, the lineages given all either come from legendary ancestral figure Coel Hên and Dyuynwal (Dyfynwal or Dumnagual) Hên. The latter was progenitor of the dynasty which ruled Dumbarton and the Clyde valley. In common with some other Welsh sources (particularly the summarised

Welsh traditions known as the Triads), the name of Gabráin and his son have been accidentally reversed in order. The section concerning them reads: Gauran m. Aedan Uradawc m. Dyuynwal Hen m. Idnyuet m. Maxen Wledic, Amherawdyr Ruuein.

Maxen Wledic, the 'Great Ruler', 'Emperor of Rome', has been intruded into this lineage and does not appear in the other segments, which end with Dyuynwal Hen. Maxen was originally Magnus Maximus, a usurper proclaimed as emperor in Britain in 383, who is conspicuous in the medieval Welsh imagination. The tract says nothing about the various genealogies given, except in one section which comments on the invincibility of three northern warband lineages when they combined forces. It hardly needs to be said that there is no likelihood that Gabráin could have been an actual son of Dumnagual Hen. The document's other incongruity is having Rhyddech, the contemporary of Áedán as Dyuynwal Hen's great-grandson (son of Tutwal Tutclyt son of Kedic son of Dyfynwal) while Áedán appears as his grandson. The suggestion that Gabráin's name lies behind the dedication to the church of Llantrisant in Anglesey (as Afran, one of three saints honoured there) is also dubious.[37]

The appearance of Áedán in the British genealogies seems out of place among these British noble kindred, though it has been explained away in several ways. Rachel Bromwich stridently ruled out a British descent, partly based on the antagonism between Áedán and the ruler of Strathclyde, Rhydderch. She interpreted his presence in the document as a deliberate joke.[38] Elsewhere the historian Molly Miller believed that the Dál Riatan rulers entered this genealogical document by mistake, through the error of a late Welsh scribe who found their names somewhere but did not know they were Irish and not Britons.[39] Even if we suppose that an earlier version of the descent claimed that Gabráin married a daughter of Dumnagual and the couple produced Áedán we would not, I think, be any nearer to the truth for this runs contrary to other British traditions and also to the Irish legend which gives Áedán a Leinster descent. The only advantage this legend has above others associated with Áedán's parentage in British circles is a certain plausibility based on geographical proximity. We have already looked at Áedán's alleged family ties with the extremely shadowy Pictish or British leader named Brachan and there is an extremely small possibility that both the Brachan story and the Clydeside descent represent genuine ties. A marriage link between Áedán and the Clyde Britons is plausible in light of the number of British names which crop up among his sons and grandsons. It's also worth noting that the contemporary British king Rhydderch Hael may also have had Irish connections, albeit the evidence is quite late. One source states that he had been baptised in Ireland.[40] There is also a tradition that his mother was Irish.[41]

Several ecclesiastic traditions mention Áedán, but it looks like the links were invented in later centuries to give various saints appropriate royal connections. St Drostan was a Pictish saint particularly venerated in the territory of that people, north and east Scotland. Like other saints his ethic origin was rewritten to give him Irish/Scottish ancestry and he was said, in the late medieval *Aberdeen Breviary*, to be 'born of the royal race of Scots'.[42] The 14th century historian John of Fordun makes the saint a great-grandson of Áedán, descended from a daughter of Áedán's son 'Griffinus'. This claim is as doubtful as his lineage on his father's side, which gives him a South Wales pedigree.[43] Other saints linked to Áedán are credited with British or part-British descent. The 12th century *Life* of St Laisren, abbot of Leighlin, County Carlow, who died in 639, says the saint's mother, named as Gemma, was a daughter of Áedán and the niece of a British king. Laisren was also known as Molaisse.[44] He is especially venerated under this name in Leinster, which is interesting, given Áedán's supposed links with that region. Laisren is linked with the island of Arran, another area which Áedán is linked to, in poetry at least. But the saint's veneration here can be traced no further back than an endowment by Ragnall of the Isles in the late 12th century.[45] Gemma may be identical with Maithgemm, called 'Noble Jewel' of Monadh. She is named as the mother of Molaisse, the 'Flame of Fire', in the *Martyrology of Óengus*. The same work also lists a similarly named Muirgein ('Birth of the Sea') commemorated on 27 January.[46] Maithgemm, according to one source, married Cáirill, father of Áedán's Ulster opponent Báetán mac Cáirell. This makes no chronological sense and it seems that the story is either untrue, or that several saints with similar names have been conflated or confused, as is often the case.[47] More significant of the supposed family connection with Irish royalty is the confirmation that there were close links between Áedán and the Northern Britons, which is mentioned in other sources.

Another saint with a supposed family connection to Áedán is Blane, who was honoured at the monastery of Kingarth on the island of Bute, and was also commemorated at Strathblane. He was nephew of St Cattán, founder of Kingarth and supposedly himself son of a daughter of Áedán.[48] Later medieval tradition names his mother as Eartha, but does not specify that she was the daughter of Áedán.[49] Blane himself is called in one Irish source *Bláán buadach Bretan*, 'triumphant Blane of the Britons', and it has been suggested that he was a British born cleric who was trained in Ireland.[50]

Records for the monastery of Kingarth (Cenn Garad) are sparse, but it seems to have played a prominent role for both Britons and Scots in the Firth of Clyde region. It may have been the principal monastery associated with the Cenél Comgaill, a kindred which became prominent in the latter half of the 7th century. Although they were descendants of Áedán's uncle Comgall they may have carried Áedán's fame with them into areas which they later controlled, along with their favoured saints, such as St Blane. Blane's commemoration at Dunblane, surely in Manau, is interesting in this respect. There are hints that this kindred were settling in the eastern part of this region, in a place termed Comgellaig, around Culross on the north side of the Forth.[51] One of the saints commemorated at Kincardine, in the region of Mentieth, was St Lolan, whose name seems to be a distorted memory of Iolán, a bishop of Kingarth on Bute who died in 689.[52] As for Bute itself, a cairn on north-east side of the island reputedly marks the burial place of Áedán.[53] This may hint at an aspiration for the Cenél nComgaill to associate the famous warrior king at its most important ecclesiastical site rather than be evidence that Áedán himself rests here.

Chapter 2

A Saint Above All Others:
Colum Cille of Iona

The most prominent figure in Dál Riata apart from Áedán was St Columba, otherwise known as Colum Cille, a saint who came to spritually dominate the Irish colony, and who was a towering figure likewise in Ireland itself and in early Northumbria. Unlike other clerics whose cults cannot be stripped back from early writings which purport to show us their lives, Colum Cille's character shines through as a fearless religious leader and secular power broker and is believably portrayed by the writing of the later abbot of Iona, Adomnán. But a sense of familiarity with his character can blind us to the fact that much about him is unknown. The most compelling interaction between Colum Cille and Áedán mac Gabráin centres around the alleged involvement of the saint in a ceremony that confirmed his kingship, and his later presence with the king at the conference of Druim Cett in Ireland. Both of these will be examined in another chapter, but there is much else to look at concerning this extraordinary cleric and his involvement in the politics of North Britain.

Colum Cille founded the monastery on the small island of Iona off the west coast of Scotland during the reign of Áedán's predecessor, his cousin, Conall, possibly around 563. Situated in the territory of the Cenél Loairn, the northernmost part of Dál Riata, the community was close to the scattered dominions of the Picts. One foundation story says that Conall agreed to the settlement, another says it was the powerful Pictish king Bridei son of Maelchon. Perhaps both versions are true, with Bridei sanctioning the arrival of the Irish monks as the over-king of Conall. Unfortunately nothing further is known about the personal relationship between Conall and Colum Cille. Conall's whole reign is something of a blank. He ruled from 558 to 574 and there are few records from his time. In 568 we have the record of a surprising event in the *Annals of Ulster*:

A campaign in I(a)rdoman (the 'Western World') [was led] by Colmán Bec, Diarmait's son, and Conall, Comgall's son.[1]

Colmán Bec son of Diarmait was a powerful king of the Southern Uí Néill dynasty based in distant Meath in the Irish midlands. The *Annals of the Four Masters* adds some interesting information. It states that Colmán sent his fleet north and pinpoints the scene of conflict as the Inner Hebridean islands of Sóil (Seil) and Islay. Another source speaks of a battle in the region at an unidentified place named Ard Tommain. These islands were probably in the territory of the Cenél Loairn and Cenél nÓengusa respectively. The impression is given that the Irish king was the senior partner in this campaign. Conall is not referred to as a king, but as *toiseach*, inferring he was regarded as a subsidiary ruler. Colmán Bec may have been assisting Conall and his dynasty to assert their authority in northern and western sections of Dál Riata, though he may equally well have been pursuing his own agenda. It was ten years since Áedán's father had died, probably while fighting against the Picts. The Cenél nGabráin were not secure against attack from other people in North Britain and nor were they yet the undisputed rulers among the Irish in the British part of Dál Riata.

Uí Néill interest in the Irish colony in Britain shows the connectivity of Dál Riata with the rest of the Irish world and it may be no coincidence that Colum Cille, a prominent representative of the Northern Uí Néill, chose this territory as his new home less than a decade later. According to one story, Colum Cille and eleven companions supposedly first journeyed from Ireland to the southern part of the Kintyre peninsula, perhaps near the secular stronghold of Dunaverty. This was the heart of Cenél nGabráin territory and folk tradition says that he chose not to settle there because he could still see his beloved Ireland in the distance. But perhaps the real reason for rejecting this area as a base was that there was some underlying distrust between the mission and the ruling lineage. Otherwise, Colum Cille may not have wanted the distraction of proximity to the main sites of secular power in this kingdom. Direct involvement in worldly politics was something he may have been wary of, at least in the short term, if the tales of his disastrous political meddling in the secular affairs of Ireland are correct. However, we should also keep in mind that a contrary tradition maintains the saint sailed directly from Ireland to Iona.

The choice of the small island of Iona, on the periphery of Irish settlement in Britain, remains intriguing. Ascetic Irish monks may already by this date have been seeking desert places in the ocean, small islands where they could live alone as hermits and commune with God. Colum Cille's ideal was not this, but he may have been inspired to find somewhere remote from the tumult of mainstream society. The Irish settlers who lived in this offshoot colony were almost certainly all Christian by the time of his arrival, even if there is barely any trace of ecclesiastical organisation in the kingdom before this time. While the connection between Colum Cille and the rulers of Dál Riata inevitably grew stronger, the monastery remained at the centre of a wider network of daughter houses, primarily in Ireland, and Iona's interests remained hardwired into the wider concerns of the Uí Néill.

The relationship between the saint and Áedán was complex and ultimately mutually beneficial, even if there are hints that it did not begin that way. Áedán features several times in the *Life* of the saint written by Adomnán, an abbot of Iona, in the late 7th century, but the work betrays little of the king's personality, although it does mention military episodes he was involved with. Nor do we get much background on the dissent that existed between the two men, albeit that Colum Cille is stated as favouring his brother for the kingship, for reasons unknown. Undoubtedly, Áedán was fortunate in having such a pious and political powerhouse as Colum Cille resident in his kingdom during his reign. It is sometimes claimed that the king's enduring fame in later Irish legend rests largely on his inclusion in Adomnán's work, but this is arguable.

The future saint was born in what is now Donegal, in the far north-west of Ireland, around the year 521, making him around a decade older than Áedán. Colum Cille, 'Dove of the Church', was a later name conferred on the boy when he entered religious training. We are informed that his birth name was supposedly Crimthann, meaning 'fox'. His tribe, the Cenél Conaill, was one of the divisions of the Northern Uí Néill dynasty who were to become the ascendant power in the north of Ireland. A descendant of kings, the cleric's understanding of the highest level of Irish society, together with his own forceful personality, gave him a unique advantage over most other churchmen as an agent of power and political force in the Gaelic world. It is unknown whether it was personal inclination or his family which directed the young man into the church.

Either way, he took to religious life quickly and had an intensive training in an institution which was flourishing in the first few decades after it had supplanted native paganism in Ireland.

After founding Derry and other monasteries, Colum Cille was the head of one of the most powerful ecclesiastic networks in the country. Although his mother was alleged by some to have been a daughter of Loarn mac Erc of Dál Riata, the connection is in doubt and should not be regarded as a reason for his choice of location for exile. The real reason for his leaving Ireland for Scotland remains disputed.[2] One legend states that he left Ireland following a dispute over a psalter belonging to another cleric which he copied without permission, but the underlying cause seems to have involved his entanglement in high level dynastic politics in Ulster. Following his participation in the battle of Cúl Dreimhne in 561, he narrowly avoided excommunication and went into exile in Britain. The earliest recorded liaison between saint and Áedán is entangled in a web of legend and literary invention, though two bare facts seem to stand out. The first is that this incomer monk is clearly credited with power as a kingmaker. The second is that he was adamantly opposed to Áedán.

As we have seen, nothing is certainly known about the career of Áedán before he became king of Dál Riata, except for faint traditions that he was associated with territory to the east of the kingdom. The choice of kingship would have included Áedán's brothers, who are named as Eoganán, Cuildach, Domnall and Domangart. Of these, Eoganán is the only one who emerges slightly from the shadows. We are told by Adomnán that the saint wanted this sibling to be king instead of Áedán. In order to agree to the heavenly decreed succession, Colum Cille was physically chastised for three nights until he sanctioned the ordination of Áedán. Eoganán himself died around the year 595. Given his later propensity for warfare it's probable that Áedán was a renowned warlord in his formative and middle years. This alone is unlikely to have made Colum Cille rule him out for leadership since he was a product himself of a militaristic aristocratic culture. Suggestions that Áedán was suspect because he had carved himself a territory among the pagan Picts is speculation, though perhaps partly correct, however there is no proof that he ruled specifically among Picts, nor that those people would necessarily have been pagan.[3] Whatever the reason for Adomnán's statement that Colum Cille thought

Áedán unworthy for kingship, this one aspect of his treatment of Áedán survived in Irish popular legend.

The 16th century Donegal chieftain Manus O'Donnell scrupulously gathered up all the surviving literary and legendary material he could find about his ancient kinsman Colum Cille to include in his prose work *Beatha Colaim Chille*. Áedán appears in this great work as a semi-villainous foil to enhance the shining qualities of the saint. His first appearance in the *Beatha* shows Áedán as inexplicably and violently hostile to Colum Cille.

On a time that Columcille was in a certain place in Alba, Áedán son of Gabhrán, to wit, the son of the King of Alba, brought two score and seven fiendish druids to practise devilry upon him and to see if they might overcome him by their powers. And so great power had they from the Devil that to whomsoever they gave blessing, he had great good thereof, and to whomso they gave a curse, he had great harm. But when they opened their mouths to curse Columcille, it befell by the miracles of God and Columcille that they blessed him and might not curse him. And not only to Columcille did their curse do none harm, but to none did it work injury thenceforth.[4]

The conflict between good saint and evil king is standard fare in Celtic saints' *Lives*. Even heroes who were later burnished into models of perfection in literature look shabby in their early roles as stooges to unblemished clerics. Colum Cille, perhaps more than many early saints, was genuinely adept at dealing with recalcitrant kings and their non-Christian retinues. Of interest here is the suggestion that the dispute between the men appears to have hardened before Áedán became king, though this detail was possibly inferred from Adomnán.

The next incident in the *Beatha* harks back before the time when Áedán and the abbot actually met. The monk Baíthéne had been sent by Colum Cille to Áedán on unspecified business. When Áedán asked the monk about the qualities of this person who was famed throughout the western world, Baithíne dutifully extolled his virtues, saying that the abbot was a virgin, untouched by vainglory, and never did any false thing. Resolving to test the saint, Áedán summoned Colum Cille to appear before him and had his own daughter, Coinchend (or Conchenn), arrayed in her fine royal robes, before him:

'Beautiful is the maiden,' saith Áedán.
'She is in sooth,' saith Columcille.
'Were it pleasing to thee to lie with her?' saith Áedán.
'It were pleasing,' saith Columcille.

The holy man said there was not a man alive who would not like to commit this sin. But anyone who rejected it for the sake of God would be crowned in the kingdom of God. He then said that he would not sleep with the girl for the lordship of the world, though his human lust wanted him to do so.

Having passed this trial of his virginity and truthfulness, the saint was further tested by Áedán. He was handed a pair of shears and refused to shut the blades when he was asked. His refusal was taken as corroboration that he scorned to use the scissors for so conceited a purpose as grooming himself. So Colum Cille overcame Áedán in the deceitful intent he had toward him.[5] Variants on the tale are found in other sources several centuries older than O'Donnell's work, such as the preface to the poem known as the *Amra Choluimb Chille*.[6] The story as we have it incorporates the Celtic predilection for three-fold elements in story-telling, but this is no guarantee of its antiquity. It is quite possible that this tale is fairly late in origin, and it may have been influenced both by Áedán's truculent character in secular stories.[7] The record of the saint's relationship with Áedán can be measured against what we know about his relations with other kings. By virtue of his blood and his personality, Colum Cille was certainly the equal of every ruler he encountered. We hear about him fiercely denouncing the Irish king Áed Dub who took refuge in Dál Riata and also having the authority to reassure the British king of Dumbarton, Rhydderch Hael, that he will not die by the hand of his enemies, which probably meant Áedán mac Gabráin. He directly confronted the northern Pictish king Bridei mac Maelchon in his own court and allegedly overcame the king's pagan advisors. We also have the tradition (detailed below) of Colum Cille, allying with an anonymous southern Pictish king against his own supporters. In legend he is also credited with disputing with his own cousin, king Áed mac Ainmuirech, and giving his assent to the succession in his kingdom. Adomnán also restrospectively credited him with foresight and power over the succession of rulership among Áedán's own ruling kindred, the Cenél nGabráin.

As already noticed, Áedán plays a role in the writings about his nation's first saint that is not dissimilar to other kings who wander in as bit part players in the tales of saints. One element of difference between Áedán's fate and those of other rulers in similar tales is that he escapes free from the fatal consequences of those who go against God's representatives. The preface to the *Amra* shows some confusion about the relationship of saint and king, for before the tale of the test which Áedán sets him, the king is described as being the king's *anmchara* ('spiritual director' or 'soul friend').[8] The exact significance of this term is somewhat undefined in early times. It was not only a relationship entered into between secular and religious rulers, but also between religious men and was not something entered into lightly. One tradition has Colum Cille refusing to become *anmchara* to the undoubtedly holy Donnan of Eigg on the basis that he would be martyred one day. As a form of patronage between king and cleric it survived for many centuries. The most famous 'soul friend' to an Irish monarch was Maelsuthan Ua Cerbhail (Maelsuthain O'Carroll), *anmchara* to king Brian Boru in the 11th century. But what this role meant particularly for Colum Cille in association with Áedán is uncertain. Whatever the commitment entailed, it must have taken place after some reconciliation between king and cleric which was established after Áedán became king.

A deeper look at the saint's relationship with the Picts gives insight into his place in Dál Riata and relationship with its king. Adomnán portrays Colum Cille's adventures in Pictland without any reference to Áedán. The saint made several trips north to the fortress of the Pictish ruler Bridei mac Maelchon. One of these resulted in a violent spiritual battle with the king's pagan uncle and adviser Broichan. The text of the *Amra Choluimb Chille*, composed shortly after the saint's death, also mentions Colum Cille in the territory of the southern Picts, 'as the teacher who used to teach the tribes of Tay,' with a gloss stating that he kept silent the tribes he was teaching there.[9] Even more striking is a further passage:

> He subdued to benediction the mouths of the fierce ones who dwelt with Tay's high king, i. e., he overcame, or he shut the mouths of the fierce ones who dwelt with the overking of the Tay; for though it be a malediction they intended, it is benediction which used to result from it…[10]

Whether or not this was what we would understand as a missionary enterprise, Colum Cille's biographer Adomnán does not mention it, nor does he show any direct connection between the saint and the southern Picts. There are few clues given by Adomnán about any effort on the saint's behalf to actively convert pagan Picts. Nor do we know that all of the Irish settlers in Dál Riata were Christian. Adomnán is again silent. In the case of the Pictish king, Colum Cille appears to have been acting in alliance with a local ruler, possibly based either at Dunkeld or further south in the region around Scone, and his activities would have been of interest to Áedán. Even if the latter was uninterested in whether the Picts were pagan or not, the spread of Irish influence in the east was obviously advantageous, as was any information about events in Pictland which the family of Iona were able to bring back to Dál Riata.

The saint's journeys to the hilltop stronghold of Bridei mac Maelchon, like the liaison with the unknown Tay king, show him equally unafraid to venture into the heart of Pictish territory to tackle its leadership. While the English historian Bede averred that Bridei was converted by the Irish saint, Adomnán says nothing of the sort. The visits were concerned with secular matters, such as the treatment of Irish people in the Pictish lands, and the only spiritual involvement was a magical contest with the king's uncle and pagan wizard, Broichan.[11]

Whether church and state ran parallel in the first decades or so of Áedán's rule, or whether each side pursued separate policies at times, is difficult to say. There is no trace of Colum Cille's involvement in the king's troubles with the Ulster overlord Báetán mac Cairell, which seems to have dominated his early reign, nor in Áedán's retaliatory pursuit of that king's settlement in the Isle of Man in the early 580s. An element of dispute between ruler and abbot can be detected in the activity of another Ulster ruler, Áed Dub, on the Scottish island of Tiree, a presence which must have been under Áedán's jurisdiction. Although this Cruithin king had apparently resigned his kingship and was attempting ordination into the priesthood, there was little love lost beween Colum Cille and himself. Áed may have been supported by Áedán when he resumed kingship again. His Hebridean period was within a monastic community outside Colum Cille's direct control, which signals a religious faction possibly having links with Áedán also.

But, as we have seen, any tension between the two prime forces in Dál Riata must have subsequently thawed, for it must have been Colum Cille who brokered the momentous summit between kings at Druim Cett in Ireland in the early 590s. It was at this meeting that Áedán was invited to the top table of Irish politics, on an equal footing with the Uí Néill potentate Áed mac Ainmuirech, who happened to be the cousin of Colum Cille. By the final decade of the 6th century there was a close alliance between Iona and Dunadd in place. In Adomnán's work we see Colum Cille magically viewing the kingdom's army from a distance as it battles against the Picts, and the holy abbot expresses concern about the fate of Áedán's sons who died fighting both that enemy and the Northumbrian English. Even if Adomnán, writing at the end of the 7th century, has radically simplified the political condition of this kingdom of the Irish in Britain by magnifying Áedán's ruling kindred, the Cenél nGabráin, it is clear that Iona and Colum Cille were personally sanctioning this lineage, even underwriting its future hold on power, with the important condition that future rulers stayed true to Iona itself and its alliance with the Uí Néill. Adomnán suggests that his holy predecessor warned that if ever the dynasty breaks covenant with the Iona-Uí Néill alliance it would find itself under the control of strangers. This happened for a time in the mid 7th century and Iona happily endorsed the new rising power in North Britain, the Northumbrians, above the native rulership. This was the result of the exile of the royal princes, sons of king Æthelfrith, who came in exile to the Scots and Picts after his death in 616. Áedán himself must have been aware that Colum Cille's support came with a parallel commitment to alliance with the saint's own dynasty in Ireland, but it was a partnership which did not cause any difficulties during his own lifetime. For his sons and particularly grandsons, dragged into the mire of Irish politics, it became a different matter.

It may be a coincidence again that Áedán's success waned after Colum Cille's death. The abbot died in 597 and Áedán himself was well advanced into old age. The warbands which he despatched beyond his kingdom would not have had him at their head, but sons and other noblemen. Áedán's own last decade possibly saw him involved in forays on two fronts, against the Picts and the Northumbrian realm of Bernicia. Would Colum Cille have been in a position to counsel against it if he had been alive? A brake on Áedán's ambition in those last years would potentially have saved him from costly defeats. There is irony in the tradition that the king himself, perhaps deposed, spent his last few years in religious contemplation as a monk. It was a fate perhaps the king would not have wished upon himself. But one can imagine Colum Cille's spirit had some part in his belated spiritual path.

Chapter 3

The Inauguration of Áedán

The rite which formally bestowed the kingship on Áedán would have been a very public event. We might envisage a crowded scene on a fortified hilltop with no space inside the ramparts. It would be visible from the surrounding low lying lands and even those witnesses unable to see would hear the ritual acclamations. Chieftains from the different kindreds of Scottish Dál Riata would have gathered to witness the ceremony. It's likely some witnesses of this transition of power would have travelled to this place from Irish Dál Riata, a short distance across the sea. The chief poet of the kingdom will have advanced to exclaim the name and ancestry of this ruler. This solemn proclamation, called *do gairm ríg*, would formally give Áedán sovereignty.[1] His bare foot would be placed into the hollow of the living rock which received his predecessor's foot, and the king before him. By this symbolic act he was seen to be connected to the land he has been chosen to rule.

So few facts are known about the inauguration of Áedán mac Gabráin that this imaginative digression may be some distance removed from what actually happened. We do not know if such a ceremony took place, and if it did we can only offer guesswork about where such an event may have happened. There are wide gaps too in our knowledge about how and why this king came to power. What we do have is a relatively substantial description of another event described by Adomnán in his book on Colum Cille. But his account is beset with difficulties based on the author's agenda, projecting his view of the divine right to rule of Cenél nGabráin back into the era of his holy predecessor.

Taking the Reins of Power

It has already been speculated whether Áedán may have returned from foreign lands in the east specifically to claim the kingship following the death of his cousin Conall in the year 574, possibly remembered in the *Prophecy of Berchán* describing Áedán as 'the distressed traveller [who] will be the red flame that awakens war'.[2] Whatever the truth of his whereabouts immediately before becoming king, it is possible that some section within Dál Riata's elite did not want him to be the next ruler. There was a battle at a place named Teloch or Delgu in Kintyre in 574, where a chieftain named Donchand (son of the late king Conall) was slain along with 'many others of the allies of the son of Gabráin'.[3] The details of the internal politics which prompted this conflict in the heart of the kingdom are likewise a mystery. There may have been outside involvement from a powerful king in Ulster, Báetán mac Cáirill, an enemy of Áedán whom we shall encounter again, having a hand in preventing him assuming authority in his homeland.[4] One realistic scenario is the arrival of Áedán from the east following Conall's death, along with a warband, and successfully attempting to strong arm his way into power. Donchand may either have been supporting Áedán's right to succeed against another faction, possibly involving Áedán's brother Éoganán, the choice of Iona, or he may have been opposing him. Whatever the political situation, it is unlikely that Colum Cille, whose religious foundation in the kingdom was relatively young at this stage, would have chosen to interfere in these internal Dál Riadan military and political upheavals.

A look at the very sparse records for the previous kings suggests that Áedán's legacy was not one of unassailable strength. His own father Gabráin ruled from around 540 and in the year of his death, 558, the Irish annals record the flight of the 'men of Alba' before the powerful king of Picts Bridei son of Maelchon.[5] This inauspicous notice is the first military record we have of Dál Riata. His successor, Áedán's cousin, Conall son of Comgall (558–574), is barely mentioned in surviving records, though we know he campaigned in the Scottish islands. Already mentioned is the campaign conducted in the year 568 Conall was campaigning in the Hebrides (Iardoman), allied with Colmán Bec, king of the southern Uí Néill.[6] It is possible this Irish ruler was bolstering the flagging military resources of this Irish colony in Britain at a time of extreme pressure, but this is conjecture. It does point to a complex and early network of dynasties connecting the Irish colony in Britain with those in its motherland, and not just with those polities nearest to it in the north. The tradition that Bridei sanctioned the gift of the island of

Iona to the Irish holy man Colum Cille, around the year 563, which was in the territory of the Scots, suggests the kingdom of Dál Riata was in client status to this northern Pictish overlord.

The Citadel of Dunadd

More unanswered questions, and some clues also, can be found on a windswept prominence above the Crinan Moss, capped by a small hillfort which has been silent for many centuries. Rising 54 metres above the valley of the little River Add, this place contains the remains of successive defended settlements from the Iron Age and later reoccupied in the Middle Ages. Nobody knows for sure whether this craggy outcrop was the capital of the kingdom of Dál Riata, though it was first identified as such in the mid-19th century.[7] If it was not the epicentre of that sea-washed kingdom, it was certainly one of its great power centres. Excavations at Dunadd have revealed an impressive assemblage of artefacts proving the importance of the site. Dunadd has the largest collection of imported European pottery from any site in Britain and Ireland.[8] Luxury goods were transported here by sea for the resident elite and the pottery type classed as E-ware was brought here from at least the beginning of the 7th century, and likely a little earlier, during the reign of Áedán. Adomnán's *Life* of Colum Cille relates how some continental sailors arrived at *caput regionis*, the 'chief place' or the region – which was likely Dunadd – and brought with them tidings of the latest natural disaster in Italy.[9] Moulds for brooches and other evidence for high grade industry were also found at the rock. One intriguing item also found in recent excavations was a small gold and garnet piece of jewellery.[10] Anglo-Saxon in origin and dating no later than the early 7th century, it could have belonged to one of the Northumbrian royals exiled in Dál Riata during the time of Áedán, or to one of his immediate successors.

Although probably located in the division of the kingdom named after Áedán's father Gabráin, the citadel also sits in a rich archaeological landscape, which raises questions about the sacred relationship between dynasty and land. If the ruling people of the Corcu Réti came here as immigrants from Ireland, would they be able to invest the monumental landscape with meaning as much as a native dynasty would? Dunadd also sits near the likely border of the territories of Cenél nGabráin and

Cenél Loairn. Such boundaries were liminal areas which had enormous significance for people in the early medieval period and earlier.

In the immediate confines of the fort there are few clues about how important this stronghold was. On the exposed bedrock surface of the summit there is the carving of a boar, which some have argued is a keepsake left over from when a Pictish army overran the citadel.[11] Dunadd features just twice in the early Irish annals. The first mention is in 638, when there is a record of a siege here, alongside a similar contemporary event at the southern Pictish fortress of Dundurn (in Strathearn, Perthshire). The identity of the aggressors in both places is unknown, though it seems probable the two events may have been part of the same extended military campaign. The second mention of Dunadd is more explicit. In the year 736 there was an invasion of Dál Riata by the exceptionally powerful Pictish ruler Unuist mac Uurguist (Óengus or Angus son of Fergus). A king in the ferocious mould of Áedán at his height, he laid waste the territory, seized Dunadd, and burned somewhere called Creic. Moreover, he bound in chains two sons of the late Dál Riatan king Selbach, Donngal and Feradach.[12] The boar carving at Dunadd is stylistically similar to representations of this animal on Pictish stones on the east and north of Scotland. Some have rightly pointed out that the Gaels re-established themselves here when the aggressors from the east went back home; in which case they would certainly have eradicated all triumphant traces of foreign occupation. Although it looks like Pictish examples the carving is likely an emblem of significance to the native people of this area. A more recent, ingenious suggestion is that the carving was left at Dunadd to commemorate a fallen Pictish warrior who had been serving in the warband of Dál Riata. It may be significant that another Pictish type symbol has been found at the British stronghold of Trusty's Hill in Galloway, again a location well outside Pictish territory.

There are other significant human imprints in the rock here. One is a scooped out basin which lies isolated near the entrance to the fort. There are two footprints in the living stone, some distance apart, with the boar symbol in between them. Near one of the footprints there is a spindly line of ancient Irish ogham writing which was only finally recognised in the 20th century. Dunadd's powerful grouping of symbols in its rock face is unparalleled elsewhere. We still have to admit that there is no overwhelming evidence that Dunadd was where Áedán's inauguration took place, supposing that there was such an event. Although the site on the outcrop was probably abandoned as a permanent residence in the 9th or 10th century there were important regional assemblies held here as late as the early 16th century, possibly in recognition of the powerful resonance of Dunadd's historic importance.

Other Possible Inauguration Sites

Footprints are found carved in stones at other sites in Ireland and Scotland.[13] The closest example to Dunadd is at Southend, near the early power centre of Dunaverty in southern Kintyre, which may be the place where the rulers of the region were installed.[14] The place where the newly-made king placed his own foot also symbolically showed the chosen ruler stepping into the footprint of his predecessors. The new leader was, in some sense, married to the land which supported him. As he flourished, so did the abundance and fertility of the territory, and vice versa. This powerful principle runs through the hidden history of Scotland and Ireland alike.

Usage of inauguration places in the north of Ireland used by minor chieftains continued into early modern times.[15] But, possibly the closest geographical and cultural parallel of inauguration, is that of the Lords of the Isles. From at least the 13th century these rulers from the Clan Donald – self proclaimed kings of the Isles – were installed as rulers at Finlaggan on the island of Islay.[16] The lords were proclaimed on a ceremonial site on Eilean Mòr, an island in Loch Finlaggan. The ceremony here involved the would-be ruler placing his foot in a hollow print in a square rock, seven or eight feet long. This act vividly symbolised that he would be walking in the footprints of previous rulers and that he was installed by right in his possessions. Clad in a white gown (which afterwards was given as a gift to the *ollamh*, the officiating officer at the ceremony), he held a white wand as the symbol of his power, which showed that he would wield authority impartially and sincerely. White wands or rods were commonly used in Irish inaugurations. He was formally presented with the ancestral sword of his fathers, a more blatant symbol of power. After his installation, mass was said and the new lord held a week-long feast for his vassals, giving liberally to monks, poets, bards and musicians.[17]

Clues from Scone and Ireland

The successor state of Dál Riata and the Pictish kingdoms had its ceremonial heart at Scone and the ritual significance of that place and the ceremonies enacted there surely throw retrospective light on earlier inauguration rituals of the Gaelic kingdom to the west. At Scone the ceremony of king making took place on the Moot Hill (or Boot Hill), also perhaps known as Caislen Credi, the Hill of Belief.[18] This mound was possibly an ancient burial site which linked the new ruler to a mythological ancestral figure. Scone seems to have existed as a central node in the patchwork territories of the southern Picts, like the spiritual boss on a shield, holding the smaller regions together. Following the unification of Picts and Scots the site was still used for inauguration for king after king, into the 17th century.

Memorably described by A.A.M. Duncan as the place 'where the salt waters of the sea… were turned back by the living waters of the river [Tay],' this was a site where the dynamic forces of Pictish and Gaelic spiritual beliefs were fused together.[19] The making of the king was his marriage, *banais ríghe*, a union both to the land and to the ancestral pagan goddess of the territory. As late as 1124, David I was crowned as king of Scotland beside the ancient mound at the heart of Scotland with a ceremony that had real echoes of ancient practice. As much a Norman as a Gael, David was fully in tune not only with his European peers as a progressive ruler, he was also (according to reputation) a 'sair sanct for the croun', too saintly for his own good. During the ceremony at Scone it is recorded that David 'abhorred the *obsequia*'.[20] This tantalising reference has been taken to mean that there was some trace of pagan sacrificial ritual still evident in the royal ceremony. Early Irish literature features repeated instances of the land of Ireland being represented by a goddess, to whom successive rulers were ritually married. In Scotland, whether in the Gaelic west or Pictish east, there were likely goddess figures which symbolised the very life of the land. John Bannerman has persuasively argued that the *ollamh ríg Alban*, 'master poet of Scotland', was a vital component of the inauguration of national monarchs here up to the installation of Alexander III in 1249.[21] On this occasion, doubtless to the surprise of some Lowland Scots of non-Celtic blood on that July day at Scone, a Highlander came forward to bless Alexander and declare him as king of Scotland. Then he proclaimed the ruler's lineage in a role which was doubtless a survival of the ceremonials which took place long before in Dál Riata. In the same way that the 9th century Scots recognised the spiritual significance of Scone in its archaeological landscape, their ancestors may have behaved similarly at Dunadd.

What other clues can we find about the likely king-making ceremonies at Dunadd? The pagan ceremony in one part of Ireland, where the king was ritually mated to his land (*Feis Temro*, the Feast of Tara) took place for the last time in the year 560, barely a decade and a half before Áedán mac Gabráin assumed power in Britain. While Christianity attempted to eradicate blatantly pagan elements in inauguration ceremonies, some practices lingered for many centuries. The Norman Welshman Giraldus Cambrensis in the late 12th century records the ritual which was current in the north of Ireland to make the new leader of the Tír Conaill. In front of the whole assembled people, Giradus says, an 'outlandish and abominable' rite was enacted. A mare was brought before the candidate for kingship. He embraced it, then it was slain and cut up in pieces and boiled in water. The king then immersed himself in the broth of the cooked beast, then drank from it. Following this, the right to be king was conferred upon him.

It is as well to remember that the exceptional event portrayed here was not viewed first hand by Giraldus and his account is further coloured by being a foreign writer who was predisposed to believe that the Irish were barbarous.[22] Even if his account is largely accurate, it need not have been happening contemporaneously, and such rituals may have differed among the many regional rulers in Ireland. The multiplicity of regional sub-kings was starkly different to the situation in the Scottish kingdom which became a remarkable, unified institution and had a long and close relationship with the national church. This closeness of church and state may have precluded blatantly heathen elements in king-making ceremonies. Despite the similarities of Ireland and Scotland, there were also divergences in culture, increasingly apparent of course in later centuries. So the extraordinary practices of regal confirmation noted in the Middle Ages in Ireland may not be exactly paralleled with those which happened in Scotland.

Adomnán's Version

The statement in Adomnán's *Life* of Colum Cille that the saint had a crucial role in assisting Áedán to power has been treated cautiously by recent historians. A 7th century description of a supposed 6th century event, this is (if it does portray an actual event) the earliest record of royal inauguration in the whole of Europe. In Ireland, where the later records of rites of king-making are abundant in later centuries, the first testimony we have of similar inauguration rites is for a king of Cashel, fully two centuries after Áedán's succession. This was the ceremony which made Arthrí mac Cathail king in the year 793. (His contemporary Áed mac Néill of Tara was specifically called 'the ordained'.) The abbot's tale is full of supernatural wonder.

The story says that the saint was in solitary retreat in the island of Hinba, deep in a mental trance, when an angel came to him bearing the 'glass book of the ordination of kings'.[23] The holy man took this remarkable book and read from it, as the heavenly being directed. With some dismay, he read that Áedán was destined to become king, not his brother Éoganán, who was Colum Cille's choice. As we have noted, apart from his death around the year 595, we know nothing whatever about Éoganán's merits as a ruler, as opposed to Áedán, though his descendants' prominence may have led to his supposed favoured status by the saint. Colum Cille's reluctance to sanction Áedán, if real, may be merely because he knew his brother better, especially if Áedán had been absent for some time carving out a territory for himself on the upper Forth. His return may have precipitated bloodshed in the very heart of the kingdom. As a seasoned warrior in middle age who doubtless had a considerable group of personal followers, Áedán is not likely to have been easily persuaded to conform to religious or political ideas promoted by Iona in the same way that a callow prince may have been. Further speculation may not lead us to any answers, but another theory may be that Colum Cille was aware of Áedán's intention to give his allegiance to the overking of Ulster, Báetán mac Cáirill, rather than his own dynasty of the Uí Néill, who were their rivals.

Áedán's propensity to lead his forces into far flung areas may not merely have been unsettling for Colum Cille in his relation to his own homeland of Ireland. The king's military attentions later turned to Pictish territory which was controlled by the powerful Pictish ruler Bridei son of Maelchon. The latter was known to the saint, who visited him at his stronghold, and if he was not actually a natural ally of Iona, he was someone who was best not antagonised.[24] On the other hand, Colum Cille may later have recognised Áedán's intense military prowess as a useful tool. At the outset of their relationship, as previously noted, he may have been reluctant to hitch his reputation to a volatile warlord. But whatever dynamics were initially present in their personal relationship, there seems to have been a powerful allegiance between the two men in the course of time. It is interesting to ponder whether the family of Iona would have attained the same prestige it did if it had been stuck in a kingdom led by a politically incompetent or unsuccessful ruler.

Adomnán's states that Colum Cille told the angel that he refused to sanction Áedán as king and so he was struck with a whip. It was alleged that he bore the scars of this until the end of his days. Did the monks who tended his body after death see the wound and link it to this event? The wound may have been inflicted during the one battle we know that the saint participated in, Cúl Dreimhne.[25] The heavenly visitor advised that he had been sent with the book to ensure that Áedán ascended to kingship, according to the command in the book. If Colum Cille refused to comply with this, he would be struck again. The angel appeared to Colum Cille on three successive nights with the same order, though we are not told if he unleashed further violence to break down the saint's reluctance. In the end, Colum Cille agreed. He sailed back to Iona, where Áedán had already arrived and he ordained him as king as the Lord commanded. During the ceremony the saint laid his hand on his head and prophesied the future of the king's sons, grandsons and great-grandsons. There has been scholarly debate about whether anointing was part of this early ceremony, and indeed whether any ceremony actually occurred.[26] It is unlikely that this biblically inspired rite was part of the ceremony on Iona, but it is irrelevant to our discussion here. Adomnán does not mention whether this king's successors were equally honoured by the Christian sanction of the family of Iona, and this is yet another question which his account raises.

Another avenue of speculation is asking whether Colum Cille retreated to the monastery on Hinba (which may have been located on the island of Jura), specifically to decide who he preferred to be the next king of Dál

Riata. We can wonder whether that carried much weight with the nobles of the territory, but serious deliberation about who was the preferred ruler would have been important for his own foundation as well as the wider kingdom. There is a reference in Irish literature, and particularly in *Togail bruidne Dá Derga*, 'The Destruction of Dá Derga's Hostel', of a rite where a man of vision ate and drank the flesh and blood of a sacrificed bull in order to have a vision of the future king. Did Colum Cille's three-day meditation parallel this atavistic, shamanistic ritual, which was known as *tarbfeis*?[27] Later Irish writers may have given shamanistic attributes to the saint, though whether he exhibited these in his lifetime is more questionable.

We are not told how the king-in-waiting knew to arrive in Iona at that moment, but may have already been chosen as the new king by the consensus of the most powerful of his own people. Did the Hinba inauguration event (with or without an angel) happen more or less as described by Adomnán? It would have been a remarkably novel intervention which broke all precedent among Gaelic speaking-peoples. Some historians think that the events around this inauguration and the role of Colum Cille with the ruling house of Dál Riata was an attempt to cast the saint in the role of an Old Testament priest, God's intermediary with the highest secular rulers on earth. Elsewhere in the *Life*, Áedán asks Colum Cille which of his three adult sons will succeed as king after him. When the king says he does not know, the saint says that all three princes would be slain in battle, but foretells that Eochaid Buide, still a child at the time, will rule.[28] A biblical parallel of Samuel choosing King David to replace Saul has been cited as the text which Adomnán had in mind here.

Yet the prophetic element of this story was in place before Adomnán wrote. An earlier, lost work about Colum Cille, written by Cumméne the Fair, abbot of Iona 657–669, says that Colum Cille prophesied Áedán's family would stay in power as long as they remained faithful to Iona and the Cenél Conaill rulers of the Uí Néill who were also the blood relations of both Colum Cille and Adomnán. The blundering military actions of the king's hapless grandson at the Battle of Mag Rath in Ireland in 637, when he fought against the Cenél Conaill, triggered this curse and brought about his downfall and that of the Cénel nGabráin as the anointed and chosen rulers of Dál Riata.[29]

If we believe that there was formal recognition of Áedán's regal authority by Iona, it must have been to the mutual benefit of both parties, even if Colum Cille's benediction was reluctantly given. Beyond the political and family relationship with the northern Uí Néill, the island saint was keenly aware of the regal power play in northern Britain and forged abiding links with Picts, Britons and other Irish rulers alike. His personal, enduring partnership with Áedán was surely something more than an alliance of convenience between secular and religious leaders. For all the facts of Colum Cille's religious integrity and moral strength, he was also a nobleman with royal blood. Alfred Smyth memorably characterised him as 'one who had the blood of countless Uí Néill warlords rushing through his veins'.[30]

The Glass Book

Was the glass book which the angel possessed inspired by some actual or legendary illuminated volume which was once treasured by Iona? It was not uncommon for later awe stricken, or naive, monks to state that the beautifully accomplished manuscripts made by their predecessors were in fact the products of supernatural beings. Rather than being entirely made of glass, however, the description may signify that the volume had ornate enamelling work on its covers. There is no consensus however, or any real way of knowing, whether Adomnán intended us to believe that the book was a physical reality or a symbolic tool wielded by the angel whom Colum Cille encountered in his visionary state.[31] We can also ask at this point why Áedán would choose to submit to a wholly novel ceremony at the behest of the abbot of Iona? Did he actively seek church sponsorship, or more precisely the support of a holy man who was in a secular sense a powerful prince in his own right, a member of an extremely powerful Irish clan? As we have mentioned, there was pressure on Áedán's position by the powerful Ulster magnate Báetán mac Cáirill, whose reach extended well beyond his homeland. Both rulers were embroiled in a dispute about control of the Isle of Man and the wider Irish Sea zone. One ancient tract states that Áedán paid homage to Báetán at Ros na Ríg on Island Magee in 575. The same source styles this ruler of the Ulaid 'king of Ireland and Britain' which blatantly advertises his ambition, if not the reality, of his geographical rule.[32] Whether or not he had some hand in the bloodshed in Kintyre immediately before Áedán's assumption of power, we cannot definitely say, though he was powerful enough to attempt to influence the affairs of the Irish in Britain. So we can recognise the advantage which Áedán saw in seeking the formal approval of the head of Iona, who was a powerful player in the politics of northern Ireland as well as northern Britain.

Divisions in Dál Riata

Was Colum Cille able to assist with political dissent in Dál Riata before Áedán ascended the throne? The relative strengths and rivalries of the main kindreds of Cénel nGabráin, Cénel nOengus, and Cénel Loairn are guesswork. Irish society here was possibly even more fragmented and complicated than we know. By around 700 there were at least seven divisions in Scottish Dál Riata. More powerful kings of the land were chosen from the *derb fine*, eligible male descendants within four generations of the previous king.[33] The term for a man within that group who was eligible to become king was *rígdomna*. At times a successor was chosen while the king was still alive and in power and was called the *tanaiste*. This finely nuanced and flexible system of succession (which I have only barely outlined) did evolve over the centuries. The practice of tanistry – the ancient system of succession – at this period in Dál Riata, or indeed later in Scotland, cannot be definitively proven, because these Irish terms do not appear in Scottish records, but it seems likely.[34] But, in the 6th century the kings seem mostly to have arisen from the Cénel nGabráin.[35] Áedán's father Gabráin had been king, but the latter had been succeeded by his brother Comgall, and the latter's son ruled immediately before Áedán. It was not until the latter part of the 7th century that the Cénel Loairn seriously challenged the hegemony of the Cénel nGabráin.

King-making at Dunadd, Iona, or Elsewhere

Considering the evidence, it has to be remarked that the Christian legend of Áedán's inauguration is equally as outlandish as the written accounts of semi-pagan acts of king-making in Ireland considered below. Beyond Adomnán's account, we have no record that he was made king at the citadel of Dál Riata at Dunadd, or anywhere else, yet there is evidence from elsewhere in the Gaelic world that such places were crucial in the public displays which accompanied the transition of power and allowed a prince to become king.

Are the written account of Adomnán and the recorded secular rituals recorded through the Irish world incompatible? Not necessarily, though there are a number of possibilities. Some scholars doubt that the laying on of hands at Iona actually occurred. The strange silence of Adomnán about inaugurations of Dál Riatan kings up to and including his own time is possibly telling. Although Dunadd is the prime candidate as capital of the Scottish kingdom, the inauguration may have happened elsewhere, possibly in one of the other power centres already mentioned. Otherwise, there were other contemporary power centres in the Scottish kingdom, notably other hilltop sites such as Dunaverty, Tarbat and Dunollie (which sits above Oban harbour and was undoubtedly in the territory of the Cénel Loairn). Nearer Dunadd there is a probably contemporary occupied site, a loch dwelling or crannog, at Loch Glashan.[36] It has also been thought that the rulers of Cénel Gabráin, or the rulers of Kintyre, may have been installed at the site in Southend near the bottom of the peninsula of Kintyre, as already mentioned.

An intriguing alternative scenario is that Áedán was obliged to return to his ancestral homeland in the Antrim region and undergo a formal initiation into the leadership of the kingdom so he could reinforce his rule in front of his people there. But imagining there were separate, secular inaugurations into kingship in Ireland and Scotland (with an additional religious confirmation in Iona possibly) is stretching the boundaries of plausibility.[37] The question of Dunadd as the place of inauguration depends on whether it is seen as the 'capital' of the kingdom, if there was such a thing. Adomnán mentions the 'chief place' of the region, *caput regionis*, without saying where it was.[38] Some have imagined that the king and his retinue travelled from place to place, gathering tribute and accessing local resources. This practice of the royal circuit was known in Anglo-Saxon England at an early date, though seems not to have been practised in Ireland. However, the later medieval kings of Scotland were highly mobile.

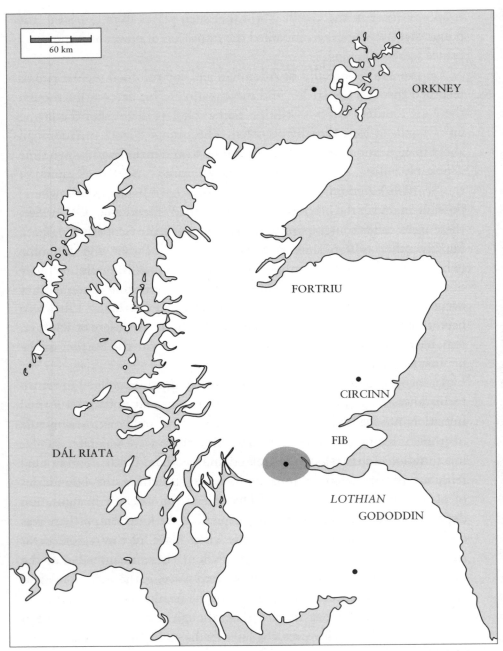

Map 4. Territories of Scotland. British and Pictish regions in the north and east. Possible battle sites marked. Shaded area approximate extent of Manau.

Chapter 4

Áedán and the War in Man

Fifty, sixty are under the water between Man and Ireland; nine here have gone to heaven; dreadful is their pilgrimage.[1]

In the last quarter of the 6th century, during the active era of Áedán mac Gabráin's rule as king of Dál Riata, there are few records about his activities and some of his known battles can't be placed in a precise geographical location. We can glean from evidence that he fought sporadic campaigns against the Picts which were in southern Pictland rather than in the north (where the powerful Bridei son of Maelchon had his power base), though one annal entry details that he mounted an outlying campaign against Orkney around the year 581. At the end of his military career he sent forces against the emerging power of English Bernicia. In the twenty years between these points there may have been two campaigns against the Picts and intermittent military activity in the British/Northumbrian zone which included the Isle of Man, southern Scotland (specifically Galloway) and northern England.

The two records of Áedán being in Ireland are recorded in areas outside Irish Dál Riata, though it seems highly likely that he would have visited the territory which he controlled. Probably near the start of his reign, either in 574 or 575, Áedán is reported to have submitted to the Ulaid (Ulster) overlord Báetán mac Cáirell, whose kingdom was centred on eastern County Down. One late 11th century tract magnifies the power of Báetán and credits him with widespread power in Britain as well as Ireland, as well as detailing his ambitions against the Isle of Man. Late information also affirms that Áedán mac Gabráin acknowledged Báetán as superior ruler at a place on the eastern Irish coast.[2] The second mention of Áedán in Ireland has him as one of the main participants in a council of kings, along with Áed mac Ainmuirech of the Uí Néill, at Druim Cett, a place some miles to the west, between Derry and Coleraine. This conference is placed in the annals around 575, but there is reason to believe it was later, around the start of the century's last decade. Evidence about this conference is discussed in the next chapter.

Báetán mac Cáirell

Áedán and Báetán mac Cáirell of the Dál Fiatach kingdom appear to have been rivals for dominance in the Irish Sea area during the years 574 to 581. Both men conducted military campaigns in a place named Manau, though there is dispute about whether Áedán fought in the Isle of Man or the more northerly Manau in central Scotland. The Ulaid king who posed such an immediate threat to Áedán was celebrated in a propaganda tract which reflected the scale of his ambitions. A poem relating his wide ranging in the late 11th century tract called *Senchus Sil hÍr* is narrated by a sorrowful speaker compelled to journey with tribute from a place named Raith Cruachan in Skye, an island which was certainly still in Pictish territory during Báetán's lifetime:

> *Even I from the pleasant dwelling of Cruachan,*
> *who have come with my tributes,*
> *long is my face after dinner*
> *in the fort of Báetán mac Cáirell*
> *Even I who have come from Skye –*
> *I have come twice and three times,*
> *to convey gems of varying hue –*
> *the Albanach [man of Britain], feel neglected.*[3]

The narrator, who conveys the impression of being a reluctant vassal, also speaks of other tributes flowing towards the ruler's stronghold in Ulster from as far afield as Connacht and Munster. From the poem we get the sense of a powerful ruler at the centre of a vast web of connections, still dissatisfied by the homage which is channelled into him. Whether this long-ranging influence contains an echo of near contemporary bardic boastfulness, or whether it is a later exaggeration constructed to favour an expansive Dál Fiatach world view is open to question. Medieval poets in both Ireland and Wales were prone at times to extend the realistic influence of their patrons to magnify their importance.

Báetán, like Áedán, may be remembered in the *Prophecy of Berchán*. This mentions a king from the north taking sovereignty in Ireland, whose power is so great that he vanquishes every family. This ruler also had control of Scotland, where he fought three battles, and was a foe to the English. While the allusions are persuasive it is possible that these stanzas refer to another, later king entirely. The following verses, describing a different ruler, may alternatively describe Báetán. Here the leader is described as the 'Furious' and the details of his sovereignty are confined to campaigns in Ireland.[4] Despite the suspicious geographical boastfulness in these various sources, Báetán clearly did enjoy a significant degree of power during his short reign (572–581). His ferocity was celebrated elsewhere in the dynastic poem which alludes to the carrion birds being fed with those he slaughtered.[5] In this poem, *Senchus Síl hÍr*, Báetán is described as king of both Ireland and Scotland, and the statement that Áedán submitted to him at Ros-na-Ríg in Semniu is given.

Áedán's Meeting at Ros na Ríg

Báetán mac Cairell was king of Eire and Alban. Áedán mac Gabráin submitted to him at Rosnaree in Semniu. He cleared Manu [of foreigners]. The second year after his death the Gaidil left Manu.[6]

The document quoted preserves the only record we have of Áedán's supposed submission to the Ulster king, a statement directly following the boast that Báetán had extended his rule to mainland Britain. As the nominal overlord of the province of Ulaid, and certainly the main power in the east of Ulster, Báetán had a case for demanding tribute from Dál Riata to the north of his own domain. Powerful as he was, it is questionable whether he commanded the resources to bring Áedán to heel quite as decisively as he may have wished, though the context of the meeting is difficult to determine. There is a possibility that the Dál Fiatach and the sept of Cenél nÓengusa in Dál Riata had ancestral links.[7] But if this is the case, there is no trace of Dál Fiatach activity in that clan's core territory, the island of Islay. There is a late legend which states that Báetán's father Cairell married a daughter of Áedán named Maithgemm (and the couple produced a cleric, St Laisren or Molaisse), but this dynastic connection looks unhistorical.[8] It is definitely possible there was long-standing ill will between the rulers of Dál Fiatach and Cenél nGabráin because of earlier territorial rivalry. There is a brief record that Cáirill died on the Scottish island of Arran in circumstances which imply some kind of defeat. But the more likely reason behind the submission of Áedán was that it was an assertion of power by Báetán and an opportunity to add to his wealth by demanding tribute. As king of Ulaid he would have expected acknowledgment of his status from the leaders of Dál Riata in Ireland, plus those sections of the Cruithin people, such as the Dál nAraide who inhabited the province of Ulster. Also, if he had his sights on renewing his dynasty's ambitions to conquer the Isle of Man, he may have demanded use of Áedán's naval resources, which must have been considerable. We should also consider whether the Dál Fiatach sought to follow the lead of Dál Riata by trying to expand into overseas territory in the east.

It is likely that the kings met soon after Áedán came to power, either in 574 or 575.[9] The location of the meeting was on the peninsula named Semniu or Semne (Rinn Seimhne), now called Islandmagee, near Larne. This chosen meeting place was at the extreme northern limit of Dál Fiatach territory. Báetán's main fortress, a place named Lethed or Layde, is sometimes equated with Knocklayd near the North Antrim coast, but his dynastic lands had their heartland in County Down, considerably to the south.

In terms of geography, Islandmagee is so easily accessible by sea from Kintyre that it looks as if it was chosen for the convenience of Áedán. The 7 mile (11 km) long peninsula lies across from Larne where modern ferries arrive from Cairnryan in Scotland. Larne Lough, a sheltered arm of the sea would probably be the place where the deputation from Dál Riata sailed into. On the eastern side of the peninsula basalt cliffs face the sea. The exact meeting site, Ros na Ríg, 'Wood of the King,' suggests it had some prior significance connected with rulership. Across the lough is the small settlement of Glynn, the traditional southern limit of Dál Riata. So the meeting was significantly near the border between Dál Riata and Dál Fiatach. The stronghold of the Mag Line dynasty of the Cruithin people was at Ráith Mór, not many miles to the west. The Cruithin may have been moving into the coastal lands here around Larne, at this time or a slightly later date.[10]

The fact that Báetán chose not to meet Áedán in the centre of his own territory, which would be important to ensure full visibility of any supposed submission before his own people, but in a place which was in the northern extremity of Dál Fiatach ruled land is extremely significant.[11] Treaties and pacts were often settled in border zones in Ireland. The later conference of Druim Cett between Áedán and the leadership of the northern Uí Néill took place in such a zone and constituted a meeting of kings, rather an abject surrender of rights, albeit one whereby Áedán had to acknowledge the power of the Uí Néill in Ireland. Given this and the exaggerated (and late) claims for Báetán's overwhelming authority in *Senchus Sil hÍr*, we might suspect that the meeting at Ros na Ríg was not the act of capitulation that is suggested by the very brief notice of it that remains. It is true that the record suggests that Áedán capitulated to the Dál Fiatach ruler (the word used, *giallais*, means 'became hostage'), but the record is late and obviously the product of Ulaid propaganda. The meeting may have been motivated by a desire to resolve inter-territorial disputes, more likely in the Irish Sea zone than in mainland Ireland, where there are no records of cross border clashes between Dál Riata and Dál Fiatach. These types of peace treaties were known as *cairde* and were formally governed by a set of Irish laws later enshrined in a now lost tract titled *Bretha Cairdi* ('Treaty Judgements').[12]

The later conference at Druim Cett is traditionally reckoned to have followed within a few years of the encounter at Ros na Ríg and on that basis would have entailed some nimble political manoeuvring on Áedán's part since he would have had to sharply renege on a submission or agreement with Báetán's Dál Fiatach and quickly commit to a similar concord with Áed's Uí Néill. To think that Báetán would have blandly accepted such a blatant disregard of his authority in his lifetime without subsequent warfare is straining credulity. If it's believed that Ros na Ríg involved Áedán's submission, it would have entailed giving hostages to the Irish king as surety for his own loyalty, plus a promise to pay tribute. Báetán may have expected this as overking of Ulaid and Áedán may have been reluctant to agree to it, yet there may not have been a great inequality of power between the two rulers. Hostage giving and tribute offering were common place occurrences which need not have entailed major loss of face. Like the later convention of Druim Cett, it was the matter of tribute and service from Dál Riata in Ireland which would have been acknowledged. Both meetings were carefully conducted because Áedán was no mere vassal, but a ruler whose greatest resources of power were beyond the fervid grasp of potentates based in Ireland. Whenever we date the meeting, following Áedán's accession in 574 Báetán had only a short term to live. He died in 581, while Áedán was alive for the next three decades. For all his authority, there may have been signs that he was entering into the final phase of his rule.

Warfare on Man

There are several records concerning contemporary events in Man which do not, however, make events entirely clear. The *Senchus Sil hÍr* informs us: 'And Manau was cleared by [Báetán] of foreigners, so that dominion over it has belonged to the Ulstermen from that time forward; and in the second year after his death the Gaels abandoned Man.'[13] Most historians agree that the Manau referred to here is the Isle of Man and not the territory with the same name in what is now central Scotland.[14] Báetán's family had a long standing aspiration to either subdue or conquer the Isle of Man, an island which sits attractively near to Ulaid land in Ireland. This strategy of the Dál Fiatach rulers, which lasted for more than a century, was highlighted by the historian Molly Miller.[15] Some of their activity is captured in a 12th century poem about the Christian kings of Ulster. Báetán's father Cáirill (who may have died around 527) is stated to have ravaged Man. After a reign of twenty-five years, however, it concedes that Cáirill suffered an apparently ignominious end to his career when he 'died of sorrow in cold Arran'.[16] This island in the Firth of Clyde, which lies to the east of Kintyre, was firmly within the orbit of Dál Riata.

There is no evidence about whether Cáirill's failed mission was aimed at plunder or territorial advantage, or whether he turned to Arran after failing to secure Man. An Irish dynasty which was able to target Arran, albeit unsuccessfully, was clearly a pertinent danger to Dál Riata. His 'plundering son' (and Báetán's brother) Demmán was apparently just as ferocious as his sibling, and ruled for fourteen years, but there is no record of him straying abroad. Like Cáirill however his career was cut short and he had an dishonourable death, being slaughtered by shepherds.[17] More than a century later, Cáirill's great-grandson Dunchad's (d. 643) 'fierce rage was directed against smooth Man'.[18] The large gap in interest directed towards Man was doubtless due to an intense period of internal military rivalry between territories in Ulster in the first decades of the 7th century. It is significant that none of the dynasty's incursions resulted in long-term domination there.

In 577 the *Annals of Ulster* record *Primum periculum Uloth in Eufania*, the 'first expedition of the Ulaid to Man'. The following year is the entry *Reversio Uloth de Eumania*, 'expulsion of the Ulaid from Man'.[19] The Dál Fiatach king died in 581 and the *Senchus Sil hÍr* states that the Gaels abandoned the island two years after this. The *Annals of Ulster* state that Áedán was the victor in a battle in Manau in 582 and it repeats the information that he fought here again in the following year. This may be a simple duplication or an echo of the events in 577 and 578. We seem to have a record of an attempt by Báetán to oust a non-Irish ruling group from the Isle of Man and a subsequent expulsion of his Dál Fiatach forces from there. Áedán's intervention against the Ulaid on the Isle of Man was timed to take advantage of the power vacuum after the death of Báetán. Whether he had any part in supporting Báetán's initial raid on Man is impossible to determine. But a raid there after Báetán's death would have benefitted whichever Irish and British groups were opposed to the Dál Fiatach on the island. It was also part of a larger power play which would have enhanced Áedán's influence in north east Ireland. His intervention may also have given impetus to his military interest in adjacent areas of mainland Britain.[20] The name Manau, as we've seen, cannot alone help us determine whether the island or the Scottish territory is intended. However, after the entry in the Irish annals which record Áedán's victory at Manau there is the death notice of Fergna son of Caiblene. Caiblene apparently gave his name to a sept of the Dál Fiatach people, which may suggest that his death was caused by Áedán, possibly while defending territory on the island.[21]

There is no certainty about the identity of the 'foreigners' targeted by Báetán as we have to admit that the island's early history is almost entirely undocumented. Despite the *Book of Lecan*'s assertion that the foreigners were English, this is almost certainly incorrect as the Northumbrians had not yet fully established dominance over British territory west of the Pennines in the late 6th century. The first recorded English presence here is when Edwin of Northumbria is recorded as having controlled the 'Menevian islands', Anglesey and Man, in the 620s.[22] But there is reason to believe there was a British population element significant enough to require ethnic cleansing by Báetán. The second ruling dynasty of Gwynedd seems to have ancestors who were attested in Man in the late 7th century. King Merfyn Frych, who came to power in Anglesey in 825 and died in 844, was a likely descendant of Merfyn Fawr, who is likely the 'Muirmin of Man', whose killing is recorded in the *Annals of Ulster* in the year 681 or 682.[23] Merfyn Frych himself was the son of Gwriad or Guriat, who is commemorated on the stone cross inscribed with his name, the *Crux Guriat* on Man.[24] This line of British rulers seems to have migrated to the island from south-west Scotland and had genealogical links with the rulers of Strathclyde and other native dynasties in what is now southern Scotland.[25]

At what stage this British line became established in Man is unclear. There are varying theories about the composition of the early population, whether originally Irish, British, or both.[26] All of the place-names on the island are either Irish or the result of later Viking settlement, and Manx Gaelic was the ultimate winner in the linguistic stakes. In one unique late antique reference in the 4th–5th century the writer Osorius says that the Isle of Man was populated by Irish people.[27] But the English historian Bede, who knew of Osorius, and commented from the vantage point of early 8th century Northumbria, seems to assert that the island was British.[28] The British dynasty which landed in Man from Galloway may have moved there in the 6th century, but whenever the date it seems they were unable to impose control over the whole territory. They either survived Báetán's attempt to clear them out, or actually migrated there from the British mainland some time in the wake of the failed Dál Fiatach invasion to bolster Irish presence on the island. There is evidence that some of the existing Irish on the island were from a different population group to the Dál Fiatach. An inscribed stone on Man commemorates a leading member of the Cruithin tribe, the Conailli Muirtheimne, whose Irish heartland was in north Louth and south Down.[29]

Was the Gaelic-speaking population on the Isle of Man predominantly Cruithin, or was it from more diverse Irish territories? Even if it was Cruithin, the suggestion that these people represented the mysterious foreigners whom Báetán cleared from the island, as some have claimed, cannot be supported.[30] The Cruithin were not regarded as foreigners despite their alleged British origins. Looking north to Galloway, the nearest mainland location to Man, there seems to have been an early Irish stratum in the population, whose distinct identity persisted into modern times. In the Rhinns of Galloway, the western peninsula facing Ulster, there was a record of an impoverished, minority class of people known as *Kreenies* or *Gossoks*. *Kreenies*, it has been argued, preserves a reference to the name of the Cruithin people of northern Ireland, while *Gossoks* derives from the Welsh word for 'servile person'. Although the very late recording of this folk name would seem to argue against its legitimacy as an early designation, the names look legitimate.[31]

It looks like the Cruithin population was unable to establish a ruling dominance in either the Isle of Man or in the west of Galloway. Irrespective of the size of an existing Gaelic population in the west of Galloway, if there was firm control of this region by a British ruling class it would explain why the Dál Fiatach were compelled to look elsewhere, to Arran and Man, for possible expansion and dominance over other existing Irish settler groups. Otherwise Galloway, which is very close to Ulster, would have seemed an ideal candidate for colonisation.[32] The Rhinns of Galloway incidentally may have shared cultural affinities with the Isle of Man from a very early period. The two places were indeed inter-visible to each other.[33] A sizeable British speaking population in Man, whose rulers had links to mainland Britain, poses questions about Áedán's reputed military presence in Galloway (which will be considered later). The short duration of Báetán's campaigns in Man suggests that the Britons weathered his invasion storm. Charles-Edwards suggests that the British and Irish occupied different parts of the island.[34] Whether this co-existence was peaceful before the interruption of the Ulaid, or indeed afterwards, is wholly unknown.

The Propaganda War for Man

> *I go freely.*
> *The pure-white morning approaches.*
> *Manannán son of Ler is*
> *the name of the man who came to you.*[35]

The strategic importance of the Isle of Man was recognized by the Cruithin and the Dál Fiatach in Ulster and some trace of their rivalry is written into legends which had a late 6th and early 7th century background. Áedán was a key player in the power struggle in this North Sea zone. Both peoples claimed affinity with the mythical founder of the Isle of Man, a figure who survived in legend as a magician, necromancer and trader. In Irish he was the god Manannán and in Welsh Manawydan, so that the twin early medieval cultures on the island both recognized him. *Sanas Cormaic*, Cormac's Glossary, a 10th century Irish text describes him familiarly in seafaring terms as 'the best pilot that was in the west of Europe. He used to know by studying the heavens…the period which would be the fine weather and the bad weather', and states that he gave his name to the Isle of Man and was a figure of repute known to Britons and Irish alike.[36] He features prominently in the later popular folklore and culture of the island, having survived the centuries of Viking dominance, and even persisted as the native Manx Gaelic language dwindled away. His grave, thirty feet long, was once shown near Peel Castle and there was a custom of laying rushes for him on certain days on two island peaks. His later stature was much reduced from its ancient position, with his most prominent power being weather control: he could raise fogs and mist which hid the island from his enemies.[37]

Among the legendary tales attached to a ruler of the Cruithin dynasty of Dál nAraide, Mongán mac Fíachnai, there is one which gives an intriguing look into the likely aspirations of his dynasty towards the Isle of Man. *Compert Mongáin*, 'The Conception of Mongán', looks like a piece of carefully crafted propaganda created by native *filid* on behalf of the Dál nAraide regime to link them to the Isle of Man by fusing their lineage onto its primal (and pagan) founding figure, Manannán. The fact that the Celtic god had such currency at the end of the 6th century among Christian Irish tribes is unexpected. In the older version of the tale, this hero's father Fíachnae Lurgan is described as a subordinate ally of Áedán mac Gabráin.[38] The latter asks Fíachnae to aid him in his war against the English which is being fought in North Britain, and in particular to combat a fearful warrior the enemy have brought against him. When Fíachnae crosses the sea to assist Áedán, his wife is visited at his stronghold by a mysterious figure who states that Fíachnae is in grave danger from the same fell warrior who cannot be slain. To safeguard him, he says she must sleep with him and that she will bear his child. Moreover, he said he would go to Britain the following day, three hours after sunrise, and stand in the front rank of the host of Áedán and Fíachnae. The image of the god physically standing in frontline military alliance with these two leaders is compelling. He appeared at the given time and told Fíachnae what had happened. The Irish army was then able to overwhelm the enemy. So it was that Mongán son of Manannán was conceived, though he was also known as Mongán son of Fíachnae.[39]

The fact that there is another literary tale which supports the idea that Mongán was the reincarnation of legendary hero Fionn mac Cumhail shows that the áes dána, the poetic 'men of art', sponsored by Dál nAraide were working hard to forge supernatural credentials for this particular dynast.[40] Mongán's life and deeds do not feature strongly in surviving annals, which frustrates efforts to disentangle his significance in regional politics at the time. As we will witness in a later chapter, he maintained a crucial personal link with Dál Riata and died in that kingdom's Scottish territory, possibly fighting on behalf of the ruling Cenél nGabráin, though the circumstances are murky. His family's close connections over two generations with Dál Riata are therefore highly relevant.

Another, more obscure ingredient to add to the mix is that a contemporary of Mongán was also credited with similar supernatural ancestry. This was Rónán son of Domangart mac Predae. His sept, the Uí Echach Arda, occupied the Ards peninsula in County Down (neighbouring Cruithin territory), and was a division of the Dál Fiatach. A verse spoken to Rónán's mother Findtan by Manannán is nearly identical with the words spoken by the god in Compert Mongáin:

> The cool clear morning approaches,
> whence men will stand forth on the battle-field;
> Manannán mac Lir
> is the name of him who has come to you.[41]

Like Mongán, Rónán is described as a hero and he has both an earthly and an otherworldly father, Manannán. The tract which details this duality strikingly divides him into these two parts lengthwise.[42] Báetán mac Cáirill's brother Demmán (d. 572), who also ruled the Ulaid as king, may have been raised by Domangart, which would make him and Rónán foster brothers.[43] The Uí Echach were therefore closely linked to the central ruling family of the Dál Fiatach dynasty at this time. The connections are all the more relevant when it is considered that it was Demmán's descendants rather than Báetán's who provided the future kings of the Ulaid. The adjacent kingdoms of Dál nAraide and the Dál Fiatach were competing for supernatural association with Manannán and claiming hereditary rights to his *locus*, the Isle of Man. It seems no coincidence either that both these heroes have names which have a connection with the sea.[44]

Whether the Cruithin tale of godly parentage was simple cultural appropriation by Mongán's lineage is unknown, but the Dál Fiatach of Ulaid certainly had an ancestral tradition connected with the sea god which underpinned their claim to his island. The Dál Fiatach claimed descent from Dáire mac Dedad. The daughter of this chieftain had intercourse with an unnamed supernatural being (*scál*), who arrived from the sea and fathered a child who was born with semi-supernatural attributes.[45] Manannán seems to be the obvious candidate. The association with divinity lingered long with the rulers of the Isle of Man. The Norse-Irish king of Man and the Hebrides, Raghnall son of Godred, ruled the island from 1187 to 1229. He is the subject of a Gaelic poem extolling his virtues and power over territories far and wide. One verse alludes to his mother and wonders about his otherworldly conception: 'What god from beside the Boyne conceived you with her in secret.'[46] It would be no stretch of the imagination to envisage Manannán again as his unearthly father.

Peiryan Vaban

Any assessment of Áedán's possible involvement in military operations in the Isle of Man in the 570s or 580s remains highly speculative.[47] Not only does the confusion between two places called Manau set a trap to confound us, but the difficulty is compounded by the lack of relevant records, particularly regarding the situation on Man. The Welsh records are one example. *Annales Cambriae* record the battle of Euboniam (Man) under the year 584, though they do not mention the involvement of Áedán or any other party. Although this is not a contemporary source, its selective focus on northern events is significant. Apart from notices of inter-British warfare in northern England/southern Scotland the only other interest in the region focuses on Áedán and his kindred. There is no interest in other events in Dál Riata, Pictland, or even the British lands of Gododdin in south-east Scotland. Admittedly this does not go far in showing that Welsh scribes regarded the battle in Manau as being in the Isle of Man rather than the same named place further north. There is adequate room for wide-ranging speculation about Irish activity on the Island of Man in these few years, not all of which necessarily have to include Áedán playing any part in them. What tilts the balance in favour of him playing a role, in my opinion, is the known association with Báetán in the first decade of his reign, the Dál Fiatach's territorial antagonism which overlapped Dál Riata's sphere of interest, plus the record of Áedán's activity in a place called Manau around the period when its is known there was warfare in the Isle of Man. Whatever the precise motivation for the Cenél nGabráin to become involved against the Northumbrians at the battle of Degsastan in 603, it is unlikely that this far flung incursion was an isolated adventure in this region, but rather the culmination of events which may have been spread over several decades. The interest of Áedán and other Irish dynasts in the British mainland adjacent to the Irish Sea is likely to have had a complex motivation which followed on from earlier expeditionary sorties to the Isle of Man.

Whatever the context of the meeting of kings at Ros na Ríg, the previous territorial ambitions of Dál Fiatach suggest that Áedán would have been on the back foot at this time. Even if the summit was amicable to some extent, Áedán as the weaker party would have been obliged to give hostages and pay tribute. There has been a suggestion that the internal conflict in Kintyre, the battle of Teloch or Delgu in 574, around the time that Áedán became king, involved Báetán.[48] The balance of power between the two men may have shifted significantly in the course of several years. A weakening regime in Dál Fiatach may have given Áedán the opportunity to throw off an unwanted overlord. He may have sought allies in Ireland in readiness to act against the Ulaid. An aspiration to support British allies associated with Galloway and the Isle of Man may have given the Dál Riatan king the excuse to intervene after Báetán's death, in Man and possibly even in Ireland with well-timed alliances. There are few known links between Dál Riata and the far south-west of Scotland before the 9th century, which does not mean there was no contact at all.

Áedán makes a surprise appearance in a Welsh poem which only survives in one mid-15th century manuscript.[49] It is the most substantial surviving Welsh source dealing with Áedán and is one of the few literary productions which purports to feature him in a contemporary setting rather than as an anachronistic character. *Peiryan Faban* (or *Vaban*), or 'Commanding Youth', is narrated by someone identified at the end of the poem as Myrddin, Merlin, though the original narrator may well have been someone else. We are not informed who the narrator is addressing, beyond him bearing the title 'Lordly', or 'Commanding Youth'. He may be the archetypal youthful deliverer or hero found elsewhere in Celtic literature.[50] A more intriguing suggestion is that the figure represents an evocation of the god Mabon, the 'Young Son,' who seems to have been especially venerated in the Solway Firth area in pre-Christian times.[51] The first part of the poem narrates the impending arrival of a vengeful force led by Áedán mac Gabráin:

> *Commanding Youth, cease your complaining.*
> *May God protect you from the Irish heathens,*
> *and on the way to Irish Hill [Galloway?], the Devil's Encounter;*
> *and the Franks and the Irish will scarcely part.*
> *Aeddan will come from crossing the broad sea,*
> *and a host from the Isle of Man will rise up with him,*
> *and the islands on the way to Irish Hill.*
> *The Devil's Encounter, as swift as a spear.*
> *Commanding Youth, cease your groaning.*
> *Aeddan will come from crossing the broad sea,*
> *and there will be neither youth nor tumult nor thunder.*
> *Many a sally, many a warrior, many an owner of arms are Aeddan's,*
> *many a long-headed spear, many a long spear-shaft,*
> *seizing land. May Gafran prosper.*
> *Many a breastplate, many a helm on head, cattle as to his intent,*
> *many a red sword, many a surly lad, a fortress of bloody conflict,*
> *many a lively steed, many a light, broad, shining shield.*[52]

The context of the impending conflict in the poem is unclear, though the narrator appears to anticipate the arrival of Áedán from the Isle of Man to Galloway to cause warfare.[53] The latter half of the poem shifts emphasis by adding gnomic lines, which change the tone of the piece. There are passing references to Myrddin's siblings and to the chieftain Gwenddolau, so possibly these references have been imported from other traditions deemed to be contemporary with the first verses. Mention of the warlord Gwenddolau signals that this section at least is linked to the battle of Arfderydd, or Arthuret, fought by British factions in 573. This battle was a famous event which accrued a wide variety of legendary material, though the many fragments of folklore which survive about the encounter do not add up to a coherent picture about the event. Famous contemporaries like Áedán and Rhydderch, the British king of Dumbarton Rock, were later sucked into the story cycle, but it is obvious that neither participated in the battle. The attribution to Myrddin, like the allusions to Arfderydd, may be additions to the poem.

In the poem we are told that 'Aeddan will come with a host across the region', and later we have a direct reference to conflict between kings: 'From the encounter of Rhydderch and renowned Aeddan so clearly it is heard from the north to the south.' No historian would seriously claim that *Peiryan Vaban* is a fully valid historical source. And although the poem has a recognisable setting and context in North Britain which would perhaps be of marginal interest to audiences in later medieval Wales, this isn't confimation that the source material goes back to a remote past. The poem's editor stated that it belonged to a small group of Welsh poems employing the Myrddin persona, all of which have material which is older than the manuscripts which contain them.[54] *Peiryan Vaban*, however, is found in a manuscript that is later than these other poems. Despite that, *Peiryan Vaban* shows that Áedán mac Gabráin retained a distinct role in Welsh legendary circles as late as the 15th century instead of becoming a shadowy, stock character. It may be that the poem is linked with earlier Welsh traditions which involved Áedán in naval warfare in the Isle of Man, possibly the same as the lost source summarised by the Welsh Triad discussed below.

A few steps further away from historical likelihood is the testimony of the 14th century Scottish historian John of Fordun who speaks of an alliance between Áedán and the Britons, and particularly with Maelgwn of Gwynedd who was certainly deceased by this period. Fordun's statement that Áedán's nephew Brendinus was a prince of *Eubonia*, 'Man', is untrustworthy and is not backed up by further detail which would substantiate it.[55]

The Strategy at Man

Clearly any mission for a Kintyre-based warband to the Isle of Man was not within the usual opportunist pattern of raids in this period, which seem mostly to have been motivated by securing moveable booty.[56] On the surface this expedition to Man may fit into the pattern of Áedán's violent incursion in the opposite geographical extreme of Orkney. But the Irish Sea was a more familiar arena for Irish activity than the Northern Isles. There are numerous tales of adventuring in this 'Irish lake' between Britain and Ireland and the impression of the storytellers is that this was an intimate area for adventure. One old Irish tale relating a joint hosting evokes the scene of a Scottish king's harbour being crowded with ships of all sizes before the expedition, and the storyteller affirms that 'betwixt Ireland and Scotland was a continuous bridge of currachs'.[57] The Irishman most prominent in Welsh literature after Áedán is a legendary figure named Cú Roí mac Dáiri. He is the subject of a poem in the *Book of Taliesin*.[58] It is significant that this Irishman too had strong connections to the Isle of Man, which might point to this place being the origin of Welsh tales about Áedán too. We have to recall also that there was a recurrent association in Irish literature alluding to Man as an Otherworld location, referred to at times as Emain Ablach, 'Emain of the apple trees'. In this context, and from other clues, it may be that Báetán and the Cruithin people at various times, had a greater interest in action in Man and the north of England than we commonly suppose. The weakened mosaic of post-Roman British states and initially weak English Northumbria might have invited predatory Irish interest.

The Isle of Man, like Orkney, may have provided little opportunity for rich, portable treasure such as cattle, though that other currency of the Dark Ages, slaves, might have been a target. Winning prestige and subduing distant opponents as a result of such long-scale exercises of power would have to be weighed against the massive expenditure of resources which any such missions consumed. Whichever mission came first, Man or Orkney, it is possible that one attack provided the template for the other. If both are given credence, it demonstrates an impressive range of power within several years. What further purpose may have been behind any attack on Man? O'Rahilly's claim that there was a Dál Riatan settlement on the island is unsupported by evidence, though it is possible that a move to protect Cruthin or other Irish inhabitants there in the face of Ulaid aggression may have given Áedán the impetus to intervene, especially if it augmented support given to British allies present on the island and in Galloway.[59] The paucity of detail about Áedán's actions in his lifetime makes informed speculation about his motivation problematic. But the following can be considered. Áedán's interventions into foreign territory, Pictland and Man, seem to have been undertaken after the major dominating leader over each area died. Each move was ultimately opportunistic.

Even if we believe that Áedán campaigned in Man, the sequence of his involvement is not easy to see. He may have been complelled to have joined in Báetán's initial invasion of the island. He may have reversed his position following Báetán's death and attacked the Dál Fiatach. Such a move would have signalled to the other Irish dynasts in the north that Áedán was a force to be reckoned with throughout the entire region and particularly put down markers for dominance on the eastern seaboard of Ulster. Different scenarios could of course be envisaged.

An Otherworld Journey?

By nature of its geography straddling Ireland and Britain and encompassing many islands, Dál Riata must have been better placed than any kingdom in Britain or in Ireland regarding sea transportation. As we related in the introduction, there were formal procedures for maintaining naval manpower in Dál Riata. One of the major mentions of Áedán outside of Ireland alludes to a Welsh legend celebrating a voyage he and his forces made by sea. It occurs as a typically cryptic mention in Welsh Triad 29, which itemises 'Three Faithful War-Bands of the Island of Britain'.[60] The Triad is a summary of a lost tale about the subject which would have been current among the noble households of Wales at some stage in the medieval period. One version of the Triad merely states that Áedán's warband 'went to sea for their lord', or possibly 'went *into* the sea'. In the context of the thoroughly maritime nation of Dál Riata, this would surely entail a more dramatic journey than in domestic, territorial waters. One would also imagine that a story about his warrior corps going to sea would involve a literary remembrance of a campaign in an area where the Welsh potentates themselves had a long-standing interest, so more likely an Irish Sea adventure rather than a far northern journey to Orkney. The two other tales alluded to in the Triad refer to other people and events relating to this Irish Sea/Solway/Northumbria zone, which may suggest the Áedán tale was set here rather than anywhere else.

The second version of Triad 29 mentions the king's warband 'when was his complete disappearance'. There is no other literary traces of a tale which concerns Áedán magically vanishing, apart from a mention by the Welsh literary forger Iolo Morganwg who states that among the 'Three Lost Parties of Adventurers of the Island of Britain' was Áedán and his men, 'who went out to sea in search of the Green Islands of the Ocean, of whom nothing was afterwards heard'.[61] Whether this was rooted in any genuine, early tradition about Áedán's warband going in search of supernatural abodes in the sea, *Gwerddonau Llion*, the 'Green Isles of the Ocean', is uncertain. But the idea was inspiring enough to be included by Robert Southey in his poem *Madoc* (1805), concerning another traveller famed in Welsh legend:

> *Where are the sons of Gavran? where his tribe?*
> *The faithful? following their beloved chief,*
> *They the Green Islands of the Ocean sought;*
> *Nor human tongue hath told, nor human ear,*
> *Since from the silver shores they went their way,*
> *Hath heard their fortunes.*

No surviving Irish story specifically associates Áedán with the Otherworld, but we might consider a tale whose name alone survives in the 12th century *Book of Leinster*. There is no certainty that *Echtra Aedán meic Gabráin* represents the same tradition which found its way into Welsh literary circles, or that it necessarily reflected actual historical events.[62] It does confirm, however, that Áedán's legend incorporated elements of Otherworldly adventure as well as more prosaic heroic tales. There were two specific classes of ancient Irish stories centred around travelling. *Immrama* were specifically stories of supernatural sea voyages with a strong Christian message, while *Echtrae* were definite journeys to the Otherworld, with secular and sometimes pagan undertones.[63] Among the various definitions of *Echtrae* is Duigan's: 'an expedition in quest of adventure', 'a warlike expedition, a hosting,' and a hero's journey 'to some supernatural realm'.[64] Proinsias Mac Cana also emphasises the hero's incursion into the supernatural in these tales, which can be set in various locations. Some of the stories involve an invitation into that shadowy reality and when the earthly hero is 'the aggressor in an act of heroic self-assertion' he encounters a class of inhabitants quite different to the serene inhabitants of the fairyland found in later folklore.[65] It should also be noted that *Echtrae* could also involve nautical journeys.

Beyond the possible link of Áedán's lost tale with the Welsh Triad, we can hardly guess about the details of the story. Judging from the stories about Mongán, these tales of contemporary Irishmen in Northern Britain seem to have been related to some extent in a loose type of cycle. Apart from Mongán, we can consider another ally of Áedán, Máel Umai, who fought as an ally at the battle of Degsastan and was the subject of his own lost tale, *Echtrae Mael Uma maic Baitain*.[66] We know nothing of that story either, though there is a hint about its supernatural adventure in another source which speaks of his meeting a hag in a dark cave.[67] On this slim evidence – one Irish tale title and one Welsh tale summary – there is not enough to say that the two traditions are definitely linked, although the possibility of a connection is tantalising.

Alliance with the Irish

Áedán's most conspicuous alliance with other kingdoms in Ireland was achieved at the convention of Druim Cett, traditionally placed near the beginning of his reign, but more likely to have taken place during the last decade of the 6th century. This meeting formalised an alliance between Dál Riata and the Cenél Conaill sept of the northern Uí Néill. This pact was most likely brokered by Colum Cille, who belonged to the Cenél Conaill. But, although the evidence is fragmentary, there may have been other alliances with the Cruithin. The Cruithin king Áed Dub mac Suibni (d. 588) achieved over-kingship in Ulster after the death of Dál Fiatach's Báetán mac Cáirill. At some stage Áed had presented himself in Dál Riata, on the island of Tiree, attempting to be consecrated as a priest following the result of some severe domestic tumult in Ireland. His presence in Áedán's realm signifies good relations on a secular level at least, as his presence must have been sanctioned by the rulers of Dál Riata, whatever the misgivings of the family of Iona concerning him. Adomnán describes Colum Cille denying the consecration and he furthermore characterises Áed in the lowest possible terms. Adomnán's character assassination of Áed is rooted in his slaying of the Uí Néill king Diarmait mac Cerbaill in the year 563, as well as reservations about his morals and return to secular rule after ordination.[68]

Whether or not Áed was in exile in the Hebrides for an extended period as a penitent after slaying Diarmait, his use as a potential ally back in Ireland would hardly have been overlooked by Áedán. Iona's dislike of this Cruithin king was based in part on a fear of an alliance between that people and Dál Riata which may have jeopardised the agreement between the Uí Néill and Dál Riata that Colum Cille carefully constructed in the same period. The fact that there are also traces of co-operation between Áedán and the subsequent Cruithin king is interesting, though again the information is minimal and should be treated with caution. Áed Dub's successor as Cruithin ruler was Fíachnae Lurgan ('Longshanks', also known as Fíachnae Finn). During his reign, which extended for several decades (he died in 626), the Dál Fiatach do not seem to have been able to seriously challenge his authority until near the end. The fact that Fíachnae was responsible for Áed Dub's death was beside the point for Áedán. There has been a recent suggestion that Áedán mac Gabráin promoted Fíachnae's rise to power and acted as overlord of the Cruithin states in Ulster.[69] If this was the case he would have been the only king of Dál Riata to have achieved this status. For all Fíachnae's longevity in power, his fame did not match the legendary prominence of his son, Mongán. The apparent Cruithin interest in Man, via links to Manannán considered above, would not have meant that either Fíachnae or his famous son actively campaigned with Áedán there, for the early 580s would be too early for either to be militarily active. But their involvement in Áedán's campaign in northern England in the following decade seems plausible.

Chapter 5

The Convention of Druim Cett

As has been told us by men that knew of it, the man of memorable life
[Colum Cille] cured the ailments of various sick people, by invocation of the
name of Christ, during those days which, when he went to the conference
of kings, he remained for a short time in the ridge of Céte.[1]

The second record of Áedán mac Gabráin's presence in Ireland is when he met the king of the northern Uí Néill at a major summit at a place named Druim Cett in the north of Ulster. There are few certainties about this momentous event, or about how or why it was arranged, though the meeting is recorded earlier and more fully than Áedán's meeting with the Dál Fiatach king. The established view is that this was a conference of kings and clerics which took place early in Áedán's reign (the mid-570s). This is based on a few brief annal entries, a scatter of mentions by Adomnán, and later legendary material about the event. The *Annals of Ulster* notes only that the convention was attended by Colum Cille and his kinsman, the Uí Néill ruler Áed, Ainmuirech's son. The *Annals of Clonmacnoise* pointedly link the event with the accession of Áed to the kingship in 587. It describes the meeting being between him and Áedán, along with spiritual and temporal nobles from both Scotland and Ireland. Colum Cille and his fellow monk from Iona, Baíthéne mac Brénaind, were noted as attending.[2] We can at least presume there were many other important lords and priests present.

A thick coating of legend has resulted in us only having a dim view of Druim Cett and its historical significance. The truth is, as historian James E. Fraser admits, that we only have sparse facts about this 'shadowy summit'.[3] Many sources agree that there were three major topics of discussion there: the status of the poetic class in Ireland, discussion on the imprisonment of a royal prince being held by king Áed and the status of Dál Riata in relation to other territories in the north of Ireland. The position of Dál Riata would obviously have been a prime concern for the rulers of that kingdom based in Britain. The discussion might have centred around whether Dál Riata should have been subject or pay tribute to the Uí Néill king, or indeed the Ulaid, and if so, what should that tribute be? And should it be from the Irish part of the kingdom alone, or from the overseas part also? Although some historians maintain there is no conclusive evidence that Dál Riata was the sole or main reason for the meeting, it's probable that the issue of the kingdom's status was an important and relevant concern that would be discussed between the kings present.[4] The anomalous duality of Dál Riata and the acknowledgment of the power of Áedán mac Gabráin were factors which had to be addressed within the framework of the competing kingdoms of the northern Gaelic world.

John Bannerman makes a strong case emphasising the apparently groundbreaking format of the conference, comparing it with the type of high level meeting prevalent several centuries later, termed the *rígdál*, which was a summit between kings. Irish sources also describe this type of meeting as *mórdail*, a great assembly. Adomnán confirms that Druim Cett was in the same class by calling it *condictum regum*, 'a discussion among kings'.[5] As stated already, the meeting between Áedán and Báetán of the Ulaid may have been along similar lines and took place some years earlier.

None of the three supposed discussion items at Druim Cett are inherently implausible, but we might suspect the recorded agenda has been influenced by the tendency in Irish tradition to group things in triads. Uncritical acceptance of the sources has obscured the fact that we know very little about the actual discussions.[6] This has led some historians to state that we cannot recover 6th century reality from the available evidence and that it is fruitless to attempt to do so.[7] Most of the written accounts focus on the attendance of Colum Cille of Iona, to the extent that secular leaders present are treated as minor characters who only merit mention through their interaction with the saint. Áedán mac Gabráin, a major player at the convention, is barely mentioned in any source. Even his later prominence in other Irish literature did not guarantee him a place in the tales about the Druim Cett. His absence from these legends could also be due to the fact that the main issue involving him, the position of Irish Dál Riata in relation to the other powers in north-east Ireland, had ceased to be relevant to later historians in Ireland because that territory lost its distinct identity by the time written accounts were compiled. If Áedán can't be described as a ghost at the feast, he remains a shadowy presence at the conference.

Even the documents centred around Colum Cille don't give us a clear picture of his activity at Druim Cett. Adomnán, writing in the late 7th century, may have omitted much that was currently remembered about the convention not only because it was irrelevant to his intention of magnifying the saintliness of his subject, but because the fame of the meeting was so great that he had no need to describe it in detail.[8] The first two mentions in Adomnán's *Life* are asides dealing with the saint's encounter with two royal princes, Domnall and Scandlán, at Druim Cett, but tell us nothing about the main purpose of the meeting. A further anecdote around the event describes how people flocked to the saint to be healed of various ailments. There is another incident when Colum Cille is described as being in the company of fellow cleric Comgall after the conference in another location. Crucially, the latter story also incidentally gives us firm early evidence that the conference was a royal meeting between Áed mac Ainmuirech and Áedán mac Gabráin.[9]

The Date and Location of the Convention

The long-held acceptance of the date in the annals for the conference in 574–575 has skewed the sequence of events involving Áedán and the other major dynasts in Ireland and the north of Britain. On the basis that a later date better reflects the chronology of the royal participants, many modern writers now accept the event actually took place around the year 590 soon after the senior king at the meeting, Áed mac Ainmuirech, became king.[10] He was from the same Cenél Conaill kindred of the northern Uí Néill as Colum Cille. The probable alliance agreed at the meeting between the Uí Néill and Dál Riata, brokered by Iona, was a defensive and strategic pact against the other major power block in Northern Ireland, the Ulaid, whose king Báetán mac Cáirill, held Dál Riata in tributary status until his death in 581, as seen in the previous chapter. Although there is no certainty about the site of the royal gathering, local people believe that it was convened at the low mound which stands in Roe Park just south of the modern settlement of Limvady, County Derry, close to the north coast. Also known as the Mullagh, or Daisy Hill, it was a conspicuous feature in the landscape, in the territory of northern Uí Néill. (More precisely, it was in Glinne Geimin, territory of the Cianachta, part of the wider territory of Cenél nEogain, in the valley of the Roe.) Such was the significance of this event that an annual commemoration was held at the site until the mid-17th century.[11]

The Three Subjects of Debate and the Two Cranes

The longest account of the gathering is in the preface of the eulogy to Colum Cille, *Amra Choluimb Chille*.[12] The main body of the *Amra* may contain material which is very early and sponsored by the saint's royal cousin Áed mac Ainmuirech following his death in 597. However, the composition itself contains very little which is relevant to Druim Cett and the preface was written in the early 11th century and is not a reliable historical record. In the preface the first issue discussed at the conference was the release of Scandlán, son of Colmáin, king of Osraige (Ossary), whom Áed was holding as a hostage to levy power over that southern kingdom. The second item was the threatened expulsion of the poets of Ireland. Their powers had allegedly become oppressive to the rulers obliged to host them because of the sheer numbers contained in their travelling retinues. An *ollamh* (master poet) had a retinue of thirty followers and it was rumoured that there were 1200 poets active in Ireland. The third cause of debate is the peace-making between the men of Scotland and Ireland with regard to Dál Riata.

Despite Colum Cille's reputation and blood relationship to Áed, his appearance at this gathering was not welcomed by all, according to one tradition. While one version of the *Amra*'s preface says that the saint's entry to the assembly was marked by some people there standing to greet him and a rush of poets eager to make music for him, another version says that the only person to rise was the king's son Domnall. All the others assembled there stayed seated, under the influence of Áed, who did not wish to discuss the matter of Scandlán or the poets. Colum Cille then blessed Domnall, who was cowardly up till this incident, but afterwards became a worthy king.

Adomnán mentions that Domnall was brought for a blessing by the saint by his foster-parents at Druim Cett. After learning his identity Colum Cille foretold that he would outlive all his brothers and be a famous king, living to a peaceful old age and would die in his own bed.[13] The saint's blessing on the boy displeased the queen, his step-mother, and she reproached Colum Cille, accusing him of being *corr*, 'crooked'. He then answered her, 'You too may be *corr*.' The second meaning of *corr* is 'crane' or 'heron', and this pun had the magical effect of instantly transforming the queen into this bird. Nothwithstanding this astonishing event the queen's maid unwisely began to revile the saint and she too was transformed into a crane. The saint ordained that the transformed women remain as birds at Druim Cett until doomsday. And from that time, one storyteller related, they were spoken of as the 'Two Cranes of Druim Cett'.

There might be something more sinister at play than punning in this humorous transformation tale. According to a gloss on an ancient law tract the term *corrguinecht* described a ritual practice where someone stood on one foot, with one eye open, and chanted a satirical verse in order to harm an opponent.[14] Such a blatantly incantory, pagan practice lies beneath the story of Colum Cille cursing the queen. We can recall that Colum Cille engaged in a fierce magical battle against the magician uncle of the Pictish king Bridei in that king's own royal fortress. It also brings to mind the three-day magic retreat on Hinba the saint engaged in while considering Áedan's accession.

The 17th century historian Geoffrey Keating made use of the versions of the story from the preface of the *Amra* and may also have been inspired by local legend which associated the continuing presence of nesting cranes or herons at a site near the location of the conference. Herons occupy a prominent place in Irish folklore and legend, but the suggestion that there was an early significant connection between the saint and this bird is probably doubtful, even if Scottish Gaelic folklore may remember a faint association connecting the saint with these birds.[15] The birds also assumed a sinister reputation in later Hebridean folklore.[16]

The Poets of Ireland

Colum Cille's reputed support of the *filid*, the poetic class in Ireland, may have given rise to the development of the tale that he intervened on their behalf at the conference. The *Amra* preface mentions the cleric responding poetically to the poets and addressing their concerns during the conference.

The poets were deeply ingrained in the social structure and the provincial and local rulers had a responsibility to support them. The privileged class of *áes dána*, 'men of art', had various classes and functions and they held enormous influence as transmitters of *senchas* ('lore, or knowledge'). The poet was *fili*, a 'seer', and had quasi-supernatural attributes. The various grades of poets, frequently accompanied by followers, and the economic burden to support these entourages was just one aspect of the burden they imposed on the noble classes. The Irish law tracts designate a number of classes of professional men who were the custodians of traditional material and the higher echelons of this literary class do seem to have supported, in some cases, a substantial retinue. Should the lord or king fail to show appropriate welcome to the poets, or incur their displeasure otherwise, he might be subjected to their satire. This was not merely a matter of rebuke leading to a loss of public face, but could lead to physical consequences, the result of an ill-wishing intent, a quasi-magical curse which was a known and feared weapon. There was a selection of ill will which *filid* could impose upon anyone who crossed them. At the sinister, darker end of the magical rebuke was *glám dícenn*, 'endless satire'. It was a thick-skinned king indeed who could flagrantly offend a poet in his own hall. Results of satire could be astonishing: 'they made three blisters in the face of any whom they satirized...' says the *Lebar Brecc*.[17] Conversely, if the satire was unjustified, those defects might immediately be inflicted upon the poet himself.[18]

The *Amra*'s preface emphasises these dangerous effects of satire, specifically the power of poets to cause ulcers and deformity on the subject of his contempt, if indeed he did not immediately die. There may have been growing dissent between the poets and the royal sponsors they preyed upon for some time, but matters seem to have come to a head when a group of them swarmed upon Ibar of Cinntracht, a place belonging to the Ulster king. When they were threatened with expulsion they appealed to Colum Cille himself and he brought some of them in person to the conference.[19] Colum Cille defended the 'wise men' of Ireland, but their overall numbers and the composition of each retinue were reduced.

The dark dangers of the skills of the *filid* were emphasised when Colum Cille became consumed with pride when he heard their praise of him. This prompted his companion to rebuke the saint, who hid his head under his cloak and repented. When he raised his head again a great mist burst forth from it and the crowd of devils which had gathered departed again.[20] The saint's actions at Druim Cett were immediately praised by the chief poet Dallán Forgaill who began to compose a poem in his praise, but Colum Cille promptly warned him not to complete this eulogy, *Amra Choluimb Chille*, until after his death, which he did. The complexity of the finished poem, with its glosses and prefaces, also attained a quasi magical quality in later centuries, giving heavenly guarantees to those who faithfully repeated it in its entirety.

Colum Cille's safeguarding of the poets here supposedly ensured that a great mass of traditional Irish native material was passed down the centuries and saved from oblivion. An effort to safeguard their remarkable cultural importance was also made by a contemporary Cruithin king who was an ally of Áedán. The Dál nAraide king Fíachnae mac Báetáin (also known as Fíachnae Lurgan) gave official refuge to the poets when they were being threatened with banishment by Áed. This tradition hints that there was Cruthin involvement in the treaty arrangements fixed at Druim Cett even though there is no official reference to their involvement. Fíachnae's sponsorship of the poets may have safeguarded the preservation of the remarkable Ulster cycle of literature.[21] It is also no coincidence that both Fíachnae and his son Mongán feature heavily in legendary tales. Some of these contemporary poets in the Ulster-Dál Riata zone may have begun the formative process of ensuring Áedán's place in legend.

The Royal Prisoner Scandlán

The circumstances around Scandlán's imprisonment are mired in folklore. He was apparently held at the court of Áed as a guarantee for tribute from Osraige and may have been a child at the time. That this northern king was able to exert power over this distant territory shows the extent of his authority. Adomnán, in his *Life* of the saint, states that the holy man comforted the prisoner, who was held in chains, but does not make any claims that the saint attempted to negotiate his release. The saint promised the boy that he would return to rule over his own kingdom for thirty years. But he does not state that the royal captive was released immediately via the intercession of the saint.[22] The preface to the *Amra* states that Colum Cille did try to petition Áed for the prisoner's release, but the king would not free him. This garbled version appears to be contradicted by another place in the preface which states that he was indeed released, 'and he bowed down to the gospel and he gave him eight score of plough-oxen. . . and therefore eight score plough-oxen are still owed [as tribute] to the congregation of Iona, by the [men of] Osraige'.[23]

The *Lebar Brecc* says that Colum Cille attempted to have him released at the end of a year, or that an alternative hostage should take his place. But Áed refused and had an impregnable enclosure made around the unfortunate prince.[24] One version of the *Amra* preface has the royal being liberated amid thunder and lightning and being magically transported to meet the saint, with whom he has a lengthy conversation after satisfying his prodigious thirst.[25] Whatever we make of the fascinating complications of the Scandlán tale, its supernatural accretions cast doubt on its historical legitimacy.

Later Re-tellings

> *Righthandwise went they*
> *Colum, Áedán, the poets,*
> *To the meeting where Áed was,*
> *In Druim Ceat of fair heroes.*
> *Thrice four mighty kings,*
> *Aed the name of each high one,*
> *Came to holy Druim of poetry,*
> *Round about Áed and Áedán.*[26]

Later Irish scholars and tale-tellers turned the bare bones of historical conference into a complex, multi-layered legend. There was still great interest in Druim Cett in the 16th and 17th centuries, which is all the more intriguing that it was a political meeting rather than a more spectacular event such as a battle. Manus O'Donnell's *Beatha Colaim Chille* was written in 1532. He informs us that Áed encamped for four months with a great host of laymen and clerics from Ireland, making laws to protect Ireland from the men of Scotland who were making war against them.[27]

Colum Cille solicited Áed to guarantee peace with Áedán, but the Irish king would not guarantee this. Manus gives various reasons for the saint coming to the meeting, including the suggestion that the Irish begged him to attend so he could bless their churchmen and common people. The commonly known legend that Colum Cille had sworn never to return to his native Ireland is also woven into the narrative. To keep faith with this oath the holy man strapped sods of Scottish turf beneath his feet and covered his face and eyes completely so that he could not see his native land. The question of the troublesome poets is also mentioned. They are said to have aggrieved Áed by mocking the elaborate golden brooch that he wore. Details of the royal hostage Scandlán are elaborated. The royal prisoner was enclosed in a doorless hut and fed a starvation diet and one drip of water daily. For further security (and to ramp up the folkloric drama), he was bound by twelve fetters and chains and guarded by fifty men. Colum Cille asked Áed for the prince's release, but he was freed by an angel and visited the saint after the conference in Derry.

The royal prince's plight forms part of the theme of antagonism between Áed and Colum Cille. Hearing of his approach towards the meeting, one tale has Áed refusing to meet him, which is again reminiscent of the manner in which the Pictish king Bridei son of Maelchon refuses to recognise the arrival of Colum Cille at his fortress. Colum Cille's dominance over his royal cousin is reinforced by miracles and prophecy. When the king's daughter drowned he beseeched Colum Cille to restore her to life, which was accomplished. He then quizzed Colum Cille about how many kings and lords of Ireland had entered heaven without a spell in purgatory and was answered, but with the assurance he would not do likewise unless he performed many good deeds and did penance. The third request, that he would gain victory over the Leinstermen he was at war with, was flatly refused by the saint on the basis that Colum Cille's own mother sprung from that people.[28]

Returning to events at Druim Cett, Áed vowed to severely punish any of his retinue who welcomed his holy relative. Áed's son Conall made the error of stirring up the rabble and the party from Iona were assaulted with stones and earth. Colum Cille decreed a curse against the prince, telling his followers to strike their bells and prophesising that Conall would never be king. This was fulfilled and he became known as Conall *Clogach* ('of the bells'). He was deprived of his senses and his memory, madness making him ineligible for kingship. To add insult to injury, he was only spared from his self-inflicted insanity in those brief times when he went to the toilet.

In contrast to Conall, Áed's other son Domnall greets the saint on his arrival and is rewarded with the promise of an extended kingship. The queen, hearing that her son Conall has been cursed and her hated foster son Domnall blessed, sent a message to the king, saying she would never agree with him again if the 'crane cleric' Colum Cille gets honour or friendship from him. Then follows the incident where the holy man turns both queen and her servant into cranes, which birds remained there as evidence of the miracle. The abbot was received by the king and they entered into a long debate regarding the treatment of the poets of Ireland. The chief of the poets, Dallán Forgaill, conversed with the saint and then came the incident where the saint was enchanted by the praise of the poets, rebuked by his monk Baíthéne, before being freed from the spell. The antagonism of Áed towards his close relative Colum Cille in later legend has no basis, as far as we know, in fact, and follows the pattern of animosity followed by friendship written into other records of the saint's association with kings.

The Position of Dál Riata in the *Beatha*

There may be little of historical substance we can usefully extract from this 17th century source. It seems clear that even the memory of the Irish territory of Dál Riata has been confused, if not altogether lost. According to the text of the *Beatha*, the dispute between the 'men of Ireland (*Erin*)' and the 'men of Scotland (*Alba*)' came because the former claimed that the land – presumably Irish Dál Riata – belonged to them and they were owed tribute for it. The parties asked Colum Cille for his judgement, but he deferred to Colmán, who was destined to give that judgement.

> Then Colmán gave judgement in this wise: The men of Erin should have rent and tribute and hosting; for rent and hosting be according to the land...

> *Hosting ever with territory,*
> *Ships across the sea with lasting tribute*
> *(My wise mouthed judgement without flaw)*
> *And compensation to kinsmen.*

And to the men of Alba he adjudged their ships and a certain compensation from them to their fellows, because they were of one stock. And whatever hosting or expedition of the men of Alba should come to Erin, the men of Dál Riata should feed them and convoy them, except they gat other help.

Then Colum Cille praised the judgement that Colmán mac Comgellan had given, and all praised it. And thus the prophecy of Colum Cille was fulfilled, touching all these things. And the poet hath verified it in this quatrain:

> Colmán mac Comgellan, without concealement,
> Gave kingly judgement concerning the Dál Riata,
> For across the Irish Sea shall come
> To the king of Erin tribute.[29]

The meaning of the passage is not absolutely clear. Possibly, so many centuries after the event, there was forgetfulness in Ireland concerning the fact that there was an Irish Dál Riata. It may be tempting to read between the lines to envisage a scenario where Áedán and the Dál Riata delegation were throwing off the traditional legal position they had towards the Ulaid king and transferring it wholesale to the Uí Néill monarch, but the later texts do not justify this. As if to confirm that the bulk of the *Beatha* account is full scale folklore, it follows a chronology whereby Colum Cille's journey to and from Druim Cett is book-ended by legendary encounters. On the voyage there his ship was beset by a sea monster which threw the ocean into tumult and threatened to destroy it. When the creature opened its huge mouth to swallow the ship, the saint's followers begged him to intervene. But Colum Cille said it was rather the job of another holy man to save them, Senach the Old Smith. Instantaneously, in Ireland, Senach cast a red hot iron ball through the air so that it slew the monster. Colum Cille then asked God to send the creature's corpse to the place where his ship would land in Ireland. It came ashore on the strand of Lough Foyle, and here the boat came to land. The iron ball was extracted from the body of the beast and used to forge three holy bells. The saint piloted his boat up the non-navigable River Roe and came to rest near Druim Cett at a place afterwards named Cabhán an Curraigh, 'Slope of the Currach'. On his way back from the conference, the saint's boat sailed near the whirlpool of Coire Brecain (Corryvreckan), between Jura and Scarba, and there the sea threw up the bones of Brecain son of Maine, son of Niall of the Nine Hostages, who had been drowned there long before. Through the spirit of prophecy, the saint recognised whose remains they were and prayed, so that he would obtain the peace of heaven, saying, 'You are friendly to me, old Brecain.[30]

Geoffrey Keating's Account

Geoffrey Keating's 17th century account of Druim Cett begins with the issue of the the poets of Ireland and the author states that nearly a third of the men in Ireland belonged to the poetic order and they imposed themselves on their hosts from Samhain to Beltane.[31] The final straw of their demands, for Áed at least, was when one band of poets demanded as a gift the golden dagger which he wore as an heirloom from previous kings. He drove them out from his domains and banished them to Irish Dál Riata. After a summary of the issues concerning the imprisonment of Scandlán and the kingdom of Dál Riata, Keating relates how Colum Cille proceeded to the convention with a large company of subordinate clergy. The folk tale of the cranes (or herons) was evidently still believed in his day, since he tells us that he has heard from many people that two herons are usually seen at the ford near Druim Cett.

During Colum Cille's audience with the king he asked for the retention of the poets in Ireland, the liberation of Scandlán, and the recognition of rights for Dál Riata. Colum Cille then asked the king for respite for Dál Riata and that he should not visit Alba in order to exact tribute, 'For you have a right only to a head-rent from them and a levy of forces on land and sea.' When Áed denied this too he was told that Dál Riata will have a respite from him forever.

The battle lines between king and cleric having been drawn, Colum Cille withdrew from the convention (which lasted a year and a month) along with Áedan. That night an angel freed Scandlán and the prince gave a tribute which was due to the successors of Colum Cille by Osraige in perpetual thanks for his freedom. Keating's information about Druim Cett tails off into a description of Colum Cille's saintliness and ancestry and unfortunately we hear no more about the circumstances of the conference.

The Position of Dál Riata and the Northern Irish Kingdoms

Even if we accept that one main topic of the convention involved the position of Dál Riata in relation to the other Irish territories, it still gives us little context for the conference. The primary purpose of the event may have been to formalise an alliance between the northern Uí Néill and Dál Riata in the face of possible threats from other kingdoms and possibly to agree the status of the Irish part of Áedán's kingdom. Although the situation of Dál Riata was an issue which may have been misunderstood by later writers, its position straddling two different countries was a matter which needed to be clarified.[32] If it is accepted that Áedán indeed attended the conference with Áed mac Ainmuirech, it must surely follow that discussion was made about obligations due to Áed as the *de facto* most powerful dynast of the province.

The later version of the supposed 'main' event at the conference suggests that Dál Riata in Ireland would be subject to the over-lordship of the Uí Néill king, which would give him an important extension of control against the Ulster kings in the east. Military service would be given to him from this territory, but possibly *muir coblach*, ship service, would stay with Áedán and his territory in Britain, as would tribute. This is one inference based on some of the descriptions of the conference and favoured by the scholar John Bannerman. However, Máire Herbert has argued that this gives too much credence to the late information and the most that can be said about any agreement between the kings at the meeting was that there was an alliance brokered between them.[33] Despite the understandable caution about depending on the much later preface to the *Amra Choluimb Chille*, many historians would agree that questions such as the military and tributary status of Dál Riata would have been discussed at Druim Cett, even if exact outcomes regarding service and tribute are not agreed.[34] The Scottish colony in mainland Britain might theoretically be subject to the over-lordship of a king in the north of Ireland, but in practical terms the latter would only be able to enforce tribute and military services from that section of Dál Riata which was in Ireland.[35]

It was noted above that the great assembly was convened at Glinne Geimin. This territory was under control of Cenél nEogain, close to the border of the neighbouring Cruithin lands in the plain of Eilne.

A recent work has looked on this location as a clue that Áed reached an accommodation with this particular people, which would have further bolstered his strength in the region, especially if the regional accord included Dál Riata.[36] In this case, or even if the agreement was just between Áedán and Áed, the main opponent they were acting in defence against was either the Ulster king Báetan mac Cáirill, or one of his dynasty. Territorial meetings to settle disputes and conflicts came under a broad class of peace treaties between kin groups and meetings called *cairde*, already mentioned when I discussed the possibility that the meeting of Ros na Ríg was an Uí Néill response to that *cairde*, again crucially including Áedán, but on a more magnificent scale. John Bannerman pointed out that *cairde* were sometimes concluded at an *óenach*, a great secular assembly, or in the latter attested *rígdál*, a meeting between kings.[37]

Áedán's Involvement

If we think the meeting took place in 586, or shortly afterwards, Áedán may have believed it was an opportune time to regulate the future alliances of his kingdom and clarify the relationship of his own Irish territories. By this date he had seen off the powerful efforts of Báetán mac Cáirill (d. 581), the Dál Fiatach king, to impose his overlordship on Dál Riata and on the Isle of Man and maybe elsewhere. Áedán then seems to have been empowered to unleash his sons in military campaigns in southern Pictland and also had the resources to make war on the northern English. Accommodation with two successive kings of the Cruithin people in the kingdom of Dál nAraide on the eastern side of Ulster would have given Dál Riata security and a position of strength to bring to the table in discussion with the Uí Néill.

One of these Cruithin kings was Áed Dub mac Suibni. Following his murder of the Uí Néill king Diarmait mac Cerbaill he had been in exile, at least for some time, in the Hebrides.[38] His slaying of Diarmait meant he became an enemy of Iona, but he may have been a useful ally for Áedán in his attempts to subdue his foremost Irish enemies, the Dál Fiatach. Following Áed Dub's slaying in 588 by another Cruithin king, Fíachnae Lurgan, Áedán transferred support to him. The passing reference in the preface to the *Amra* suggesting Fíachnae gave shelter to the poetic class may be a clue about the involvement of this Cruithin leader in the political negotiations surrounding the conference at Druim Cett. There is no reference to Fíachnae or any other secular leader of the Cruithin being at Druim Cett, but the chief cleric in his kingdom, Comgall, seems to have been present. If Áedán was in a position of dominance over the Cruithin leadership, his place as a paramount king in direct negotiations with Áed of the Uí Néill at Druim Cett would have emphasised his authority. A source relates that the Dál Fiatach king Fíachnae mac Demmáin, nephew of Áedán's adversary Báetán, *do ghabh righi n-Ulad,* 'seized the kingship of Ulster,' in the early 7th century. Was Áedán able to achieve the same several decades earlier without the dignity of the title?

This would still be the situation, slightly modified, if the traditional date of 575 is accepted for Druim Cett. Áedán would have been smarting about accepting terms with the Dál Fiatach leader Báetán mac Cáirill at Ros na Ríg, which would need to have occurred very soon before the second meeting at Druim Cett. This scenario would have Dál Riata almost immediately reneging on any alliance imposed by the Ulaid and forging new alliances with the northern Uí Néill and possibly the Cruithin powers also. It is hard to believe that such an about face would not lead to battle in Ireland. But the only trace of possible Dál Riata-Dál Fiatach armed conflict comes after Báetán's death in 581, when Áedán attacked Man. A later date for Druim Cett also makes sense in terms of the chronology of Áed son of Ainmuirech, who ascended to wider power some years after 575. It also frees us from believing that the start of Áedán's reign was crowded with logistically difficult events.[39]

The almost complete silence concerning Áedán at the meeting is frustrating but it can be compared with the slender record of the most powerful ruler there, Áed mac Ainmuirech, whose primary role in the later literature about Druim Cett revolves around his stubborn refusal to free Scandlán mac Colmáin. Adomnán's account is crucial 7th century confirmation that Áedán was believed to be at the meeting, a corroboration of some (but not all) of the annals.[40] The conviction that the conference lasted for an extended period and that Colum Cille, Áedán and the party from Iona departed at an early stage possibly contributed to the scarcity of material about the Dál Riadan king in the later retellings about Druim Cett.[41] A long conference may point at a more complex agenda being discussed, most of which is lost to us.

Colmán and St Comgall

Little is known about the involvement of two other men at Druim Cett who must have been important contributors. One of them at least is credited with a decisive part in the most crucial matter being decided at the meeting. Colmán mac Comgellán of Dál Riata pronounced his opinion regarding the status of his own territory, saying that their expedition and their hosting should go with the men of Ireland, 'for there is hosting always with possessions of land; but their law of tribute and their tax with the men of Scotland'. Following the theme of recognising great things in children he encountered, the *Amra* preface then tells us that Colum Cille had met Colmán when a boy and foretold he would make peace between the men of Scotland and the men of Ireland.[42] The saint is stated to have brought the young man Colmán specifically to the assembly and it has been thought that he belonged to Irish Dál Riata, the land under dispute, so he could give fair judgement on the matter.[43] The grooming of Colmán for later greatness has led to the suspicion that he was acting as the mouthpiece of Colum Cille and delivering a judgment which had been formulated by the Iona faction.[44] There is scant mention of Colmán in the sources and therefore no proof that he was a representative of the Irish Dál Riata, let alone that he was a member of the learned legal class in that territory, as has been claimed.

We can tentatively trace Colum Cille's footsteps in Ireland around the time of the conference. Some of the tales which involve Scandlán place the saint in Derry following or even during the meeting Druim Cett, suggesting that he resorted to Derry, which was one of his own foundations for respite during the lengthy proceedings. Another tradition says that he founded a church at Easdara in Sligo at the time. This may point to an extended stay in Ireland by the Iona party and possibly an intinerary that had Colum Cille busying himself with other church matters between repeated attendances at the conference. There is no reason to doubt Adomnán's account that he travelled east after the close of the conference, journeying along the coastal plain in the company of St Comgall, a saint who had previously visited him in Scotland. Their leisurely passage was broken by an interlude which turned into a visionary nightmare. While the two clerics sat and relieved their thirst on the hot summer day, Colum Cille had a dark glimpse of the future and said the well they drank from would be polluted with human blood, for the headless corpse of one of his kinsman would be found in the water. He foretold that the place would be near the site of a battle (Dún Cethirn, near the present Sconce Hill), fought in the year 629.[45] The opposing sides would be his own kindred, the Uí Néill, and Comgall's own Cruithin people. Albeit that the corpse polluting the well was one of Colum Cille's own kinsmen, the Uí Néill would be victorious that day.

As one recent historian has highlighted, the message of the prophetic vision signified Colum Cille warning the succeeding generation of dynasts in the north-east of Ireland not to unstitch the civilised accord which had apparently been carefully agreed at Druim Cett.[46] Seen from the perspective of clerics writing later in the 7th century on Iona and elsewhere the apparent relapse into barbarity was seen in the repeated bloody battles which ravaged the province of Ulster in the first half of the century. The battle of Dún Cethirn, as foreseen by the saint, was a specific warning to the Cruthin people of the terrible price they would pay by not fulfilling the terms of an earlier agreed peace.

Though the records omit the participation of the Cruithin at the event, this again suggests they had a place in the discussions. But what role, if any, was played by the Cruithin there? The inferred presence of Comgall at the convention suggests there was at least high level religious representation. Comgall's monastery at Bangor on Belfast Lough was founded around 555 and was within Cruithin territory. There may have been fairly close links between the religious houses of Bangor and Iona, which is implied by Adomnán, but if so most of the fine detail of this connection has been lost.

Comgall's control extended to a number of other religious houses and he had the equivalent status to Colum Cille in his own province. The significance of the two saints being together immediately after the conference is reinforced by the route taken. Colum Cille could have left by sea immediately, embarking from Lough Foyle, but chose instead to take a longer, land route. From the site of the future battle, Colum Cille journeyed down the valley of the River Bann to Coleraine. Here he was met by a multitude of people, including the local bishop, and offered a feast in recognition of his holiness.[47] The church was deep in the heart of Cruithin territory and the abbot's conspicuous presence here reinforces the belief that he was winning hearts and minds as a result of discussions undertaken at Druim Cett and partly at least at the behest of Dál Riata. It is only a short distance from Coleraine to the sea and this presumably marks the point of departure for the Iona party.

The Aftermath of the Conference

What was really discussed at Druim Cett and what did it mean for Áedán and Dál Riata? Leaving aside the tales of captive princes and burdensome poets, we are left with the vexed area of the position of Dál Riata, the uniquely divided kingdom. This still remains a probable subject for discussion, even if we may question whether the debate centred around the tribute and service due from either or both parts of Áedán's territory. The possible decision at the conference to put the the Dál Riatan fleet, based in Britain, at the disposal of Uí Néill kings may be evidenced by 7th century events in Ulster. Some writers have insisted that the conference actually sealed and ratified the 'independence' of Dál Riata in Britain.[48] But who would it achieve independence from? Báetán of the Ulaid may have claimed sovereignty over some part of Dál Riata's British lands on the basis that they ruled Ulaid and Dál Riata in Ireland was part of Ulaid and theoretically subject to the Dál Fiatach, but was he able to enforce his over-lordship overseas? One historian has detected a family link between the Dál Riata sept of Cenél nÓengusa and the Dál Fiatach.[49] Similarly, we have the record of Uí Néill activity among the Western Isles in 568, so they may have had a continuing presence there. Even the Cruithin king Fíachnae mac Báetáin is reputed to have extended rulership to some part of Britain, though admittedly the source for this is a folk tale rather than a solid source.[50] It might suggest an interest in North Britain by his dynasty, even if he was not able to achieve any kind of territorial dominance there.

In the decade following the convention, several of its major attendees were either dead or in altered circumstances. The great Colum Cille succumbed to death in 597 and his successor as abbot of Iona, Baíthéne, died around three years later. Áed mac Ainmuirech was slain in battle by a king of Leinster the year after Colum Cille departed and was succeeded as king of the northern Uí Néill by Colmán Rímid of the Cenél nEógain. For Áedán mac Gabráin, the last ten years of the the century were different. There was a stepping up of his military activity in the 590s that contrasts with the sparse record of his early reign. His warbands were sent on a major campaign against the southern Picts and he also commanded enough resources to attack the new power in North Britain, the English kingdom named Bernicia which would grow into one part of the mighty realm of Northumbria.

It might be wondered why Áedán did not extend his military ambition to mainland Ireland, especially if we suspect that he was in a position to exert authority over some of the Cruithin territory in Ulster. Prudence may have played a part in his decision to avoid entanglement in the complex territorial power play inNorthern Ireland. But his absence here may also have been a condition imposed upon him by the Northern Uí Néill, who would not have been keen to accommodate such a formidable, but unpredictable, dynast on its own doorstep. Whether that was the case or not, the alliance between the Uí Néill and Dál Riata wouldlast for several decades, only to be fatally undone by the military choices of Áedán's grandson Domnall Brecc, who ventured into the fatal waters of Ireland and paid the price for it.

Participants at the Convention of Druim Cett

Áedán mac Gabráin, king of Dál Riata in Britain and Ireland.

Áed son of Ainmirech. Ainmuirech was Colum Cille's first cousin. Áed was king of Ailech, from the Cenél Conaill kindred, part of the northern Uí Néill. He died in the 598.

Baíthéne mac Brénaind, monk of Iona. Successor of Colum Cille as abbot. Died 600.

Colmán mac Comgellan. Possible member of the Dál Riata in Ireland who gave judgement on the relationship between the kingdom and the over-king in Ireland.

Colum Cille, abbot of Iona.

Comgall mac Setna. Irish saint, contemporary and friend of Colum Cille. His major foundation was Bangor.

Dallán mac Forgaill. Poet and composer of the *Amra Choluimb Chille.*

Domnall mac Áed (Domnall II). He was high king from 628 until his death in 642. Among his victories was his defeat of Congal Cáech at the battle of Mag Rath in 637, where Áedán's grandson Domall Brecc was on the losing side.

Scandlán mac Colmáin. Son of a king of Osraige who died in the year 607. Scandlán himself became king around 613 and died in 644.

Alleged Participants at the Convention of Druim Cett

The *Amra* says that twelve kings and twelve bishops attended the convention of Druim Cett. Every one of the kings was named Áed. The fact that there were a number of contemporary rulers with that name in Ireland does not lessen the suspicion that all attended.

John Keating's list of twelve royal attendees is also dubious. It includes Illand, son of the captive Scandlán, plus other later figures such as Congal Cennmagair, who died in 710.

The names of the parties from Irish and Scottish Dál Riata and the various Irish kingdoms represented are mostly unknown.

Chapter 6

Campaigns Against the Picts

The people known as the Picts only gained that collective name from the Romans, as far as we know, in the late 3rd century AD. We don't know whether the people referred to applied that title (which may mean something like 'the Painted Ones') to themselves, or whether it was a nickname imposed on them. Roman contact and pressure may have had something to do with the apparent unification of the tribes north of the Forth-Clyde line. In the 2nd century the Romans noted sixteen distinct tribes in the area now called Scotland, including non-Pictish areas, but most of these were subsumed in larger groups. Only one grouping, called the Maetae, who were mentioned at the start of the 3rd century, allegedly maintained their tribal identity and surprisingly crop up again as Áedán's military enemies in the late 6th century.

Whatever the peoples of northern and eastern Scotland called themselves, we know that they spoke a similar form of Celtic (P Celtic) to the Britons in the rest of the island, rather than the Gaelic (Q Celtic) which the Irish spoke. There are traditions of Irish incursions and possibly settlement in eastern Scotland in the centuries before the settlement of Scots in Dál Riata, but the stories are not secure enough to be treated as historical. Similarly, the tales and clues which link Áedán and his father Gabráin to specific areas within Pictland are unsound as evidence, but remain intriguing. We do know that Áedán conducted an operation in Orkney in 580 or 581 and is credited with at least two battles in mainland Pictland more than a decade later, but the motivation for his aggression in each case is not apparent. Another subject of uncertainty is whether any of Áedán's sons, or other descendants in the 7th century, were able to rule any part of Pictland. There is some evidence that they fought there and may have attempted to claim territory, but again it is not conclusive.

The relationship between Áedán mac Gabráin and his Pictish neighbours also has to be viewed through the later lens of later Scottish state perception. After a fluctuating balance of power for several hundred years, marked by periods of intense aggression, the Scots and Picts united in a kingdom which would later be called Alba. Pictish language and identity quickly died following the union of leadership achieved by Áedán's descendant Cináed mac Ailpin in the mid 9th century. The union of peoples came to be seen as a takeover, with lurid Irish tales celebrating a massacre of Pictish nobility at Scone. To support the claim of righteous dominance over the Picts, later writers invoked powerful ancestral figures, such as Áedán himself. It is possible that Cináed's supporters consciously fused the conquering military traditions of Áedán with the aspirations of Cináed.[1] Ninth century propagandists supporting Cináed would have been aware of Áedán mac Gabráin's place in the annals and in Adomnán's *Life* of Colum Cille. Despite this fame and his repeated incursions into different parts of Pictish territory, there is no real evidence that Áedán's aim was to permanently occupy that land. His campaigns were not motivated by any national or ethnic aim as an 'Irish' or 'Scottish' ruler. Rather, they were motivated by desire for wealth, fame and power, the common aspirations of a successful Dark Age king.

The probably 10th century *Tripartite Life of St Patrick* imagines an encounter in 5th century north-east Ireland between the saint and the ancestors of the Cenél nGabráin. Patrick enters the land of Dál Riata and is greeted by the twelve sons of the ruler Erc. Fergus (noted elsewhere as the first king of them to rule in Britain) approaches the cleric and announces that, if his brother would respect him in dividing his land, he would offer that land to Patrick. The saint foretells that he will be king, and, 'The kings in this country and over Fortrenn shall be from thee forever. And this was fulfilled by Áedán mac Gabráin, who took [the throne of] Scotland by force.'[2] Fortriu or Fortrenn was, until recently, viewed as a southern Pictish province centred on Strathearn, but is now generally believed to have been in northern Pictland. Irish writers sometimes regarded the province name as being synonymous with the whole of Pictland. The story serves to legitimise the right of the Irish settlers to the bulk of the land which later became Scotland and it also dynamically links the medieval line of Gaelic kings of Alba with noble and notable ancestors such as Fergus Mór and Áedán mac Gabráin. The special sancity of the royal segment founded by Fergus is also noted in a prelude incident in the *Tripartite Life* when the less enlightened other sons of Erc steal the horses of St Patrick. He summarily relegates their descendants by saying, 'Your offspring shall serve the offspring of your brethren forever.'[3]

We have already seen that there are traditions of Áedán associated with the the upper Forth area, which may have been Pictish, and other traditions placing his father Gabrán further east, conquering Gowrie in Perthshire. Leaving aside Scottish settlement or incursion on the upper Forth or in Perthshire, Áedán's geographical interest in Pictland was split into three distinct areas: Orkney, Circenn (present day Angus) and a territory around modern Stirling. Military events in the latter two areas may possibly be part of an extended campaign or strategy, but the Orkney mission was an isolated one. Áedán's relationship with the Picts needs to be seen in context of what we know about the Pictish leadership during his reign. Bridei mac Maelchon ruled for thirty years, from around 554 to 584, a comparable length to Áedán's own reign.

Bridei's reputation was known to the Venerable Bede, via the tradition that he sanctioned the settlement of Colum Cille and his Irish monks on the island of Iona:

Columba came to Britain when Bridius the son of Meilochon, a most powerful king, had been ruling over the Picts for over eight years. Columba turned them to the faith of Christ by his words and example and so received the island of Iona from them in order to establish a monastery there.[4]

Bede's statement, which he may have had from the Picts themselves, runs contrary to the assertion that Iona was gifted to the incoming saint by Conall son of Comgall, the ruler of the Irish colony in Britain.[5] Whether this means that one statement is false, or that Bridei was in effect the over-king of the northern part of Dál Riata at least, is unknown. Even if it was wishful thinking on the Pictish part to have the gift of a southern Hebridean island in their power, Bridei's presence was close enough and large enough to cause a concern. The *Annals of Tigernach* record two items in one entry which may be related to the year 559:

The death of Gabran, Domangart's son, king of Scotland. Flight of the Scots before Bridei, Maelchon's son, king of the Picts.[6]

We do not know if the two items are directly linked, but we may strongly suspect that they are. The inauspicious entry is the first which notices this Irish colony in North Britain. There seems to be an inference here that Bridei was the aggressor, but whether that means he entered the territory of the Scots or violently repelled them when they entered Pictish lands is unknown. Whether or not Bridei was responsible for his father's death, he was still a forceful reality who had to be accommodated when Áedán himself became king in 574. But there was no meeting or military clash between the two rulers that we are aware of. All we have are encounters between Bridei and Colum Cille, related by Adomnán. Adomnán does not say that the saint converted the powerful warlord to Christianity. The Irish saint's aims were freeing Irish slaves and asking Bridei to underwrite the safety of Irish monks on Orkney.[7]

It is possible that Áedán's expedition to Orkney was also connected with guaranteeing Irish rights and expanding his influence in Pictish territory. Áedán's journey to Orkney is recorded by the *Annals of Ulster*.[8] This military campaign stands apart from the rest of Áedán's other, often wide ranging ventures. Áedán may have been acting on behalf of Bridei as an agent to force a recalcitrant regional underling back into line. Bridei's authority was perhaps a template for Áedán. The Picts appear to have achieved, or were aiming to achieve, a unified kingship ahead of all the other northern peoples.

Bridei kept hostages at his court from the Orkney ruler, a standard safeguard to keep an underling in line, but their arrangement may have deteriorated.[9] Such a successful raid would have magnified Áedán's fame far and wide. Orkney's impressive place in prehistory may have left a residue of renown which lingered through the post-Roman period. While the islands were not a legendary place of wealth and magnificence, their plunder would still have bolstered Áedán's reputation. The reflected glory would have augmented the integrity of his warband also, though whether they were able to share in any spoil, such as slaves, from the mission is unknown.

Summary of the Battles

Relations between Dál Riata and the Picts remain a blank following the death of Áedán's father. There is no mention of Picts in the reign of his cousin and predecessor, Conall, whose reign started in 558. But there are traces of religious contact between Colum Cille and the Picts who ruled around the River Tay, as already mentioned. The Irish annals record the death of a Pictish ruler named Cennalath (or Cendalaeth) around the year 580. His death is unlikely to be linked to Áedán's action in Orkney. Another source states that 'Galam Cennalath shared Bridei's kingdom for one year.'[10] Different sources credit him with a short reign length. Little further can be gathered about this king, though Margaret Anderson thought that Cennalath looked like an Irish epithet, meaning something like 'with parti-coloured head', possibly a reference to a facial birth-mark?[11] The exact situation in southern Pictland in this period cannot now be easily discerned. Áedán's two battles in the mainland territory of Pictland are placed toward the end of his career, in the 590s, and both had uncertain results for Dál Riata. There is a chance that these battles have been confused and the campaign was more convoluted. There is conflicting evidence about them.

The Irish annals variously record the series of battles in the 580s and 590s as follows, excluding the entries which specifically mention war in England and relate to a campaign which resulted in the battle of Degsastan in 603. The first two entries are recorded similarly in the *Annals of Ulster* (*AU*) and the *Annals of Tigernach* (*AT*):

582. Battle of Manonn, in which Áedán mac Gabráin was the victor.
590. Battle of Leithreid (Leithrigh) fought by Áedán mac Gabráin.

The next event is entered differently in the two sources:

AU. 590. The slaughter of the sons of Áedán, Bran and Domangart.
AT. 590. The slaughter of the sons of Áedán, Bran and Domangart and Eochaid Find in the battle of Circenn in which Áedán was the victor.[12]

Based solely on these sources we could reach for some tentative conclusions. Manonn is either the Manau in central Scotland (around Stirling) or the Isle of Man. There is no consensus among historians about which place is meant. Modern Scottish writers favour the Scottish location, partly because it seems supported by other action in Pictland. I have made a case in this book for stating that this action was in the Isle of Man based on Áedán's association with the Irish king Báetáin mac Cáirill who invaded the island. Lethreid has not been identified, though it is likely to be somewhere in the north. The name means 'smooth side' or 'smooth slope'. A tentative suggestion has been made that the site might be hidden in one of the many place-names in Lennox, the British district around Loch Lomond, which have the element *leth* or *letir* in them.[13] The battle designated in Circenn was probably in the Pictish province of that name, Angus/Mearns in east central Scotland. It is a relatively long way from Dál Riata and there are questions about Áedán's sudden aggressive appearance in this area. There is evident confusion about which sons of Áedán died fighting the Picts and one or more of them seem instead to have died in wars against the Northumbrian English, as will be examined later.

It should be added that there are incidents during the reign of Áedán which do not feature in surviving annals. One of these is the record of his submission to the Ulaid leader Báetáin mac Cáirill in Ireland during the early part of his reign. An argument that the above list of battles must be definitive because contemporary annals kept on Iona would surely have commemorated every military event during his reign is weak. Information could easily fall out of records during their repeated copying and transmission.

Adomnán's Account

More information is provided by the abbot of Iona, Adomnán, who lived from around 624 to 704. He wrote his book about Columba or Colum Cille, the founder of his monastery of Iona, *Vita Columbae*, towards the close of the 7th century. It contains several passages relating to Áedán mac Gabráin's warfare against the Picts. Nobody could claim that Adomnán's book contained the sum of knowledge about Dál Riata's wars with its eastern neighbours during the lifetime of the saint. We have nothing, for instance, from Adomnán about Áedán's adventure to Orkney. The purpose of his work was to magnify the sancity of Colum Cille and to do so he selectively used the material available to him. Even some information relating to his subject's interface with the Picts is omitted, such as his journeys into southern Pictland. His closeness to the period concerned, relative to the later period in which the annals were committed to writing, still make him a compelling source, albeit that his own sources were a mixture of oral and written material.

The first mention of the Pictish wars in Adomnán comes in a chapter headed 'Of the battle with the Miathi'.[14] He tells us that the saint was in church in Iona and instructed his servant Diarmait to ring the bell. When his brethren were summoned he knelt down and instructed them to the pray to God 'for this people and for king Áedán, for even now they are going into battle'. A short while later he went outside, looked at the sky, and announced that the 'barbarians' had been put to flight. Áedán was victorious, though it was not a happy victory, the saint said. Adomnán states that 303 men from Áedán's army died. This too, Adomnán says, was foretold by the saint. The 'standard' number of 300 for a warband occurs elsewhere and the variant 303 appears in the Welsh *Gododdin* poem as the number of British warriors who died in the expedition which is the subject of the verse.[15] This suggests that Adomnán gleaned his material for this battle from a poetic source.

The next section of Adomnán's book deals with Colum Cille's prophecy about Áedán's successor.[16] When asked by the king about which of his sons will be king after him, the abbot says that Artúr, Eochaid Find and Domangart will be slain by enemies in battle and that Eochaid Buide would succeed. The first two princes, Adomnán says, died soon afterwards in the battle against the Miathi, while Domangart was killed in a battle in England.

Miathi and Manau

There are problems trying to equate the battle of Manau in the annals with the battle of the Miathi mentioned by Adomnán. The first is a location which could be either of two places, as already mentioned, while the second evidently refers to a people only otherwise referenced long before the 6th century. The Miathi (or Maiatai) appear in Roman records within a very restricted time frame, the end of the 2nd and beginning of the 3rd centuries.[17] Cassius Dio, referring to the years 197–200, says the Maetae tribe initiatated hostilities against the Roman Empire and that the Caledonians broke promises and aided them. They are supposed to have lived near the Wall; apparently the Antonine rather than Hadrian's

Wall. The governor Virius Lupus was forced to buy peace from them. Herodian and Cassius Dio refer to renewed northern warfare in the period 208–211 when the emperor Severus pursued warfare against the Maetae and Caledonians. The barbarians were defeated, but later revolted before peace terms were agreed. This is the last mention of this people. Roman sources refer only to Caledonians and Picts in the first half of the 4th century and Picts, Dicalydones and Verturiones in the latter half of that century. Were the Miathi the same people recorded by Adomnán as the Maetae? There is no mention of Miathi by any source after Adomnán either and so they vanish again long before the extinction of the Picts. The Miathi, like the Caledonians, may be the name of a confederation rather than an ethnic tribe. The name may mean something like 'the larger part of the people'.[18] If they were a small confederacy rather than a single people, this may raise questions about their ability to maintain an identity between the period of Dio Cassius and Adomnán.

Where were the Maetae originally located? They are commonly assigned to the central Scottish region of Manau. Here the tribal name may be incorporated in two hill names, Myot Hill, south of the River Carron (and west of the present town of Denny) and Dumyat, one of the most southerly of the Ochill Hills, north-east of Stirling. The two places are around 16 km from each other. There is nothing to say that the same recognisably distinct people were still there in the late 6th century.[19] Geographically the name of Manau is evidenced both north and south of the River Forth, most notable in Clackmannan, the 'stone of Manau,' which formed into a later small Scottish county. Beyond a few passing mentions in later sources, notable Welsh poetry, we do not know if this territory was inhabited by people who styled themselves Picts, British, both, or something else. The region is recorded in the 9th century Welsh *Historia Brittonum*. A very brief notice states that a chieftain named Cunedda came to North Wales from the region of Manau Gododdin and drove out the Irish, 146 years before the reign of his descendant in Gwynedd, Maelgwyn.[20]

Some writers have wrongly assumed that Manau Gododdin was the full title of the British kingdom of Gododdin. But it appears that the writer of the *Historia Brittonum* used the term to distinguish this Manau from the insular one. Manau Gododdin was a region immediately to the west and the north-west of Gododdin proper, adjoining the Gododdin territory later known as Lothian. It was either Manau belonging to or neighbouring Gododdin. Whether there was a British part of Gododdin and a more northerly Pictish part is unknown but not impossible. The area of Manau and its surroundings was an area of immense strategic value, fought over repeatedly in the Early Medieval period by Britons, Scots, Irish and Picts. It was in this region that Áedán's grandson Domnall Brecc was slaughtered in the year 642 by the Dumbarton Britons.

Adomnán doesn't say that the Miathi were definitely Pictish. His mention of them as barbarians may mean that they were pagan, but it definitely means that, to him, they were outside the civilised context of Dál Riata, as Richard Sharpe notes. Sharpe also makes the point that the Miathi were forced to flee in the battle, which could imply they were not on their home ground.[21] Barbarism seems a strange accusation applied to a people who inhabited the lands next to the definitely Christian territories of the northern Britons. It would be surprising if Christian missionaries had left the Picts living here the most untamed and pagan. It is worth considering possibilities that the Miathi had migrated elsewhere or that another population group was involved in the battle. Richard Sharpe's suggestion that the conflict was between the Scots and 'some isolated highland group' is worth considering.[22] If the battles of Circenn and the Miathi are envisaged as one event, recorded from different perspectives, it is easier to imagine the Miathi having moved north into Angus rather than suggesting, as some historians have done, that the province of Circenn has been somehow misplaced or that there were multiple Pictish places with this name. Accepting that Adomnán's battle of Miathi and the annal's battle in Circenn are identical is a workable solution, though not a perfect one. There is no difficulty imagining that the Miathi had been forced out of Manau and migrated to Angus some time before the late 6th century based on the pressure of other peoples to control their home region.

But Adomnán makes the Miathi battle a hard won victory for Áedán while the other Irish sources indicate that Circenn was a defeat for him. This is not a major obstacle in reconciling the two apparently conflicting records. At least one Irish annalist declared that the battle of Degsastan, Áedán's last battle, was a victory for him rather than a win for the Northumbrians as other sources claim. Narrowly contested results in warfare made for disputed victories.

War and Succession in the East

Áedán's Pictish campaigns open to a number of interpretations, including a supposition that Áedán's aggression against the Picts was pursued over an extended period. The *Prophecy of Berchán*'s figure of thirteen years fighting against the Picts comes to mind. The eminent historian John Bannerman places the deaths of Eochaid Find and Artúr around 590 in Pictland, then further warfare in Circenn after the death of Colum Cille in 597.[23]

One possible outline of the known military activity of Áedán might be as follows.

580. Expedition to Orkney against Pictish sub-king based there. Death of pictish king Galam Cennalath.

582. Further seaborne mission. This time to the Isle of Man, attacking allies of the Ulaid King Báetán Mac Cáirell following his death. There may have been associated military activity in British held territory in Galloway, and possible also in the north of England.

584. Death of Pictish King Bridei son of Maelchon.

586? Battle of Circenn.

590–594? The convention of Druim Cett in Ireland. Áedán and Colum Cille meet Uí Néill King Áed.

591. Áedán fights in the battle of Leithreid, location unknown.

The *Annals of Tigernach*'s battle of Circenn was distant from the border of Dál Riata, so the encounter cannot have been defensive and nor is it likely to have been for territorial gain. A raid which penetrated so deeply into the land of the Picts would have had major risks as an invading army would have had to cross a large tract of enemy territory before it entered this region. Rather than hazarding the mountainous and potentially hostile Pictish held central Highlands, Áedán may have travelled by sea around the northern coast and attacked on the Angus coast.[24] H.M. Chadwick pertinently pondered what it was about this area which attracted the attention of Áedán. Was the region the chief centre of Pictish power down to the 7th century as he supposed?[25] One intriguing suggestion is that Áedán was pursuing a policy in the south which had the tacit approval of allies based in northern Pictland.[26] The powerful Bridei was certainly based in the north of Pictland, somewhere near present day Inverness, and there is a clue in the records that he tried and failed to bring the south under his sway. The entry in the *Annals of Tigernach* appears under the year 752, but it appears to have been misplaced by two 84-year cycles.[27] The entry reads:

> The battle of Asreth in the land of Circenn, between Picts on both sides; and in it fell Bridei, Maelchon's son.[28]

This would dovetail with the annal entry correctly entered under the year 584: 'The death of Bridei, Maelchon's son, king of the Picts.'[29] Even if Áedán was not specifically avenging Bridei's death, he might have been taking advantage of chaos among the Picts to pursue his own agenda. One possible date for the battle of Circenn is 586, just two years after the battle of Asreth (though the dating is by no means certain). We can also wonder whether there's any possibility that Áedán's battle in Circenn was actually the same battle of Asreth.

It has been noticed that there are a number of indications of Irish settlement in eastern Pictland. Apart from Irish literature about legendary incursions into eastern Scotland, it was believed that place-names may indicate early settlement. First among these is the provincial name Athfhotla, Atholl, noticed in Irish annals under the year 739.[30] It was long thought that this name denoted a region or sub-kingdom and meant 'New Ireland'.[31] But current thinking rejects this and gives an alternative, native meaning, something like 'North Pass'.[32] Although Áedán's own alleged formative involvement in Pictland, on the upper Forth, is nowhere near Angus/Circenn, his father Gabráin allegedly had control over western Strathmore and gave his name to this area, Gowrie, which adjoins Angus. However, the evidence for this is open to other interpretation.

Gartnait son of Áedán

There were several Gartnaits who were prominent in Pictland during the 7th century. The king of that name who died in the year 601 may have been the son of Áedán. The *Annals of Tigernach* call this ruler 'king of the Picts'.[33] Whether or not this is so, the Gartnait mentioned as Áedán's son in the genealogies is his only child with a demonstrably Pictish name. The name itself may mean 'noble champion'.[34] Much of this evidence is complicated by a family from Skye, prominent in the annals from the mid 7th century onwards. Áedán mac Gabráin makes an anachronistic appearance in the 9th century *Scéla Cano meic Gartnáin*, the 'Tale of Cano', which involves this kindred. I will return to this tale towards the end of the book, but also consider this family's connection with the Cenél nGabráin below.

The Pictish king Gartnait is associated with the foundation of the monastery of Abernethy, not far from the south bank of the River Tay, though another foundation legend links it with an earlier king named Nechtan.[35] Beyond that, Gartnait is unknown to the annals. He is credited with a reign of either eleven or twenty years. One genealogy states that Áedán had a son name Gartnait.[36] The latter had a son named Cano and grandson called Nechtan who may be present in the records.[37] The king who died around 601 is recorded in some Pictish king lists as son of Domelch, which might be his mother's name. Reckonings of his reign may roughly fit into the period 584 to 599. The *Chronicle of the Kings of the Picts* make Gartnait succeed Bridei as king.[38] It is possible that a primary aim of Áedán's Pictish wars was to install and retain this son as a ruler over a large part of southern Pictland. However, the identification of this Gartnait as a son of Áedán has been disputed on the basis of conflicting evidence and various related and non-related Canos and Gartnaits in Pictland.[39]

There is other evidence regarding dynastic links with Pictland in this period. Áedán's son Eochaid Buide succeeded his father as king in Dál Riata and was described at his death in 629 as 'king of the Picts', the first Gaelic king to bear this description, which raises interesting possibilities about his rule if the description was not merely a scribal error.[40] His descendants too are reputed to have ruled part of this area, for they are described as *fir ibe*, 'men of Fife'.[41] But there is no record, legendary or otherwise, of Eochaid campaigning against the Picts. During his reign the most significant military theatre for Dál Riata was in Ireland, which continued to be the case into the early reign of Eochaid's own son, Domnall Brecc. It is possible also that there was confusion between the Picts of Britain and the so-called 'Irish Picts', the Cruithin, and Eochaid was associated with the latter.

A contemporary ruler of Dál Riata was Connad Cerr. Connad, the 'Left Handed', was either Eochaid's own son or the son of Áedán's predecessor, Conall mac Comgaill. Both Eochaid and Connad died around 629, but several years earlier Connad Cerr was being termed king of Dál Riata. The suggestion that Connad ruled in the Irish part of the kingdom while Eochaid remained to govern Britain is possible.[42] If Eochaid in effect relinquished active rule over part or the whole territory of Dál Riata, it would be an interesting parallel with his own father Áedán who was not an active ruler when he died. Another possible son of Eochaid Buide was Dicull, who died in battle alongside Connad Cerr and others of Dál Riata. He was called 'king of the kindred of the Picts', using the term Cruithin, which may imply he was a claimant to their territory in Ireland rather than a ruler of Picts in Britain.[43]

Based on this, it seems likely at least that Gartnait, a son of Áedán, ruled in Pictland, even if the case for Eochaid Buide's rule there is dubious or unproven. There were a number of kings of Picts in the 7th centuries who certainly had foreign fathers, which has been ascribed to the unusual succession system operating in Pictland. These included Bridei son of Beli (a Strathclyde Briton) and Talorcan son of Eanfrith (the latter son of Northumbrian king Æthelfrith). Eochaid Buide's own son, Domnall Brecc, may have been the father of Pictish kings Gartnait and Drest.[44] Garnait's accession was not necessarily an innovative foreign intrusion either, since some have argued that Bridei son of Maelchon was actually son of the king of Gwynedd, Maelgwn, extraordinary as that seems, given the geographical distance between northern Pictland and north Wales.[45] The rule of foreign kings in Pictland did not equate with wholescale takeover of the top layer of society by the nation which provided the non-Pictish king. Jonathan Jarrett makes the observation that the sons of Áedán are conspicuously front and centre in the surviving records about the Pictish wars, suggesting that the campaign here was motivated by their personal intention to sieze territory and power in the east.[46] This may have overridden Áedán's previous policy. If it was a campaign by the rising generation of Cenél nGabráin dynasty to claim parts of Pictland for themselves, it had mixed results. The deaths of several of Áedán's sons would almost certainly have entailed the wholesale slaughter of their warbands also. The fighting strength of Dál Riata as a whole would have been greatly reduced. If the battle against the Miathi was a different encounter, it would have been a dearly won and possibly pointless victory, with over 300 men left dead on the field. Gartnait's rule has left behind an ambivalent record. The Irish annals record his death under the year 601, but it may have occurred a few years earlier. It is tempting to view his death in conjunction with Áedán's failure in the east, but that may not be the case. His possible relationship to Áedán and his own achievements remain an enigma.

Even if the Cenél nGabráin was able to control parts of southern Pictland in this period it was not a conclusive or permanent gain. During the 8th century ferocious Pictish leaders were able to rampage through Dál Riata and it would have seemed unlikely at that time that the settler kingdom would have won the cultural lottery for overall control of the country which eventually became Scotland. A Scottish attempt at land grabbing in Pictland also runs counter to our perception of Áedán as an opportunistic raider rather than a conquerer, unless he had a late career change in procedure. More likely that his sons had a different agenda in Pictland than he did. Their gamble in Pictland may have dangerously overstretched the kingdom's military capacity and led to a lack of manpower in Áedán's last campaigns against the Northern English.

The Prophecy of Berchán

We should at this point cautiously return to the *Prophecy of Berchán* to see whether it can shed any light on the later Pictish campaigns. As we've seen, the verses which may relate to Áedán begin with a reference to a king coming eastwards and causing woe to the Picts. The king's ambition is stressed; he is not content with Irish being subject to the Picts. This may be an anachronistic view imposing ethnic antagonism between people at a period when there was none. It may be significant that the 'Áedán verses' are directly followed by ones which celebrate his descendant Cináed Mac Ailpín, famous for his supposed obliteration of Pictish power. Berchán does not assist us much with the details, even if we suppose that he is employing later traditions remembered about Áedán. There is reference to this king rising in the east, possibly referring to events before 574. We are also told that the king will control the Picts for a short while and that he makes a pact which he will not break. Mention of his considering an attack against the Picts at a time when he was not king either refers to his early career or at the end of the 6th century when he was apparently ousted from the kingship of Dál Riata. Specific details are added about Áedán's death, tied in with the information that he fought for thirteen years against the Picts.[47]

Map 5. The area of eastern Pictland associated with Áedán and Gabráin. Approximate modern extent of the county of Angus detailed. Circenn comprised Angus and the Mearns (Kincardineshire to the north-east).

Contemporary Rulers in Northern Britain

Pictish Kings

Bridei mac Maelchon. Powerful king of the Picts, based in the north. Ruled c. 556–584. Defeated Dál Riata in 558. Possibly killed in civil conflict in southern Pictland.

Gartnait son of Domelch. Reigned from 584 to around 599–602. Possibly a son of Áedán. Domelch was his mother's name.

Galam Cennalath. King of southern Pictland, whose rule overlapped for a short period with Bridei, who was possibly a rival. Died in 580.

British Kings

Rhydderch Hael. King of Allt Clud (Dumbarton), from around 580 until his death in 612. Associate of St Kentigern of Glasgow.

Urien of Rheged. May have ruled in north-west England or south-west Scotland. Fought against Bernicia and led a British coalition at one stage. Possibly died in the 590s.

Gwenddolau. King in the Solway Firth region. Died at the battle of Arthuret in 573, a conflict between Britons.

English Kings

Æthelfrith. Ruler of Bernicia (northern Northumbria), he defeated Áedán at the battle of Degsastan in 603. Slain by English opponents in 617.

Chapter 7

Áedán and the Britons

Áedán's relationship with the Britons who inhabited most of the Scottish Lowlands south of the rivers Forth and Clyde, and all of what is now Cumbria, is restricted by a lack of written material which gives any kind of timescale for events which happened in the 6th century. There is almost no record of interaction between Scots and Irish in Britain before Áedán's time and what clues we have are contradictory and fragmentary. If we look at his contact with the Picts, Áedán had both friendly and aggressive relations with them, acting as the opportunities arose. The same may be true regarding his southern neighbours. A close connection with these Northern Britons is hinted at by Áedán's multiple appearances in Welsh literature, some of which may be based on direct contemporary traditions. Several Welsh sources brand him as a 'traitor'. Áedán's double sided reputation should not surprise us. In some sources he is credited as facing the might of the Bernician warlord Æthelfrith on behalf of unnamed British allies; in another he is held guilty for raiding the great British fortress of Dumbarton. In order to examine these difficulties we have to have a closer look at these Northern Britons themselves.

The fortress of Dumbarton looms over the Clyde from a vantage point overlooking the north bank of the river. Known in earlier times as Allt Clud (or Alclud), the Rock of Clyde, sometimes also called the Fort of the Britons, the stronghold overshadows not just its own hinterland, but is an imposing landmark which overshadowed the eastern part of Dál Riataas the primarily fortified power base. The fortress stands close to the boundary between the Britons and the Scots. It is only a short distance westward up the Clyde coast to Gare Loch, which has been suggested as another boundary between the Britons and the Scots, though Loch Long to the west of this makes a more plausible boundary.[1] To the north, the Britons controlled the lands around Loch Lomond, more or less the later region called Lennox. A border stone, Clach-nam-Breatann, in Glen

Falloch, north of Loch Lomond, and traditionally marked the boundary between the peoples. Another possibly boundary stone is Clach nam Breatunnaich near Lochgoilhead.

So close is the settler kingdom to the British heartlands that historians have wondered how both coexisted peacefully.[2] Did the Dumbarton Britons encourage the transfer of the ruling dynasty from Antrim to their own doorstep in Kintyre?[3] A strongly established territory on these archipeligoes and islands with a naval resource could control not only the navigational routes through the Hebrides, but also access to the Firth of Clyde which would have been crucial to British interests. Any Kintyre kingdom may plausibly have blocked marauding Pictish fleets coming from the north and harrying exposed British coasts around the Firth of Clyde and further south.[4] The barbarian conspiracy of the late 4th century which had undermined the Roman province in Britain had involved concerted attacks by the Picts and the Irish which seem to have involved a degree of sophisticated communication and alliance. If the Britons on the Clyde did allow the Irish Scots to settle on their western flank, they may also have taken some care to ensure that the new kingdom's policies were aligned with their own. The Britons in the south had allegedly invited English tribes as mercenaries to protect them, with disastrous consequences.

Alternatively, the Britons may have been forced to accept a neighbouring permanent Irish presence by aggression. An army from Connaught is alleged to have raided British lands on the Clyde at some point in the mid-5th century. The Irish dynast Nath Í mac Fiachrach (also known as Dath Í) was said to have led the assault, though another source credits his son, Ailill Molt, with this invasion.[5] The same force is said to have penetrated into Circenn, the eastern mainland of Pictland. Whether or not this actually occurred, it would not necessarily mean that there was a pact in place which linked Connaght with the tiny Irish territory of Dál Riata. The latter of course may have independently taken advantage of British weakness which resulted from other Irish aggression on the Clyde. But the sources for this period are hardly to be relied upon for any kind of historical accuracy.

Leaving aside the tale of Áedán's raid on Dumbarton rock, there is no record of warfare between the Britons and the Scots until a sudden, brutal raid by the latter in the Scottish midlands, when Áedán's grandson

Domnall Brecc was slaughtered and decapitated by the British king
Owein at Strathcarron in central Scotland in the mid 7th century. Until
that time the relationship between these northern peoples seems largely
peaceful if we choose to judge it by the lack of evidence which proves
otherwise.

The Identity of the Britons

The Britons between Hadrian's Wall and the Antonine Wall existed in
a twilight zone following the end of Roman Britain in the 5th century.
Never fully embraced by Rome, the two northernmost British tribes of
the island nevertheless emerged in the Early Medieval Period as both
Christian and pseudo-Roman in their outlook. The Damnonii of the
Clyde and the Votadini in Lothian recognisably survived the fall of
Rome, unlike some of the other British tribes further south. The
duality of the tribal identity centred on Dumbarton was captured by the
British St Patrick, complaining to the warband of the Clydeside regent
Coroticus (Ceredig). His epistle identified them certainly as Christians
and self-conscious 'citizens', heirs of Rome, but it also castigated them
for the barbarian practice of raiding north-east Ireland and enslaving his
Christian converts. A dynasty capable of ravaging Ulster was a major
power in the region and the slaving raids may also be connected with the
establishment of Dál Riata in mainland Britain. Ceretic's dynasty would
last into the 11th century and the kingdom itself survived aggression
from Scots, English, Picts and Vikings. Following a major devastation by
Scandinavians in the late 9th century the territory rallied and expanded
massively, taking over former British controlled regions in south-west
Scotland and in Cumbria.

Áedán in Welsh Tradition and Family Connections

The strands of tradition which link Áedán with the Britons fall into
several categories: genealogical traditions, poetic sources, plus remnants
of lost prose material which survive only as summaries in surviving
material like the Welsh Triads. As mentioned earlier in this book, there
are several strands of Welsh tradition which insist that Áedán had British
blood. He certainly features more consistently in Welsh material than

any other Irishman, appearing in genealogies, the Triads, and as the only early Irish king, apart from his own father, whose death is noticed in the *Annales Cambriae*. While the attempts to give Áedán British ancestry are individually unconvincing, they demonstrate an effort to integrate him into Welsh traditional material. His wider fame may partially explain his intrusion into Welsh literature, but the cumulative amount of material linking him to the Britons is interesting. Most important is the firm evidence that a collection of British names turn up among his sons and grandsons: Artúr, Rigullán, Pledan. The appearance of these names, unprecedented in any other Irish royal dynasty's genealogy, signifies a firm bond with British culture.

Y Gogled, The Old North

The poltical shape of the the British successor states to Rome is difficult to read in the north of England and southern Scotland. In the south-east of this large area, British kingdoms, such as one established in Lindsey, Lincolnshire, fell quickly to English incomers. Deira too, in eastern Yorkshire, was lost at an early date and became the southern half of what would be the long-lasting kingdom of Northumbria. But the Pennines also harboured pockets of resistance, such as the small British kingdom of Elmet. Areas elsewhere still retained British speech, culture and rulership into the 7th century: places such as Tweedale, Lancashire and Cumbria. The shadowy kingdom of Rheged survived too, though we do not know whether it was centred in Cumbria or Galloway. British rulers in Dumbarton may have had influence or rule over Ayrshire and the Gododdin rulers based at Edinburgh certainly controlled the Lothians.

When it comes to outlining the history of these British lands through the late 6th century, we are similarly in the dark. There are few dates marked in the annals, Welsh or Irish, to give us guidance. Some time toward the middle of the century an English ruler called Ida established a coastal kingdom at Bamburgh and is credited with being the founder of a kingdom named Bryneich or Bernicia, the northern half of Northumbria. It was his descendant, Æthelfrith, who Áedán would battle half a century later. In the meantime, the British warriors of Gododdin went south to do battle at a place named Catraeth, possibly Catterick in Yorkshire. This may have been against an English enemy, or it may have been against other

Britons. We do not know exactly when this battle took place. Whether there was any relationship between this military campaign and Áedán's own operation against Æthelfrith is another question mark. From west of the Pennines perhaps, the Britons from the kingdom of Rheged launched sporadic attacks against Bernicia. By the end of the century, Æthelfrith was taking over British territory in the Pennines and driving out the native British aristocracy and landowners.

The Battle of Arthuret

If Áedán's ascent to power in Dál Riata probably entailed factional fighting at the battle of Teloch or Delgu in Kintyre in 574, there was similar internecine conflict among the northern Britons in the previous year at a place called Arthuret (originally Arfderydd) on the Solway Firth, near the present English-Scottish border. The battle was an all British affair and may have been restricted to factional infighting between different segments of the descendants of the legendary chieftain Coel Hên. The result of the encounter was the death of a locally based warlord named Gwenddoleu, but the cause of the conflict and its wider results are not known, although Gwenddoleu's opponents evidently raided his fortress of Caerwhinley. An array of historical, but mostly little known characters are associated with the battle, as befits an event which inspired a wide range of legendary literature. First among the famous was Myrddin, or his northern cognate Lailoken, who lost his senses there and fled to the remote fastnesses of the Caledonian Forest in the Southern Uplands of Scotland. Beyond the lesser participants, there are several leaders whose participation was due only to their wider fame in Welsh legendary material, coupled with the fact that they lived in the same northern millieu – Y Gogledd – which was an inspiration for later poets and storytellers. The British ruler of Dumbarton, Rhydderch Hael, looms large as a persecutor of the wild man Myrddin/Lailoken in poetic material supposedly set in the period after the battle. But his association with Arthuret is late, even if there was a possibility of participation of forces from the Clyde area in the encounter.[6]

Áedán mac Gabráin was also dragged into association with the battle, albeit there is even less likelihood that he fought there than Rhydderch did. The most mundane objection against his participation is that the battle immediately preceded his own assumption of rule in Dál Riata and he was surely preoccupied with consolidating control in his home territory. The Welsh Triad 84 cites Arthuret as one of the 'Three Futile Battles of the Island of Britain' and states that it was fought because of a lark's nest.[7] This cryptic reference has been the subject of speculation for centuries, as has the wider circumstances of the conflict.

The Welsh antiquarian Robert Vaughan of Hengwrt (d. 1667) left some notes about the battle (added to later by Evan Evans) which may reflect earlier traditions about the encounter, but the story is sadly garbled. According to his tale, Áedán allied with a British leader named Morgan Mawr ap Sadyrnin against Rhydderch Hael, who fled to Ireland, and Áedán possessed Dumbarton. Some time after Rhydderch returned, his shepherd and Áedán's shepherd entered into an argument about a lark's nest. Áedán then solicited the aid of the British lord Gwenddolau and they were defeated at Arthuret, which forced Áedán in turn to flee the country.[8] There is no certainty about whether Vaughan and Evans were in fact drawing on a now lost strand of legend about the battle. However, material from the Old North was subject to reinterpretation and speculation by successive Welsh writers into the modern period. In the 18th century Lewis Morris (c. 1765) wondered whether the reference in the Triads to Áedán's warband going to sea entailed a retreat to the Isle of Man after the defeat at the battle of Degsastan in 603.[9] Not all interpreters were so judicious, as in the example of Iolo Morganwg (d. 1826), whose supposed antiquarian Welsh materials also touched upon the battle of Arthuret and were almost certainly forgeries.

Modern authors have speculated whether this 'lark's nest' can be equated with the name Caerlaverock, a medieval castle and pre-existing parish on the Scottish side of the Solway Firth.[10] Not only would this supposition involve a transmission in meaning from an original Cumbric place-name to English, it is not backed up by any other evidence.[11] The name Caerlaverock is alternatively and plausibly derived from a Welsh personal name, Llywarch,[12] so there is no real proof that it represents the 'lark's nest' alluded to in legend. The latter may not even have been intended as an actual place in Welsh tradition.

As discussed earlier, Áedán mac Gabráin features in *Peiryan Vaban*, a 15th century Welsh poem, which speaks of his avenging Gwenddoleu with an invading army. If there is any earlier Welsh tradition contained in the poem, it seems likely not to refer to the battle of Arthuret or its immediate aftermath, but possibly to a slightly later period when Áedán may have been militarily involved in the Isle of Man or later in the north of England. Arfderydd's aftermath, now hidden from us, may have had repercussions in the wider regional balances of power which allowed keen eyed Irish carrion kings like Áedán and Báetán to make moves in the area.

Rival Kings. Áedán and Rhydderch Hael

Áedán's contemporary ruler as king of Dumbarton was Rhydderch Hael, whose epithet means 'the generous'. Rhydderch seems to have been active as a ruler between around 580 and the first decade of the 7th century. In some genealogies he is styled *hen*, 'ancient', which may be a reference to the perception that his ruling house was perceived as stretching back into antiquity. His reign is still full of obscurity. The fullest source about him is a 12th century *Life* of the important saint, Kentigern, who seems to have operated in Rhydderch's territory, but we can still cautiously claim to know more about Rhydderch than about Áedán's other great contemporary and rival Bridei son of Maelchon, king of the Picts. He figures, for instance, in some of the poems associated with Myrddin, cast in the role of his persecutor. The concept that he was a Christian ruler determined to defeat lingering paganism as represented by Gwenddoleu may be a later misconception. Forgotten in the north after Strathclyde lost its Welsh language and identity, he was remembered as a magical figure in Wales as possessor of a wonderful sword which would burst into flames if an unrighteous man drew it.

The most pertinent evidence for relations between Dumbarton and Dál Riata comes in a passage from Adomnán's *Life* of Colum Cille.[13] Rhydderch, we are told, sent the Iona monk Luigbe moccu Min back to the saint on a mission to enquire whether or not he would be killed by his enemies. Colum Cille questioned the envoy carefully about the king, his kingdom and his people. But Luigbe expressed some scorn about the foreign king and asked Colum Cille why he was asking so many questions about this unhappy man. Colum Cille vowed that the king would never be delivered to his enemies, but would die at home on his own pillow. His predictions about Rhydderch were fulfilled. He is reputed to have died peacefully, several years after Áedán, around the same time that St Kentigern of Glasgow died.

The passage in the *Life* implies regular high-level communication between the neighbouring kingdoms, which is not unexpected. This particular diplomatic episode can be read in a number of ways, but most likely can be taken as an appeal to the cleric to mediate with the secular authority of Dál Riata to prevent an attack. There is no record whatever before the reign of Áedán of any contact, good or bad, between the two territories.

The Raid on Dumbarton

The story or saga in Welsh tradition which purported to show that the Rock on the Clyde was violated by the Scots as Triad 54 asserts:

> And the third Costly Ravaging [of the Island of Britain] was when Aeddan the Treacherous came to the court of Rhydderch Hael at Alclud; he left neither food nor drink nor beast alive.[14]

This event is unknown in Irish or Welsh annals and we can only speculate about its meaning. Whether or not there were blood ties between the dynasties of Alclud and Dunadd, there seems to have been an implicit alliance between them. The contemporary background for any assault on Dumbarton is limited. While Rhydderch's association with the battle of Arthuret is unhistorical there is a more credible record that he joined a coalition of other British leaders in an attack against the growing threat of Anglo-Saxon Bernicia, the northern half of the nascent Northumbrian kingdom.[15] This was possibly an extended campaign rather than one military hosting, with Rhydderch in the company of leaders named as Urien (of Rheged), Morcant and Gwallawg. The *Historia Brittonum* later states that Urien blockaded the English enemy in Lindisfarne for three nights, then he was assassinated. Whether Rhydderch was present during this event is not stated, but an absence for an extended period would possibly allow the opportunity for an unforeseen attack on Dumbarton Rock.

The poem *Peiryan Vaban*, which we have already looked at, specifically mentions hostility between the kings Áedán and Rhydderch. Can it be related to Áedán's aggression at Dumbarton? It is almost impossible to say. Looking at the likely period when Áedán might have chosen to attack the Britons is also fraught with difficulties. Any time between 574 and 597 is possible, with the decades of the 580s and 590s looking likelier, in light of other known activity in Orkney, Pictland, possibly in Man, and visits to Ireland. The Irish annals are singularly reticent about matters in North Britain which did not take place either in Dál Riata or the land of the Picts despite the facts that the monks on Iona were keeping annals during this period. Áedán's actions against the Northumbrian English which culminated in the battle of Degsastan in 603 must have involved some liaison with the Britons, if not active alliance, which may have been the background for his subsequent reversal in policy and attack on Dumbarton.

The question as to why he chose to attack the citadel is also irredeemably obscure. Although he looms large in Welsh legend, Áedán was also branded with the unflattering epithet *Vradawc*, the 'Traitor', which appears to give a clear indication of opinion about his conduct.[16] The description is appended to him in both the Triads and Welsh genealogies. The suggestion that he earned this infamy as a result of the termination of a long-standing alliance is attractive.[17] It would accord with the view of Áedán as a relentless opportunist who took advantage of any perceived weakness in all of the nations encircling Dál Riata, perhaps militarily acting against each of them in turn as the opportunities materialised. But there are other possibilities. If the other suggested meaning of *Vradawc*, 'Wily', is considered, it aligns him with his contemporary (and opponent at the battle of Degsastan in 603) Æthelfrith. This Northumbrian king was also a formidable foe of the northern British and was given the byname *Flesaur* (or *Ffleisawg*).[18] If this epithet is early and indicates the reputation of a treaty breaker, a 'twister', he may have been regarded in the same way as Áedán.[19]

Apart from Áedán mac Gabrain's possible raid there is no record of outside aggression against this exceptionally well situated citadel until the year 870 when it was besieged by an enormous Viking horde which arrived from Ireland in 200 ships. This latter event was the possible subject of an epic tale in Ireland because of the scale of the disaster. The siege by Olaf and Ívar lasted for four months until the fortress was starved into surrender and its well dried up by miraculous means. After

Dumbarton was plundered the Vikings devastated the area and carried away a massive cargo of human misery: British, Pictish and Irish slaves back to their base in Ireland.[20] Alfred Smyth seems to have correctly suspected Dál Riadan complicity in the event since all the other nations of northern Britain had their people enslaved, but there were no Scots among them.[21] The Scots of the coastal kingdom were in the ascendant after having achieved a takeover of (or a merger with) Pictland, by fair means or foul. Two years after the fall of Dumbarton, the Scottish king Constantine mac Cináed arranged the assassination of the British king Artgal.[22] The seismic affects of the raid did not destroy British power in the region, but the ruling dynasty relocated to Govan near Glasgow and managed to survive with a new name, Strathclyde, into the 11th century.

If the hilltop stronghold of Dumbarton could only be devastated by one of the greatest sieges known anywhere in the medieval period it is pertinent to ask how Áedán managed to breach its defences with resources which must have been much more modest 300 years earlier. Granted that the defences of the hillfort were improved and augmented in the intervening period (and there is evidence this was begun around the year 600), but it still would not have been a place which was easy to overcome unless some 'wily' subterfuge (as possible suggested by his Welsh nickname) was involved. James Fraser's reading of Triad 54 has led him to suggest that the meaning relates more to an abuse of hospitality and that this implies that he held Rhydderch in submission at some stage and that he came to Dumbarton on one occasion at least and demanded too much tribute from him.[23] This would make an attractively and plausible solution to the Triad. The other two 'ravagings' summarised in Triad 54 similarly refer to violation of formal hospitality and excessive consumption of food and produce at royal courts by outsiders.[24] If this scenario is accepted we could imagine an opportunistic Áedán happily reversing the position he may have been forced to accept at the meeting with Báetán of the Dál Fiatach. By the 590s, fighting on several fronts, the resources of Dál Riata may have been overstretched. Sending demands for considerable tribute from Dumbaron as a price to pay for a war on Northumbria might have seemed entirely appropriate to Áedán, though was possibly perceived as an outrageous burden to Rhydderch and the British elite, especially if they did not want to antagonise the English.

We have one stray Irish tradition of a great bloody raid on the British lands around the Clyde, but we don't know if it relates to Áedán's time or a later period. Unfortunately we only possess the title of this lost story from a list in the *Book of Leinster*: *Orgain Sratha Cluada*, 'The Slaughter of Strathclyde'. It may well refer to the 9th century devastation of the area.[25] We have a possible parallel in another lost tale which dealt with the supposed murder of Pictish nobles by Scots at a feast held at Scone. This tale too dealt with 9th century events, and was known as *Braflang Scóine*, the 'Treachery of Scone,' and is a title contained in the *Book of Leinster*.[26]

Other Welsh Traditions

We have seen that Triad 29, 'Three Faithful War Bands of the Island of Britain,' exists in two variants.[27] The first speaks of Áedán's warriors going to sea for their lord, while the second, more mysteriously, refers to their loyalty 'when was his complete disappearance'. The original tale behind this has long since vanished, but it would seem to allude to a naval mission over a medium or long distance from Dál Riata, so would not refer to the Dumbarton attack. Various guesses have been made about the subject of this Triad, with some linking it to Áedán's last battle at Degsastan, around the year 603. More likely is a connection with an expedition against other Irish in the Isle of Man in the early 580s. This may also be connected to the poem *Peiryan Vaban*. If this remembers Irish military activity near the Solway associated with conflict in the Isle of Man, it would more likely have taken place in the early 580s than immediately following the battle of Arthuret in 573. However it may also remember warband activity sent from Dál Riata towards the close of the century, associated with raids against the English of Bernicia.

Summary

There is no fundamental reason to disbelieve the Venerable Bede when he states that Áedán went to fight the Northumbrian English at Degsastan, somewhere in southern Scotland or northern England, to support the flagging dynasties of the British in this area. But accepting this fairly plausible reason leaves more questions unanswered. If we also take account of H.M. Chadwick's belief that Áedán broke a long-standing treaty with the dynasty of Dumbarton, it would then mean that he would have subsequently had to have repaired this bond at some stage in the 590s, or else come to separate treaty terms with other British powers in the region, such as the shadowy territory of Rheged. Dumbarton's disinclination to battle Bernicia might not have been typical of other British powers who had the English breathing down their necks. A fluid attitude to treaties with the various parties of the Britons may have underscored the Irish action in the Degsastan campaign. There are clues that Áedán was capable of making the same shifts in allegiance earlier in Ireland when he was allied (perhaps under duress) to the Ulaid people and then gave his support to the Cruithin in the eastern part of Ulster and the Uí Néill dynasty more widely in the north of Ireland. Consideration of the circumstances in Northern Britain which led Áedán to the battle of Degsastan will be considered in the next chapter.

Even to give a tentative outline of Áedán mac Gabráin's interactions with the Britons is to immediately enter speculative territory. A measure of the general confusion about events in the North British zone can be seen in the fact that some historians, up until the late 19th century, chose to confuse the battle of Degsastan with either Arthuret in 573 or the undated Gododdin defeat at Catraeth.[28] Several recent historians have attempted to offer different contexts for the Irish activity in this region at the turn of the century, but there has been no consensus about events. Despite these and other efforts from historians there is a cultural hangover which lingers on from a disregard of the Northern Britons. While Welsh historians kept alive the heritage of the Old North for generations, the history of the Britons was ignored by Scottish historians until relatively recently, with consequences for our understanding of this people and its place in the formation of Scotland.

Áedán's seepage into later Irish tradition has been blamed to an extent in his prominence in Adomnán's work of Colum Cille. However credible that is, the same source cannot be responsible for Áedán's frequent, if fragmentary, appearances in Welsh literature. The founder of Iona was not widely venerated in Wales. Beyond the memory of him in those places we have cited there were other, fainter tributes to his renown in isolated mentions of the name Áedán in the *Gododdin* poem and in a verse in the *Black Book of Carmarthen*. Even if the heroes mentioned here were not the king of Dál Riata, they were probably echoes, real or actual, of the king of Dunadd.

Chapter 8

The Last Battle, Degsastan

From that time no Irish king in Britain has dared to make war on the English race to this day.[1]

This decisive description of the battle of Degsastan, which took place around 603, was written nearly 130 years after the event and is our main source of information about it.[2] Its author was the Northumbrian monk Bede who remains one of the primary authorities for the history of North Britain in the Early Medieval period. While Bede's blatantly anti-British sentiments make him a partial source, he fully acknowledged the massive contribution which the Irish made to his own kingdom's learning and religious life. A reader looking at his description of Degsastan, fought between the English of Bernicia and the Scots of Dál Riata under Áedán mac Gabráin, might accept that it was a crushing victory for the former, or even venture further to believe it set in stone his own people as the dominant power in the north. These conclusions can be questioned.

Both the site and the renown of the battle were well known in Bede's day. In his work the encounter stands as the first significant event following the formation of the kingdom of Bernicia. He states that it was a well known event which was remembered in oral retelling, but he may have also used a written source, now lost. Although there may have been territorial gains before his time, the supposed victor Æthelfrith was the first English warlord of Bernicia who is recorded as successfully expanding out of the coastal enclave of Bamburgh to conquer adjacent territory. His acquisition of British lands, with the holders either being dispossessed or exterminated, made Bede admiringly compare him to a ravening wolf, albeit one whose extreme violence was sanctioned by parallels from the Old Testament. On the surface it would not be inaccurate to compare his career with Áedán's. But the picture of two Dark Age heavyweights slugging it out for the spoils of the north may not be entirely accurate. The finer points of Æthelfrith's policies may be hidden under Bede's admiration for this pagan dynast's cutthroat victories in the same way that Áedán's character is hidden beneath the hagiographic gloss of Adomnán. If we were to point to obvious differences between the two rulers it would seem that Æthelfrith was intent on expanding the territory of Northumbria while Áedán's military career was not conducted near his own borders, suggesting his aims were motivated more by acquisition of wealth and renown.

Áedán's offensive is stated by Bede to be a direct response to the growing power of the Bernician king, a motivation perhaps more believable than a desire to assist beleagured British kingdoms. In light of Æthelfrith's success, Bede says, 'Áedán, king of the Irish living in Britain, aroused by his successes, marched against him with an immensely strong army; but he was defeated and fled with few survivors. Indeed, almost all his army was cut to pieces in a very famous place called Degsastan, that is the stone of Degsa.' But Bede does admit that Æthelfrith's brother Theobald was slain there with his entire army.

But, while Æthelfrith may have been gaining territory in British lands west of the Pennines and pushing north into what is now Scotland, he was nowhere near land which was under the direct control of Áedán's Irish in Britain. Áedán's long-range action was not motivated to counter an immediate threat to himself. Even given Æthelfrith's spectacular ascent, Áedán would have needed uncommon foresight to envisage that Northumbria would be a direct danger to Dál Riada. Any expedition against the English would hardly have been a purely altruistic military venture. There may have been an underlying alliance to help the British, but this would have been at the price perhaps of enforcing Áedán's status as over-king or on the understanding that the British would recompense him for his aid. The ambivalence of surviving information about the relationship between Áedán and the Clydeside Britons at least makes the situation hard to determine. The battle was probably fought either on British territory, or on English ground bordering their control. But there is no mention of their participation or co-operation in any early legitimate source.[3] There is so little known of the history of the Northern Britons during this period that we can't infer that they definitely did not participate in the campaign at Degsastan. Additional factors for committing to war would have included more general aims for the participants as securing glory and booty, a prerequisite for any self respecting warband, and one which is demonstrated by the *Gododdin*, set in this same time and space.

The Location of the Battle

The site of Degsastan has not been satisfactorily identified, though the most widespread suggestion that it was Dawston in Liddesdale was made as long ago as 1692.[4] The link was made on the basis that the two names somewhat resemble each other, though the modern place-name cannot be derived from Bede's name of the site. 'Degsa's Stone' signifies an upstanding monument which is also missing from the landscape at Dawston.[5] Dawston remained the favoured site through the 19th century, via writers such as W.F. Skene,[6] but other Borders places have been suggested, including Dalston near Carlisle and Dawstone near Jedburgh.[7] A more recently favoured, though still not a generally accepted battle site, is Addinston in Lauderdale, Berwickshire. It has been conjectured that a number of cairn burials could represent the disposal of the dead after the battle.[8] But, for all we know, the encounter could have taken place anywhere in a vast swathe of land from the Clyde valley to Tyneside.

Other Evidence: Fordun and the Anglo Saxon Chronicle

We are unfortunate that we don't have any full scale Scottish source about the battle earlier than the 14th century work of John of Fordun, which either derives from an elaboration of Bede or uses sources which no longer exist. He states that Áedán co-ordinated the campaign with British allies, leading his army by land from the north while the Britons approached from the south. Before the two armies could meet however, Æthelfrith surprised and overwhelmed the Scots who were surprised when they were engaged in burning and despoiling English territory.[9] This brings to mind the campaign of devastation that the Welsh king Cadwallon of Gwynedd waged against Northumbria in the 630s. Fordun may have borrowed details of this campaign and ascribed it to Áedán. Cadwallon's later attack against Northumbria was part of a power play to redress the historical tide of English ascendancy in what became the north of England, so that Bede accused him of attempting to eradicate the English race from the region.

While Áedán and his Irish army are likely to have had more pragmatic reasons for operating in the area, targeting the English population may also have been one aspect of their mission. The acquisition of slaves would have been a legitimate aim for any leader of the era, primarily because slaves were a commodity which could be readily exchanged for luxury and prestige goods to enhance personal glory and status. Long range transportation from Dál Riata for the sake of conducting a single, orderly battle does not accord with the behaviour of Early Medieval warlords either. Powerful leaders of that era were prone to conduct plundering raids deep into enemy territory which sometimes extended over a period of months.

The Death of Aedan's Sons

There is a hint in the record of the deaths of Áedán's sons that there was a longer campaign against Northumbria than a solitary encounter at Degsastan. However, there is conflicting information about which of his numerous sons died where. A few years before the English records of the battle of Degsastan the *Annals of Ulster* record 'the slaughter of the sons of Áedán, namely Bran and Domangart'. The *Annals of Tigernach* places the deaths of four sons at a battle in Circenn, in which Áedán was defeated. These are named as Bran, Domangart, Eochaid Find, Artúr.[10] Conflicting evidence is given by Adomnán in his *Life* of Colum Cille.[11] According to this tale, Áedán approached the saint to enquire which of his adult sons would succeed him: Artúr, Eochaid Find or Domangart. Colum Cille replied that none of them would follow him as king as they would all fall in battle, slain by enemies. The next king, the saint said, would be Eochaid Buide. Shortly after the prophecy, Artúr and Eochaid Find were killed in the battle of the Miathi against the Picts and Domangart was slain 'in a rout of battle in England [Saxonia]'.

From this it can be gathered that Eochaid Find and Artúr died fighting the Picts, as this is stated by two separate sources. Bran may have been killed by them also. Domangart's death may have been misplaced by the Irish annals and he likely died fighting the English.

Domangart appears to have died fighting either at Degsastan or in an unrecorded incident in a wider campaign against the Northumbrians in the north of England. It is likely that either Bede or the *Anglo-Saxon*

Chronicle would specifically mention the death of a son of Áedán, had it occurred at Degsastan, as other high ranking casualties are mentioned, but it is unwise to assume so from negative evidence.

English and Irish Allies

The expedition to England would have been mounted only a few years during a major campaign against the Picts, which must have depleted Áedán's resources significantly even if we assume that the northern warbands were primarily comprised of the personal retinues of several of his sons, at least against the Miathi.[12] Faced with the loss of many able fighting men in the east, Áedán might have been compelled to call upon other allies. While there is evidence of similar long range military expeditions in the 7th century, Áedán's mission is the earliest one recorded and gives an impressive picture of resources at his disposal.

One recension of the *Anglo-Saxon Chroncle* adds to Bede the information that one part of the army was led there by Hering son of Hussa.[13] Hussa can be equated with the ruler of that name who is entered as the seventh king of Bernicia in the anonymous notes added to Bede's work known as the *Moore Memoranda*.[14] He was also remembered by British sources, appearing in the 9th century *Historia Brittonum*, and given a seven year reign over Bernicia.[15] The 12th century chronicle ascribed to Florence of Worcester states that Hering was the first king of the Northumbrian English to rule after the Britons. But father and son are otherwise unknown. The wording of the entry in the *Anglo-Saxon Chronicle* does not make it clear which side Hering was fighting on. It is possible that he represents a dynastic segment which had been deprived of power and chose to oppose Æthelfrith by allying with the Irish. Such pragmatic alliances contradict the perception that Early Medieval conflict was drawn entirely across ethnic lines. High ranking individuals at least could transfer their skills to neighbouring peoples. The core of the Edinburgh based army in the *Gododdin* poem were native Britons, but also in the ranks were prominent English and Pictish heroes.[16]

There are also traditions that Áedán deployed several Irish factions against the Bernicians. Personal or tribal obligations to Áedán mac Gabráin would not seem to warrant the massive commitment required to fight in this foreign land, though the prospect of gathering large amounts of booty and associated glory from their exploits would have been a significant part in their participation. The great distance which any Dál Riatan warband had to travel to fight the Northumbrians is a measure of the capacity of that kingdom to reach far beyond its immediate borders. Accepting the nearest identified site of the battle, Dawston Rigg, would mean that the Kintyre force travelled over 160 miles (260 km) to the encounter, while the Northumbrian force, if it came from Bamburgh, would have journeyed only 50 miles (80km).[17] The logistics of Irish forces travelling to the Borders or Northumbria would of course be equally considerable, if not more so, given the necessity for sea transportation. Practical need for sustainance would mean a warband harrying and raiding near the point of arrival, especially if the native Britons were uncooperative with this Irish adventure. This scavenging behaviour may be reflected in John of Fordun's account.

The *Annals of Tigernach* record of Degsastan states that Æthelfrith's brother Eanfrith was personally slaughtered by Máel Umai mac Báetáin.[18] It is possible that the annal is mistaken in the name of Æthelfrith's brother and that it was actually Theobald who was slain. There is no known brother of Æthelfrith named Eanfrith, though he did have a son of that name who died several decades after Degsastan.[19] Máel Umai himself survived the fray, since his death is recorded around the year 610. A prince of the Cenél nEógain branch of the Uí Néill, Máel Umai's father Báetán mac Muirchertaig (d. 572), was also king of Tara. His presence in arms under Áedán marks the continuance of strong relations between the northern Uí Néill and Dál Riata. Máel Umai was called *Garg*, meaning 'hero' or 'the fierce' and was also styled *Maelhuma in rīgfẽinnid*, signifying that he led a group of young warriors.[20] A lost tale title of Máel Umai is recorded in the *Book of Leinster* as *Echtra Máel Uma meic Báetáin*, grouped in a list next to titles relating to both Áedán and the Dál nAraidi prince Mongán.[21] This proximity suggests that there was a cycle of interlinked stories about Irish heroes fighting in the north of England. The fact that each of these heroes has his own *echtra*, instead of being grouped together in a single *cath*, 'battle', tale suggests that the lost legendary material referred to a more extensive military campaign rather than a single military encounter at Degsastan.

Yet another lost tale has been seen as indicating the participation of another royal Irish hero. The story is recorded in the same list of the tales just mentioned (though not adjacent to them) as *Slúgad Fiachnai maic Báitáin co Dún nGúaire i Saxanaib*, 'The Hosting of Fiachna son of Báitán to Dún Gúairi in the land of the Saxons'.[22] The hero here is the father of Mongán, Fíachnae mac Báetáin (whose own father is not to be confused with other contemporary rulers of the same name), who we have already encountered as an ally of Áedán. The tale concerning Mongán specifically mentions Fíachnae fighting the English in northern Britain, having been summoned there to assist Áedán, though it cannot be regarded as historical proof. Assuming however that he did fight in England with Áedán, when would that have been?

Despite the association linking his Cruithin dynasty with the Isle of Man, Áedán's military action there in the early 580s looks too early a date for Fíachnae to have been actively involved. But he might have been involved in a campaign which culminated in the battle of Degsastan.

Dún nGúaire appears similar to the Din Guayrdi mentioned in the *Historia Brittonum*, which states that king Ida joined this place to his own realm of Berneich, Bernicia.[23] The place in question would be the Irish version of the stronghold called Bamburgh. But historian Kenneth Jackson pointed out there is also an entry in the *Annals of Ulster, Expugnatio Ratho Guali la Fiachna mac Baetain*, stating that Fíachnae destroyed Ráith Guali, 'the fort of Gualie,' a fortress in Ireland probably belonging to the Munster ruler Áed Bolc in the year 623.[24] There is a chance that the two places have been confused and that the description *i Saxanaib* was added to the tale in error. There is also the fact that adventures in England are not mentioned in the poem detailing the eastern Ulster kings, *Clann Ollaman Uaisle Emna*. Yet the lost tale may still refer to a place in Britain, wherever Fíachnae's later career took him. There is also the possibility that Ráith Guali is not in Ireland at all, but somewhere in Scotland.[25] It should also be noted that Munster, a province of south-west Ireland, is as remote an area of operation for an Ulster king as Northumbria. The collective evidence only leads to a stalemate.

While Bede may be accused of exaggerating both the huge size of the invading army and the scale of its casualties, we can surmise that there were distinct contingents within the ranks on both sides. Apart from the levy from Dál Riata itself and Máel Umai's Uí Néill force, there may have been Cruthin men fighting there, plus an exiled English warband under Hering son of Hussa. Each distinct *comitatus*, or warband, would be commanded by its own leader as part of the greater host. This practice was evident also in Æthelfrith's army, where one division was led by Theobald. The British at the same period also mustered larger forces along the same organisational lines.[26] With Áedán likely too old to personally lead his host into battle, this role may have been taken by either one of his sons, such as Domangart, or by a high ranking nobleman from Dál Riata.

The Aftermath

Bede mentions that Æthelfrith's brother Theobald was killed in the battle along with his entire contingent.[27] This points to a substantial slaughter on the Northumbrian side as well as the Irish. Highly committed warriors could and did fight to the deaths alongside their leaders, sometimes even when there was an option to retreat or otherwise save themselves. This was the expected price of their loyalty which would otherwise afford them tremendous shared prestige if their lord led them to victory.[28] The *Annals of Clonmacnoise* alone states that Degsastan was a victory for the Irish. The *Annals of Ulster* documents it as a defeat for Áedán, though a case has been made for amending the ambiguous notice in the *Annals of Tigernach* to show that a victory for Áedán was intended in the text.[29] A martial adventure on such a scale might have been difficult to determine as either a victory or a loss. The loss of face resulting in anything less than a magnanimous victory would have been magnified by the presence of other Irish contingents in the army. A less than obvious victory may also have damaged the delicate web of alliances between Dál Riata and other Irish powers.

We hear no more about Æthelfrith's characteristic belligerence in the British lands between the Roman walls after Degsastan. His next aggressive action was turning south against Æthelric and adding his territory of Deira to his own Bernicia to form Northumbria, which possibly suggests there was no further threat from the powers to the north of Bernicia. His most famous victory was the battle of Chester in 616, when he annihilated an army from Wales and slaughtered a large contingent of hapless monks who were praying for a British victory.[30] Yet, if Degsastan had been an overwhelming victory for the Northumbrians, we might have expected them to sweep northwards and westwards into

Participants at the Battle of Degsastan and the English Campaign

Due to his age it seems unlikely that Áedán himself would have physically fought at Degsastan and may not have been present. Uncertainty also extends to some of the other supposed participants, particularly the Irish allies who are supposed to have fought alongside the host from Dál Riata.

The Irish and their Allies

Bran and Domangart. Domangart was recorded by Adomnán as being slaughtered 'in England' and it is likely that his brother died there also. The fact that no source states that he died at Degsastan suggests he fell somewhere else during a campaign against the English.

Fíachnae mac Báetán. Also known as Fíachnae Lurgan and Fíachnae Find. Cruithin king of Dál nAraide in Ireland from the late 6th century until his death in battle in 626, slain by Fíachnae mac Demmáin of the Dál Fiatach.

Hering son of Hussa. Hussa ruled Bernicia for around seven years, possibly between 585 and 592, and was succeeded by Æthelfrith. Hering was probably an English *ætheling* allied with, or exiled in, Dál Riata.

Máel Umai mac Báetán mac Muirchertaig. Prince of the Cenél nEógain branch of the northern Uí Néill. Both his father and his brother, Colmán Rímid, were kings. He died around 610.

The English

Æthelfrith, king of Bernicia, 592–604 and Northumbria, 604–617. Son of Æthelric and grandson of the first king of Bernicia, Ida. Killed in battle by king Rædwald of East Anglia.

Eanfrith, brother of Æthelfrith. Killed at Degsastan by Máel Umai. Although there is otherwise only a record of a son of Æthelfrith named Eanfrith, this should not rule out the possibility that the first Eanfrith existed.

Theobald. No other information survives about Theobald, brother of Æthelfrith, who died in the battle.

enemy territory and take it over. As it happened, the chief seat of the Gododdin Britons, Edinburgh (Din Eidyn), did not fall to the English until 638. This is not to say that Æthelfrith's power could not have been magnified by even a marginal victory. A neutralising effect on the military capacity of the neighbouring Britons is a realistic possibility. Even if he did not have the resources to immediately annex more territory to the north he may have demanded tribute from these rudderless British states in the Scottish Lowlands, but whether he was able to extort it from Dál Riata is debateable.

Chapter 9

Death and Progeny

Thirteen years, face to face, against a Pictish army, fair the emblem; at the hour he will die he will not be king, on a Thursday, in Kintyre.[1]

If this stanza in the *Prophecy of Berchán* refers to Áedán, it opens up speculation about possible reasons for his retirement.[2] The Irish annals record the death of Áedán mac Gabráin in either the thirty-seventh or thirty-fourth year of his reign. It was more likely the latter, and a reign of that length would mean that he died in either 607 or 608, though the year 609 has also been argued. This length of personal rule stands in comparison with his older contemporary, the Pictish king Bridei mac Maelchon, who ruled from 554 to 584, and also with the Irish Cruithin king Fíachnae Longshanks, who supposedly reigned for thirty-eight years. One annal entry states that Áedán was aged seventy-four at the time of his death, which is more credible than the alternatives of eighty-six or eighty-eight given in other sources, but still represents a prodigious age in the Early Medieval period.[3]

It is likely that Áedán's advanced age and the repercussions of his defeat at Degsastan were elements which contributed to Dál Riata choosing another king. His age may have made him physically unable to fulfil some of the active functions of kingship. Past renown was not a defence against accusations of physical incompetence for elite, warrior driven societies. We might have an indication of the attitudes in a contemporary court via the reference to mockery being bestowed on the renowned leader of the British kingdom of Rheged because of his age.[4] If Áedán was no longer king, did he abdicate or was he forced to relinquish authority? Penalties for decrepitude, along with deformity, were extreme in some cases. But at least one historian has discerned a possible point of cultural difference between Dál Riata and mainstream Irish kingship. Molly Miller detected that both this people and indeed the Picts 'sometimes deposed and did not kill unsatisfactory kings'.[5]

Several writers have thought that Áedán's final years were spent in religious retirement. A passage into monastic life may seem incompatible with his former warlike behaviour, but it was a route which may have become possible through the enormous cultural influence of his *anmchara*, or 'soul friend', Colum Cille. In this respect he may have set a recent precedent, though it is interesting that the Dál nAraide king Áed Dub's attempt to assume the priesthood while in exile on Tiree was personally thwarted by Colum Cille, according to Adomnán. Marjorie Anderson considered that the annalistic death notice of Áedán's own grandfather, Domangart, who died around 507 in Kintryre, points towards a withdrawal from active kingship and entry into religion. If there was an established monastic community on the peninsula at this date, there is no record of it, whether or not it survived until Áedán's time.[6]

In the centuries following Áedán, there were other rulers who chose contemplative Christian retreat as an alternative to secular leadership, albeit religion did not harbour some of these leaders for long. A prominent early example in Ireland was Adomnán's friend Finsnechta Fledach, who abdicated as king of Tara in 688, though he only lasted a year in monastic life. In Scotland examples of royal entry into religion include Selbach, king of Dál Riata, who took the tonsure in 723, plus the Pictish king Nechton son of Derilei, who entered a monastery in 724, but later re-entered society and assumed the kingship again, as the Ulster king Áed Dub also appears to have done. Irish tracts recognise a class of 'ex-laymen', who entered religion later in their lives, called *athláech*. In some cases these men are described as former warriors who may have sought refuge in religious settings out of necessity in old age, or as a means of sanctuary following unlawful acts. They were not highly regarded by the mainstream establishment of the church and were only grudgingly accepted into monastic establishments.[7] It is possible that the date of Áedán's death actually can be pinpointed. The 8th or 9th century *Martyrology of Tallaght* lists Áedán son of Gabráin among the honoured religious figures of Ireland and gives his feast day as 17 April.[8] If, as some think, he died in the year 609, this date would have been Maundy Thursday. In a monastic setting, his brothers would be preparing for the duties which led up to the celebration of Easter.

The 14th century historian John of Fordun states that Áedán was buried at Kilkerran, on the east side of Kintyre, near the present town of Campbelltown. While there is no certain early medieval occupation site identified here, there is a cave several miles away, at Achinhoan Head, said to have been the residence at St Ciarán, a 6th century saint. The cave is one of several on the Achinhoan peninsula. The associated medieval church here is possibly no earlier than the 13th century.[9] There is a possible early Christian stone inside, marked with a decorated cross.[10] This, however, may not be earlier than the 8th century and there are few other clues about possible locations of very early Christian settlements in the peninsula of Kintyre. The dearth of knowledge regarding monastic settlement here is notable, but the small island of Gigha, off the west coast of Kintyre, has been postulated as a likely site for early monastic settlement.[11] The relative isolation of Kilkerran from well-known religious and secular power centres in the kingdom reinforces the impression that the king was removed, voluntarily or not, from playing a part in its political functioning. There was a *dun* at Kildalloig, south of Campbelltown, base of a local, minor potentate. It is tempting to think that the religious community and the ex-king himself may have been under the watchful eye of its occupant.

None of the sons of Áedán have any clerical associations, though his supposed daughters are associated with saintly lineages. It is difficult to gauge the truth of these connections, thought it must be suspected that they are echoes of Áedán's own supposed descent from St Brychan. This connection is alluded to in a late work about St Laisren, whose mother Gemma is Áedán's daughter and the niece of a British king, which suggests that Áedán married the sister of Rhydderch Hael or some other British potentate who ruled between the two Roman walls.[12]

We do not know for certain where the remains of the old king were laid to rest. Not at Iona, probably, for the first record of a ruler being buried there was later in the 7th century, when Northumbrian king Ecgfrith was interred here after being slain by the Picts at the battle of Dunnichen in Angus. One very late tradition states that Áedán was buried beneath a cairn on the north-east of Bute. The cairn was called Rulicheddan and was known in the 18th century as Realigheadhean, which was interpreted as 'Relics of Áedán'. The cairn was mostly destroyed between 1841 and 1858. A stone cist was found in its centre, but no relics which might have belonged to a king, Áedán or otherwise.[13] Excavation in the mid 19th century seemed to confirm that the great cairn was prehistoric and another warning about the veracity of a connection with Áedán is that the place had another folkloric tradition as the site of a battle between local families, the Spences and the Bannatynes. Like many other conspicuous monuments it was said that:

> The cairn covered the remains of a great hero. He was wont to wear a belt of gold, which, being charmed, protected him on the field of battle. One day however, as he rose a-hunting accompanied by his sister, the maid, coveting the golden talisman, prevailed upon him to lend it to her. While thus unprotected he was killed – whether by enemies or mischance the attenuated tradition does not clearly indicate; and this cairn marked the warrior's grave.[14]

It is possible that the Cenél Comgaill, whose territory included Bute, promoted a link with the renowned chieftain in the century after his death.

Renown and Achievements

The fame of Áedán spread through the Gaelic world in his own lifetime and was magnified by bards for many generations across both Ireland and Scotland. In Wales too he won renown, despite his impolitic infringement on the hospitality of the fortress of Dumbarton. His place in the Welsh Triads and in poems like *Peiryan Vaban* tell us that his reputation rested alongside other native heroes of *Y Gogledd*, the old North, which was an extraordinary achievement for an Irish ruler. The result of his many military campaigns was less lasting in all probability. If his forces had decisively overturned at Degsastan it might have assisted the survival of British, that is to say Welsh culture, throughout what is now southern Scotland and northern England. It is more difficult to say which of the other nations may have ended up as the cultural winner in what is now Scotland. In Ireland, Áedán pursued or was forced to accept, a hands-off position where Dál Riata accepted the overlordship of the Northern Uí Néill dynasty there, but were still able to exert some control themselves over the other major players in Ulaid, the Cruithin people and the Dál Fiatach. Despite the best intentions of Iona, the alliance between Dál Riata and the Uí Néill gradually withered away over three or four decades following Áedán's death, as we will see shortly.

Successive generations of war leaders unwittingly followed Áedán's career trajectory over the next two and a half centuries until, by some means, his descendant Cináed mac Ailpin (Kenneth mac Alpin) united the thrones of the Picts and the Scots. Despite later Scottish propaganda 'victory' over the Picts was by no means a foregone conclusion. Right up until the reign of Cináed there were periods of Pictish dominance over Dál Riata and even times when British rulers of an expanded Strathclyde kingdom achieved dominance in the north. Áedán mac Gabráin did not live in a time when personal success on the battlefield would have ensured that his posterity was destined to set future generations on course for an assured future. Having said that, it was not forgotten by later kings that he was a figure of unique achievement and tenacity on the field of battle.

Sons and Successors

The kingdom of Dal Riata probably passed, on the death of Áedán, to his son Eochaid Buide (the 'Yellow'), whose future rule was given the prophetic benediction by Colum Cille after many of his elder brothers died in battle against the Picts and the English. But there is confusion about the position of Connad Cerr, a king whose reign may have overlapped with Eochaid's or run parallel with it. We don't know whether he was a son of Eochaid or a son of Áedán's predecessor, his cousin Conall.

Whoever ruled Dál Riata after Áedán's death would have had a hard act to follow. We look here about some of his sons and grandsons before, in a following chapter, we consider the disaster and defeats which befell the kingdom later in the 7th century. There is little known about Eochaid Buide. He seems to have reigned for a creditable twenty-one years and died in the year 629.[15] The annals give few direct clues about his time in power, but this is also true of his grandfather Gabráin whose meagre annalistic record belies the fact that his kindred was named after him. Lack of records does not mean failure, especially when Eochaid's apparent reign length is considered. Still, the lack of information about him is disappointing when we remember that Eochaid was supposedly singled out from a stable of sibling princes and hand picked to rule the kingdom by Colum Cille. Eochaid's naming as successor to the kingship during his father's time may in fact have been an early instance of the *tánaiste* system, designed to stop internecine bloodshed in a scramble for power when Áedán died.[16] The battle of Delgu, in Kintyre in 574, may have been partly motivated by factional competition after the death of Áedán's predecessor Conall mac Comgaill.

We are left scrambling for meagre scraps of information of information concerning him. Both Eochaid Buide and his brother Eochaid Find bore given names which stem from the Celtic word for 'horse'. This may be a conscious link to the tribal name which occupied Kintyre centuries before, the Epidii, 'horse people'. Beyond that, Eochaid's appears as the grandfather of Cruithin king Congal Caech in the tale *Fled Dúin na nGéd*, 'The Feast of Dún na Géd', is unhistorical because they were contemporaries. However, in the light of events during his later lifetime, the connection may have been prompted by events in Ireland that concerned Dál Riata.

Towards the end of it there are records of involvement by Dál Riata's men in a spate of warfare in Ulster. Eochaid himself did not participate, as far as we know, though whether this was deliberate policy or because he had no power base in Ireland is unknown. His kinsmen, from his own generation and the next, who did battle in Ireland gained only limited success and their campaigns were brought to a bloody and disastrous conclusion by Eochaid's son and successor, Domnall Brecc. As mentioned in a previous chapter, Eochaid Buide was described in his death notice as 'king of the Picts', the first Gaelic king to bear that description, which raises interesting possibilities about his power if the description was not merely a scribal error.[17]

The rule of foreign kings in Pictland did not equate with wholescale takeover of the top layer of society by the nation which provided the non-Pictish king. That being the case, the intriguing issue is what the relationship was between the two Gaelic brothers, Gartnait and Eochaid Buide, who supposedly ruled in Pictland. The latter was certainly much younger than Gartnait and was perhaps able to succeed to part of the territory which he ruled. The possibility that their father Áedán also had sons by British and English women is discussed below.

The Drowned Prince of Dál Riata

The other princes of the Cenél n Gabráin who immediately followed in the wake of Áedán, his sons and grandsons, inhabit a half light beyond his dazzling personal fame. This is partly due of course to the arbitrary nature of history rather than the particular merits of these immediate descendants. We can still find bright beacons to light up small parts of those succeeding generations, and among these the following must rank as the most affecting:

> Conaing, son of Áedán, Gabráin's son, was drowned. This is what Ninnine the poet sang:

> *The great clear waves of the sea reflected the sun's rays;*
> *they flung themselves upon Conaing, into his frail wicker coracle.*
> *The woman who threw her white hair into Conaing's coracle,*
> *her smile has beamed to-day upon the tree of Tortu.*[18]

The prince who died, presumably in the Hebrides, must have been a man of importance to have his death recorded in the annals, following the composition of an elegy to mark his passing. It's possible that the verse represents a portion of a contemporary elegy to Conaing composed after his death.[19] If we know little about Ninnine the poet, there is even less certainty about Conaing. We do not even know for sure whether he was the son of Áedán of Dál Riata, though it appears likely. The verse tells us little more about the fate of this Conaing. We know of course that the northern kingdom he came from relied heavily on sea transport, but we don't know whether he died on a military mission or if it was merely a maritime accident. The suggestion that his demise can be linked to the Welsh Triad which records the fame of his father's sea-going warband, 'who went to sea for their lord', is unfounded, since it specified the father and not his son.[20] Beyond that, we know that Conaing was the founder of a recognised branch of the Cenél nGabráin.[21]

The woman alluded to in the verse seems to be the supernatural being called the Mórrigan and we are reminded that the dreadful whirlpool named Corrywreckan in modern times had the alternative name of the 'Cauldron of the Old Woman' in *Cormac's Glossary*. The Tree of Tortu (Bile Tortan) mentioned in the poem was a revered tree in the territory of the Uí Tortan tribe in County Meath. This tree was one of the three landmarks and one of the five great trees of Ireland and seems to have had deep mystical associations stretching back into the pre-Christian period. When it fell it stretched across Ireland. In the 11th century poetry

of the *Metrical Dindshenchas*, there is a description about the collapse of
the tree which contains a reference to a similar female spirit in Conaing's
elegy, a spirit who 'gleefully laughed' at its destruction.[22] This poem
may link the tree's end to the fall of a specific king, or line of kings.
The Mórrigan was notorious for gloating on the death of men on the
battlefield.

The surviving lore around Conaing's death channels him into the
mainstream of early Irish legend and culture, and the information hints
at a detailed death legend. His name also provides a clue towards the
aspirations and connections made by his father. The name Conaing is
a borrowing from the Old English *cynyng*, meaning 'king', and Áedán's
son is the first Gael we know to have borne this name.[23] He was not
alone among his brothers to have a non-Irish name; other sons (and
grandsons) of Áedán took their names from other peoples of Britain.
Mention was made in the previous chapter about the possibility of an
exiled Northumbrian noble named Hering fighting for the Scots at
Degsastan. We know also that there were several English monks on Iona
during Colum Cille's time and that some of the sons of Æthelfrith sought
refuge in Dál Riata after his death in 616. While Eanfrith of Bernicia
went in exile among the Picts, his brothers went to the court of Dál
Riata. It may seem surprising that they sought the friendship of a nation
whose king had fought their own father, but the diplomacy of the day
meant that alliances were fluid and there was little ethnic animosity yet
between different peoples. Also, there may have been a Saxon presence
in Áedán's court during the intervening time. It has been suggested that
the Osric (Oisiricc mac Albruit) who died at the battle of Fid Eóin in
Ireland in 728 was a grandson of Áedán, the result of a union between
a Northumbrian and Áedán's daughter.[24] Beyond that, we know next to
nothing about him as an individual. One crucial fact, however, is known
in addition. This is that his son was called Rigullán, and that name is not
an Irish Gaelic name, but a British Celtic one.

Strangers in the Family?

The fact that Áedán had a grandson with a British name, Rigullán,
hints at a close connection (though not necessarily a blood relationship)
between the ruling family of Dál Riata and the Britons, probably the

Britons of Dumbarton or the Clyde valley. One source informs us the name of a son of Eochaid Find mac Áedán was Pledan, which means 'Briton', reinforcing the connection between neighbouring kingdoms.[25] Áedán's own possible British descent was examined in an earlier chapter, and this name evidence may suggest that either Áedán or one of his sons married a British royal woman.

Facts about Rigullán (or Rígullón) are just as scanty as those about his father, Conaing. His name equates to the Welsh Rhiwallon (Old Welsh Riguallaun from Early Celtic *Rīgo-vellaunos*, meaning 'most kingly') and he seems to be referenced in the early Welsh poem *Peiryan Vaban* (which also mentions his grandfather) in the context of being brother of the legendary Myrddin.[26] The *Annals of Tigernach* tell us that Rigullán died around 630, in the battle of Fid-eoin in the north of Ireland. A fellow casualty was another grandson of Áedán, Failbe son of Eochaid, and the king of Dál Riata, Connad Cerr.[27]

There is another grandson of Áedán with a British name: Morgand, who bears a name which crops up in several north British genealogies (as Morcant) and was borne by later generations of Gaelic Scots.[28] Morgan(d) is named as the son of Eochaid Find, son of Áedán, in the tract called *Míniugud Senchesa fher nAlban*.[29] Two British names in the lineage might possibly be taken as cultural coincidence. The fact that there was a third surely says that the connection between the Irish and the British was very close indeed at this time. But the very name of this third Dál Riatan prince with a British name adds a huge strata of complication because of its historical significance: his name was Artúr (Arthur).

Artúr of Dál Riata

The Artúr, or Arthur, who was either the son or the grandson of Áedán mac Gabráin, is fully as obscure an individual as any of his kinsmen previously mentioned.[30] But the enormous significance of his name has meant he has been unhappily dragged into orbit around the Arthurian legend, to the benefit of neither the history of Early Modern Scotland nor Arthuriana in general. We are compelled to examine this association, even though it is largely a modern phenomenon which has marginal relevance to the family of Áedán. Despite repeated warnings from historians some modern writers have continued to wrongly equate this Arthur with the Arthur of legend.[31]

Several facts should be noted about this northern Arthur initially. One of the earliest men in the British Isles or Ireland who bears this name, he is mentioned in the late 7th century by Adomnán, in his *Life* of Colum Cille, who states that Artúr died in battle against the Picts, along with several of his brothers, around 590. This source makes him Áedán's son. The later *Míniugud Senchesa fher nAlban* calls him a grandson of Áedán, which would transfer his lifespan into the early-mid 7th century.[32] There is no reason that there could not have been two Arthurs, uncle and nephew, in the same lineage. Given names were bestowed on closely related men within the ruling lineage at this time. One example is that two of Áedán's sons were named Eochaid.

Did Áedán choose to name this prince after an actual British warrior, a legendary folk hero, or someone else? Unfortunately there can never be any definitive answer about this. Some have claimed that he was named after an entirely imaginary folk hero famous among the Britons.[33] This can be ruled out on the basis that no other Irish royals were named (as far as I know) after fictional foreigners, however famous they may have been in popular tales. The only two 'actual' royal Arthurs we know about crop up, roughly contemporaneously, in the genealogies of the kingdoms of Dyfed and Dál Riata, several generations after the original Arthur is supposed to have existed as a Celtic British warlord fighting the English somewhere in post-Roman Britain. The name Artúr, a son of Pedr, in the genealogy of the rulers of Dyfed, possibly suggests a late 6th century lifespan. Curiously, both these kingdoms were formed by Irish settlers which should be placed alongside the extraordinary fact is that no known person of Welsh descent bore the name Arthur until the 16th century.

Leaving aside the possibly equation of Áedán's son or grandson being the prototype for the legendary hero for a while, we can ask whether the real warlord Arthur was in fact based in the northern part of Britain. Like everything Arthurian, there is no clear answer to this. The list of Arthur's battles, which some have chosen to believe as an early indication of his geographical military range, contain only one certain location which can be placed within the area which later became Scotland: the battle at Celyddon Forest, which was likely somewhere in the Southern Uplands of Scotland.[34] The other battles in this list might be located anywhere from Cornwall northward.[35] Despite this, the name of the real Arthur may still have had currency as a remembered warrior in the far north.

The *Gododdin* poem, which recounts the military campaign of an Edinburgh-based British army in the 6th century, features a throwaway comparison about one of the fighters involved, who, though he was brave, 'was not Arthur'.[36] The date of this passage in the poem is contentious, but if we accept that the mention of Arthur is among the earlier material incorporated in the poem it would go some way to indicating (in conjunction with the Dál Riatan Arthur), that this hero was well-known in the north. Honourable mention in support of this should also be made of Arthur son of Bicoir, described as a Briton (though perhaps it was his father who was the Briton), who killed the famous Ulster king Mongán son of Fiachna in (Scottish) Dál Riata, around 625.[37] He will be mentioned again below. The suggestion that the little known prince from Argyll who died in battle against the Picts was in fact the man who became famous as 'King' Arthur has grown in recent years. The fact that this can be refuted at a number of levels has not stopped a number of authors fervently asserting that this is the truth. Points against this northern Arthur being 'King Arthur' include the fact that he was the wrong race, lived too late, and does not seem to have accumulated any trace of personal fame we know about during his own lifetime.[38]

Having disposed of King Arthur, we can ask why were there so many foreign names in the Dál Riata dynasty at this period? There is no comparable record of this happening with any other ruler of any nationality within the British Isles where we can see instances of names from several other nations within various generations. Whether the names in Áedán's family tree are mere borrowings from other nearby peoples which mean no more than his awareness of them and desire to be seen as a possible overlord over all the north is debatable. It may well be due to a combination of inter-marriage with neighbouring peoples and his desire to invoke some degree of authority over them. The non-Gaelic names mostly have royal connotations, but are not specifically named after known heroes, with the possible exception of Artúr. The contention that the latter was so named after his father as a genealogical insult to the Northumbrian English,[39] against whom he would be sent in warfare, falls down due to the lack of evidence and the knowledge that the Dál Riatan prince lost his life fighting the Picts and not the English.

It's more likely, I believe, that there were different marriage connections between Áedán's kindred and other ethnic groups. The names may show there was a delicate and extensive outreach of high level alliance and diplomacy initiated by Dunadd. Part of this involved Áedán involved in personal relationships with royal British, Pictish and English women.[40] Such unions were important for short term alliances even though the respective races united might still partake in habitual hostility against each other. A pertinent example is the British royal woman Rienmellt of Rheged who seems to have married Oswiu of Northumbria, a union that did nothing to stop Northumbria annihilating Rheged in short measure.[41]

The fact that English and perhaps Pictish names occur within several generations in the Cenél nGabráin speaks of a complicated interconnectivity of people in North Britain. The court of Dunadd at the turn of the 7th century can be seen as a multicultural place, the result of a policy to connect itself strongly with other ruling centres throughout Britain. In this we can suspect that Áedán was at the forefront of insular diplomacy during his era.

The Legend of Guaire

Some caution must be given when ascribing offspring to kings when the names of the children are transmitted in different sources. Apart from those sons and grandsons considered above there is another possible candidate who is not specifically named as Áedán's son but may be just that. In Adomnán's *Life* of Colum Cille there is a tale concerning a man named Guaire, said to have been the son of the strongest man in Dál Riata.[42] His father is named as Áedán, though it is not specified whether or not he was the king. Guaire's tale deserves examination for its own intrinsic worth and the light it sheds on other subjects.

Adomnán states that Guaire went to Colum Cille and asked him how he would meet his death and was told that he would not die in war, nor at sea. An echo here perhaps of the prophecy involving Áedán's other sons. One of Guaire's companions, the saint said, whom he would not suspect would cause his demise. Guaire then wondered whether one of his entourage would plot to murder him, or whether his wife would plan it through witchcraft if she fell in love with a younger man. Colum Cille denied it would happen that way and responded to Guaire's questioning by saying knowledge of his killer would cause him great trouble until the time when his death actually happened. One day, Guaire was sitting under an upturned boat, whittling the bark from a stick (or a spear perhaps), when he heard an argument among some men nearby. He jumped up quickly in order to stop the fight, but his knife penetrated his knees and the wound became badly infected, directly causing his death some months later.

Adomnán gives other occasions when Colum Cille engaged in prophesy on behalf of royal associates. Most notable was the instance when he asked Áedán which of his three adult sons would be king after him. When the king stated he did not know which one, the saint responded that the kingship would be conferred on Eochaid Buide, then a child.[43] Another example follows that story in the *Life* when the saint encounters Domnall mac Áed in Ireland and foretells that he will outlive all of his brothers and be a famous king and die in old age in his own bed. Similarly, Colum Cille grants knowledge of his personal future to the prince named Scandlán who was being held as a prisoner.[44] Other individuals, royal and not, are granted insight into their own ultimate fate by Colum Cille, but the covenant seems more striking when it is between the saint and a king or future king. The closest parallel to Guaire's circumstance in the work is that of the British king of Dumbarton, Rhydderch Hael, who specifically asks for the boon of knowing how he would be meet his end and is granted it.[45]

The exact nature of the story has obscured its meaning to scholars because of its obscure Latin in the original. David Woods believed the incident involved Guaire scraping barnacles from the bottom of a wooden vessel.[46] The death of Guaire seems to incorporate strong mythic elements and the tale may have accrued these by oral transmission before it was incorporated by Adomnán into his *Life* of Colum Cille. Examination of the tale has revealed similarities with other 'wounded kings' in traditional Celtic material.[47] The most notable character in that category is the elusive Fisher King, but it would perhaps be unwise to use that similarity to throw Guaire into the whirlpool of Arthurian speculation in the same way as his possible brother Artúr. Better that his story is considered as a intriguing addition to the fabric of material about the other progeny of Áedán.

Children and Grandchildren of Áedán

Various sources give different accounts of the names and relationships of the sons and grandsons of Áedán. The *Míniugud Senchesa fher nAlban* mentions seven sons: Eochaid (Buide), Eochaid (Find), Tuathal, Bran, Báithéne, Conaing, Gartnait. Adomnán names four sons: Artúr, Eochaid Find, Domangart, plus Eochaid Buide who succeeded as king. The list given here is not exhaustive. Names with disputed descent in italics.

Artúr. Killed in battle against the Picts (*c.* 590?), according to Adomnán, who names him as a son of Áedán. But *Míniugud Senchesa fher nAlban* states he was a son of Áedán's son Conaing.

Báithéne son of Áedán. No details are known about him.

Bran son of Áedán. Died in battle against the Picts, according to Irish annals. But there is a possibility he died fighting the English.

Conaing son of Áedán. Drowned, *c.* 622.

Conchenn daughter of Áedán. Mentioned in *Amra Coluimb Chille.*

Domangart. Died in battle in England, according to Irish annals. His death also mentioned by Adomnán. D. *c.* 598. Adomnán makes him a son of Áedán, but *Míniugud Senchesa fher nAlban* calls him a grandson.

Eochaid Buide son of Áedán. Succeeded Áedán as king. D. 629.

Eochaid Find son of Áedán. Killed in battle against the Picts, according to Adomnán. Died *c.* 590.

Gartnait son of Áedán? King of the Picts. Died *c.* 599?

Gemma. Mother of St Laisren. *Vita Sanctorum Hiberniae.* Possibly identical with **Maithgemm.** Allegedly married Cairell, of Dál Fiatach.

Guaire son of Áedán? Possible son mentioned in Adomnán's *Life* of Colum Cille.

Morgand son of Eochaid Find.

Oisiric mac Albruit? Described as rigdomna Saxan, an English prince,' who died with other descendants of Áedán at the battle of Fid Eóin in Ireland in 629. It has been suggested he was a grandson of Áedán by a daughter of his.

Rigullán son of Conaing. Died at the battle of Fid Eoin in Ireland. *c.* 629.

Tuathal son of Áedán.

Chapter 10

In the Wake of a Mighty Lord

I saw an array that came from Kintyre
who brought themselves as a sacrifice to a holocaust...
And it was Domnall Brecc's head that the ravens gnawed.[1]

During the 7th and 8th centuries it has to be admitted that Dál Riata did not outshine its fellow nations in North Britain, the Picts, British, or English. There was little evidence that it would eventually take over that entire region and form the basis for the eventual kingdom of Scotland. Even Áedán's own kindred lost dominance within Dál Riata, or at least were obliged to share its rule. The king's immedieate successors were partly responsible for the loss of pre-eminence after his death though other kindreds were keenly waiting to take advantage in the north.

This chapter examines two major themes which are relevant to the legacy of Áedán mac Gabráin and explain some part of his place in history. The first is the bare bones of Dál Riatan history in the 7th century and the second is the undercurrent of tales and legends which seem to have been first formulated, at least in part, during this area.

The Death of Mongán

The shadowy early history of the kingdom of Dál Riata includes fragments of verse and prose legend which can give a sense of the connectivity of the northern world, British and Irish, at this time. This legacy of important links was forged, to a large extent, by the political and military efforts of Áedán himself. An example of the complex relationships evident during this period is the death of Mongán, the Cruithin ruler whose father, Fíachnae mac Báetáin, was a key ally in Áedán's war against the English at the turn of the century. Although we don't know the full details, Mongán's death around the year 625 was regarded as a momentous event and was marked in the annals and in verse. The *Annals of Tigernach* gives an account of the event and an excerpt of a poem about it composed by a Dál Fiatach king of Ulster who died a century later:

> Mongán, son of Fiachna Lurgan, was struck with a stone by Arthur's son, a Briton, and perished.
>
> And hence Bec Boirche said, *'The wind blows cold over Islay; there are youths approaching in Kintyre: they will do a cruel deed thereby, they will slay Mongán, son of Fiachna.'*[2]

The *Annals of Clonmacnoise*, confusing the father and son, states: 'Mongán, Fiachna's son, a very well-spoken man, and one much given to the wooing of women, was killed by one Bicor, a Welshman (Briton), with a stone.' Another poem adds that he was slain 'at the meeting of the boundaries'.[3] In the legendary tale *Immram Brain*, the 'Voyage of Bran', Mongán's 'true' supernatural father, the god Manannán, laments the death of his son, who will meet his end in Islay at a predestined hour:

> *He will be – his time will be short –*
> *Fifty years in this world:*
> *A dragonstone from the sea will kill him*
> *In the fight at Senlabor.*
> *He will ask a drink from Loch Ló,*
> *While he looks at the stream of blood,*
> *The white host will take him under a wheel of clouds*
> *To the gathering where there is no sorrow.*[4]

Despite these evocative descriptions we know almost nothing about this hero's actual life. In hindsight, and although he was not a native Dál Riatan prince, his death on behalf of them and in their territory looks like an unconscious elegy which ushered in a more brutal, less poetic period. Individual heroism is overtaken by grim, mass carnage in successive, increasingly meaningless battles. The 'Death of Mongán' was perhaps a specific tale which has not survived and the fragments are some way short of the whole. What was Mongán doing in Islay, the territory of the Cenél nÓengusa, in Dál Riata? And who was the Briton Artúr (the second person we know about in Dál Riata with this famous name within a generation) who slew him with a slingshot? It might be guessed that, if Artúr was coming from Kintyre, he was attached to some faction of the Cenél nGabráin and opposed to the native kindred in Islay (or their Irish Airgíalla allies), but we can say no more. The policy of outreach which was evidently begun by Áedán mac Gabráin to his British neighbours may ultimately have resulted in this warrior's presence in the core Dál Riatan territory. In light of the changing alliances which affected the major power groupings in the north of Ireland in these decades it is also possible that Mongán was leading a force hostile to his family's former allies in Dál Riata.

As we have seen earlier in this book, Mongán was conceived by a liaison between his mother and the god Manannán while his royal father, a subordinate ally of Áedán mac Gabráin, was fighting the English in North Britain. The god himself appeared on the battlefield and fought a fearsome English champion. If the divine fatherhood of the hero was partly inspired by the aspirations of his own Cruithin people to contest their right to the Isle of Man against the Ulaid, it also powerfully implies much about Áedán, an Irish king who could summon an ancient god to stand alongside him on the battlefield. Are there other hints about an underlying connection between Áedán's aspirations on the Solway and the Mongán-Manannán legend? One strand of tradition says that Mongán was carried off into the Otherworld at three days old. As Proinsias Mac Cana has pointed out, there is a direct parallel between this and the fate of the Welsh hero/god Mabon son of Modron as an infant of the same age.[5] Mabon was specifically honoured in the Solway Firth area between modern England and Scotland, where Áedán was reputedly militarily active.

The Cauldron of War and Legend

The same multi-ethic complexity of legend and facts runs through the mainly frustrated ambitions of Dál Riata as it involved itself in the wars of Ulster and beyond in Ireland throughout the first few decades of the 7th century. King Fíachnae Find (or Lurgan), may have died soon after his son Mongán, but this fact does not get in the way of the legend that Mongán avenged himself upon his father's killer. This killer was, confusingly, another king named Fíachnae. He was a Dál Fiatach ruler of Ulaid, son of Demmán and nephew of Áedán's old adversary, Báetáin mac Cáirill. This Fíachnae was also known as Fíachnae Dub, 'the Black', possibly to distinguish him from his enemy, Fíachnae Find, the 'Fair'.

Battles on Irish soil were something which Áedán notably avoided, but for a variety of reasons his successors were drawn into the wars which scarred the north of Ireland in the first half of the century. The first known battle they took part in was an encounter at Fidnach Eilegg in Dál Riata itself, in 615 or 617. Nothing is known about the participants or the outcome of this battle. In the year 627, Connad Cerr of Dál Riata slew Fíachnae mac Demmáin at the battle of Ard Corrand, which one source says was directly in retaliation for the killing of the Cruithin king Fíachnae in the previous year. It was a battle which took place between different factions of the Cruithin in 629, named Fid Eóin, which proved to be the first disaster in Ireland for Dál Riata. Connad Cerr himself fell, as well as his close kin, grandsons of Áedán, named as Rigullán, cousin Failbe and another possible cousin, Oisiric. One annal speaks of a very great slaughter of the men Oisiric had there. All the warbands commanded by the fallen leaders from Dál Riata must have similarly suffered.

The bloody battle which Colum Cille had visions of following Druim Cett was next in the sequence of encounters which Dál Riata were involved with. This was the battle of Dún Ceithirn, which took place soon after the fight at Fid Eóin. Here the main combatants were the Uí Néill and the Cruithin. The latter were defeated and Dál Riata was in alliance with the victors. The last major battle which Dál Riata participated in during the first half of the 7th century was a disaster for its standing among the kingdoms of the north. It marked a major personal setback for the new king of Dál Riata, Domnall, the son of Eochaid Buide. Domnall, known as *Brecc*, 'the freckled' (or 'pock marked'), took part in five battles that we are aware of. The range of his ambition seems to have paralleled his famous grandfather, Áedán mac Gabráin, but his capability, or his luck, led to disaster for him personally and badly dented the power of his dynasty.

Mag Rath (or Moira), which took place in County Down in 637, was reputed to have been the largest battle ever fought in Ireland and one tradition has the fight lasting the course of a whole week. These are probably exaggerations and part of the legends associated with the

event, which are considerable. The battle was a culmination in the decade
long power struggle between the Cruithin king Congall Cáech, who was
established as overking of Ulaid, and the leadership of the Cenél Conaill
branch of the Uí Néill. The Cenél Conaill king who was victorious in the
battle was the same Domnall son of Áed who was singled out for great
things as a child by Colum Cille at the convention of Druim Cett. His
victory effectively sealed the dominance of the Uí Néill in the north of
Ireland and it is significant that he was the first ruler properly designated
as high-king in Ireland.

Many of the legends surrounding this bloody battle centre around a
supposed Cruithin king Suibhne, who was driven mad by the experience
of Mag Rath. *Suibhne Gelt*, 'the Wild,' is the subject of the 12th century
saga *Buile Shuibhne*, which is based on poetic material circulating in earlier
centuries. Two associated tales which deal with events leading up to the
battle touch on an alliance made between Dál Riata and Congal's Dál
nAraide dynasty, which abruptly ended the traditional links between Cenél
nGabráin and Cenél Conaill to unleash the forces of Dál Riata against the
Uí Néill. The 12th century Irish tale *Fled Dúin na nGéd* states that the
defeated Congal Cáech fled to Britain after his defeat at Dún Ceithirn
and sought refuge at the court of his maternal grandfather, Eochaid
Buide, who dwelt at Dún Monaid. While there is a possibility that this
relationship may be real, we have to start doubting the story when it next
states that Congall's maternal grandmother was daughter of a fictitious
king of the Britons, Eochaid Aingces. King Eochaid would not personally
assist his grandson against the Uí Néill king, for he had promised Domnall
when he was exiled in Scotland that he would never oppose him. Yet he
said his four sons would join in an expedition to Ireland. Congall's uncles
were named as Aedh of the Green Dress, Suibhne, Congal Menn, and
Domnall Brecc, the eldest. Apart from Domnall, the brothers named here
seem to be fictitious. There was a dispute between the brothers about
who should give hospitality to Congall, which also involved the siblings
laying claim to a magic cauldron from the king's house which never
became empty of meat. This magic heirloom of the Cenél nGabráin was
named *Caire Ainsican*, though we never hear about it again in any source.
A council was then called and the king's chief druid, Dubdiadh, and all
the other druids discussed the merits of the invasion. But a dire warning
was issued to the men of Scotland:

Ten hundred heads shall be the beginning of your slaughtered.
Around the great fair king of Ulster,
This number shall be slaughtered of the men of Alba,
And ten hundred fully.
Wolves and flocks of ravens
Shall devour the heads of your heroes...
When the obstinate are on the brink of destruction!
Your men shall be separated from sovereignty,
Your women shall be without constant goodness.

Despite this stark prophecy, Congall persuaded them to go on expedition to Ireland. He then went to solicit aid from the British king, said to have been the son-in-law of Eochaid and also Congall's grandmother.[6] The tale obviously does not convincingly explain the dramatic policy change by the ruling Cenél nGabráin. The alliance between the Dál Riata and the Uí Néill had held firm for almost half a century, following the agreement between the kings, Áedán and Áed mac Ainmuirech, at the convention of Druim Cett. Cenél nGabráin had fought against Congall at the battle of Dún Ceithirn, and some of Domnall's close relatives had also been slaughtered by Congall's brother at the battle of Fid Eóin. An earlier tale, *Cath Maige Rath*, at least addresses the anachronism in the rulership of Dál Riata at this time and states that Congall went to visit Domnall Brecc, who was ruling in Argyll. But it gives us no details of any discussion, historical or legendary, which may have taken place in Dál Riata.[7]

Traditional accounts which say that Domnall Brecc's invading army contained not only his own Irish or Scots, but also Picts and Britons, may in fact have a kernel of truth in them. If he commanded such multi ethnic resources (which he then wasted in a profligate fashion) it was due to links made by his father and grandfather. Thanks to the policy of Áedán, the court at Dunadd had become somewhere which actively encouraged relationships with neighbouring foreign powers. Literature also gives evidence about the cultural interchange across the Irish channel. The wildman Suibhne, who loses his senses after the subsequent battle in 637, is a reflex legend very probably borrowed from the British figure of Lailoken or Myrddin Wyllt, who similarly went mad after the battle of Arthuret in the year 573. There seems to have been a transfer of legendary material from North Britain to Ireland around this time, which may have been a byproduct of Dál Riata's engagement with the Britons and their campaign in Ulster. The position of eastern Ulster as a landing place and confluence of traditions and people brought over from Britain at this period has been noted. It's likely that the monastery of Bangor on Belfast Lough was a power house creating or magnifying the traditions associated with Mag Rath and also the cycle of stories associated with Mongán.[8]

The negative repercussions of this breach in alliance at Mag Rath were enormous for Domnall Brecc's dynasty. This last Irish defeat signalled the end of his effective control of the Irish homeland. With the benefit of hindsight, the powerful religious institution based on Iona wrote a version of history which promised that the Cenél nGabráin would prosper and maintain the kingship of Dál Riata as long as it worked in alignment with the rulers of Cenél Conaill in Ireland. This solemn oath had been given by Colum Cille to Áedán, according to Adomnán. The breach in agreement led Cumméne Find, abbot of Iona in the 7th century, to blame the fact that Dál Riata in his day was under the sway of foreigners (probably the Northumbrian English) on the betrayal of this traditional alliance.

The Battle of Sailtír and the Fate of Domnall Brecc

The particulars of Domnall Brecc's involvement in the battle are mired in the surviving legendary accounts. Neither Adomnán's account (which states that he ravaged Cenél Conaill lands), nor any other source, gives concrete proof that he was personally present on the battlefield. One tradition has him being confronted on the field by two sons of Domnall, Áed's son, which compelled him to surrender. One version of *Cath Maige Rath* has the entire contingent of Dál Riata being slaughtered on the field, except one man who lived only long enough to relate the awful tidings.[9] There was also a simultaneous battle, named Sailtír, fought on the same day. This seems to have been a naval encounter off Kintyre and possibly added insult to injury for Domnall. Abbot Cumméne's tale of Domnall's treachery was spelled out in no uncertain terms in Adomnán's work of Colum Cille.[10] We have an anachronistic story about the saint vowing that the Cenél nGabráin will be all powerful unless their rulers betray Iona and his own kindred the Cenél Comgaill. This prophecy, and the saint's resultant curse, fell upon Domnall when he laid waste the territory of Domnall son of Áed. This may mean that Dál Riata's forces raided Donegal, in which case they were perhaps pursued back to Kintyre by sea. Personally present on the field that day in Ireland or not, the result for Domnall was a calamitous loss of prestige.

On the surface, the parallels between Domnall Brecc and his illustrious grandfather abound. Not only did he find a place (though hardly a happy one) in Adomnán's great work, he also figures in some legendary material. Like Áedán also, we have a record of a handful of battles ascribed to this grandson. The first we hear of Domnall is around the year 622 when he is recorded fighting alongside the Southern Uí Néill king Conall son of Suibhne in Meath. An echo here, in reverse, of the battle in the Hebrides in 568 which saw a Meath king fighting in the Dál Riatan islands. This first battle was his only recorded appearance on a victorious side. He was defeated at a place named Calathros (which may mean 'harbour point'), probably on Islay around 635, which may have led to a diminishing of his authority within Dál Riata. Worse was to come after Mag Rath, which likely resulted in him losing control of his Irish lands. His army was put to flight at another unidentified place, Glend-Mairison, around 640. This was apparently on the Scottish mainland somewhere, though we do not know if his opponents were Picts, Britons, or fellow Irish.[11]

His end was not long in arriving. In 642 he came head to head with the British men of Dumbarton at Strathcarron, somewhere near the present town of Falkirk. This was in the contentious midland plain of Manau and his opponent was Owein son of Beli, British king of Dumbarton. The geography of the encounter is somewhat surprising. Domnall was a considerable distance outside of Dál Riata. If his diminished warband was still based in his homeland, he would have made the journey east through the region of Menteith, a place associated with his grandfather. There is an indication that he may have been forced to share power in Dál Riata with Connad Cerr's son Ferchar. If Mag Rath meant the effective annihilation of his power base in Ireland, the defeats of 635 and 640 greatly lessened his authority in Scotland. The move eastwards looks more like an act of desperation than a resolute attempt to capture the plain of Manau. It followed the fortuitous deaths of his likely overlords, Domnall in Ireland and Oswald in Northumbria. There had been a collapse in British power in south east Scotland and the English takeover threatened Manau and also made both Dál Riada and the surviving British kingdoms vulnerable to Northumbria for much of the rest of the 7th century. Domnall may have decided that one rash military act could help him stake a claim to the vital central area of Scotland. The *Annals of Tigernach* state that the battle occurred in December, which is hardly the ideal time for a long-range military expedition, and this information adds to the sense that it was an ill thought out reaction to some unknown advance by the Britons.

A victory poem composed for the Britons of the Clyde which has fortuitously survived affords us detail about the circumstances of Domnall's demise. With his array of men from Pentir (Kintyre), the Cenél nGabráin warband apparently took the Britons by surprise at dawn. Although the Strathcarron area was also not within the core area of these Britons, but a considerable distance to the east, the fragment of poetry implies that they had made inroads into the area and indeed had established settlements there. The region of Manau was a tempting territorial prize up for grabs at this time as the kingdom which controlled it, British Gododdin, had collapsed and its chief citadel, Edinburgh, had fallen to the Northumbrian English only a few years previously. The verse describes the Britons descending from an established township in Strathcarron to confront the invaders. The result, for Domnall at least, was annihilation, his severed head being gnawed by ravens on the battlefield. Ironically, like his more successful grandfather, he won some degree of eternal fame through being remembered in Welsh verse. Unlike the Mag Rath verses, or even the poem *Peiryan Vaban* about Áedán, we can be certain that the chilling victory song crowing over his death echoes a contemporary British celebration piece about the battle.

Bad luck may have played a part in the downward trajectory of Domnall's career, but to lose four major battles in less than ten years speaks of something more than carelessness. His power began to be eroded internally within his lifetime, giving an opportunity to the Cenél nComgáill segment from Cowal to dominate. Following Domnall's death the rising regional superpower, Northumbria, took the upper hand in the north for several generations and was not ultimately subdued until heavily defeated by the Picts at the battle of Dunnichen in 685. It was Áedán himself, through his own hard experience, who opened the door for the first Northumbrian refugees at his court before the exiled sons

Kings in the North of Ireland, 6th to 7th Centuries

Dál Fiatach Kings (Ulaid)

Demmán mac Cairill. Died 571.

Báetán mac Cairill. Opponent of Áedán. Died 581.

Fíachnae mac Demmáin. Also known as **Fíachnae Dub**. King of Dál Fiatach dynasty. Opponent of the Cruithin for power in Ulaid. Killed king Fíachnae Lurgan. Slain by Connad Cerr of Dál Riata at the battle of Ard Corainn in 627.

Cruithin Kings

Áed Dub. Died *c.* 588. Killer of Diarmait mac Cerbaill, king of Tara. Possibly ally of Áedán.

Fíachnae mac Báetáin. Also known as **Fíachnae Lurgan** and **Fíachnae Find**. Possibly came to power in 588. Ally of Áedán in English wars. Killed by Dál Fiatach king Fíachnae mac Demmán at the battle of Leithet Midind in 626.

Congall Cáech. Grandson of Fíachnae Lurgan. Killed by the Uí Néill at the battle of Mag Roth in 637.

Cenel nÉogain Kings (Uí Néill)

Colmán mac Báetáin (or **Colmán Rimid**). D. 604. His brother Máel Umai led a contingent of troops for Áedán at the battle of Degsastan.

Cenel Conaill Kings (Uí Néill)

Áed mac Ainmuirech. Ruled c. 586 until death in 598. Attended convention of Druim Cett with Áedán.

Domnall mac Áedo. Son of Áed mac Ainmuirech. Defeated and killed Congall Cáech at Mag Roth in 637. Died in 642.

of Æthelfrith fled north following the death of their father. Within Dál Riata, the Cenél nLoairn saw their opportunity to take control of the whole kingdom following Domnall's disastrous reign, though their ascent was only a temporary aberration in the long run. The kingship passed again to the rulers of Cenél nGabráin, who celebrated their descent not from Domnall, but from the illustrious Áedán mac Gabráin. It would be left to other kings, like the ill-remembered Áed Find, who reigned for thirty years, and the celebrated Cináed mac Ailpin in the 9th century, to restore the lineage to its former glory created by Áedán.

Appendix

Áedán mac Gabráin in Legend

How did the legend of Áedán develop in the centuries after his death? His name would certainly have been remembered as an honoured ancestor by those lineages which descended from him. We know there were several side branches in the Cenél nGabráin which did not compete for kingship, so he may have had many descendants through his multiple children. Áedán's fame also seems to have been honoured by those not directly descended from him, such as the Cenél nComgaill, and his reputation of course widely circulated in Ireland. Decades ago the perceptive late historian Molly Miller noted that 'a thorough study of the growth of the Áedán legend in Irish material was needed'.[1] This still awaits and hopefully when such an academic study arrives it will shed further light on the fascinating array of material which mentions this ruler. What remains is a fragmentary, frustrating record of the king through the looking glass of legend, but we should perhaps celebrate the fact that anything at all survives from his remote lifetime.

Legends which reference Áedán are of course only a miniscule part of the great national history of Wales, broadly termed *ystoryaeu*, and the oral traditional history of Ireland, *seanchus*.[2] Given the poor survival of early material from Scotland, it is hardly surprising that we don't have any written material about Áedán from that nation. Much of what does survive elsewhere exists in piecemeal form. We only have the title of the tale named *Echtra Aedán meic Gabráin*, and the Welsh tales about Áedán and his warband in the Triads exist only as short summaries. It is easy too to blame the garbled qualities of some of the surviving tales on the monks who wrote them down first, or on later copyists. But, by the time the religious scribes took town some of these tales, they had doubtless been through the mill of oral repetition for several hundred years. The flaws and omissions in the manuscripts may be as much due to the defects of the tale tellers as those who scratched out the words on the page. Early professional story-tellers were highly honoured and peripatetic, carrying tales from one kingdom to another. Their repertoires included specific categories of tales they had to remember in order to entertain aristocratic courts. The *filíd*, or poets, had to learn a rota of primary and secondary tales.

Many of the actual texts are lost, but we have lists of the headings they were grouped under. According to medieval Irish manuscripts, the highest grade of poets had to commit to memory 250 major tales and 350 minor ones. They were classified as *togla* (destructions), *tána* (cattle raids), *tochmarca* (wooings), *catha* (battles), *uatha* (terrors), *immrama* (voyages), *aite* (deaths), *fessa* (feasts), *forbassa* (sieges), *echtrae* (adventure journeys), *aitheda* (elopements), *airgne* (plunderings).[3] We are told specifically that the audience for these primary tales were chieftains and kings.

There is no certainty when the Irish tales of Áedán began to circulate orally, but there is no reason to suppose that it was long after his death, since a tale like the *Echtra* was doubtless a secular independent tale of adventure which magnified the character of Áedán more than Adomnán's *Life* of Colum Cille. The 'Tale of Cano', one of the primary tales, features an anachronistic guest appearance by Áedán, and references real events in the Hebrides in the late 7th century. The primary tales manuscript list contains another story from the same century and also set in the Western Isles: the slaughter of St Donnan on the island of Eigg in 617.[4] This legend exists in various short versions[5] and demonstrates that stories set within the orbit of Scottish Dál Riata must have formulated at an early period, though the date of their transmission to Ireland is unknowable.

Áedán's appearance in Welsh legend is tied up with the great abundance of material which concerns North Britain found, sometimes in fragmentary form, in Wales itself in later centuries. There is a case in stating that a lot of this Northern material was manufactured in Wales itself to serve an abiding fashion for material set in *Y Gogledd*, the fabled 'Old North'. Some tales and genealogical material supported the claims of Welsh rulers who promoted ancestors from that region. But the sheer amount of tradition from North Britain suggests that some of it represents a body of tales and poetry transmitted to Wales which then evolved and changed over several centuries. Nobody in medieval Wales would have invented tales of Áedán out of the ether unless there was some pre-existing knowledge about him. These traditions must have come from either Ireland or Scotland. When exactly the traditions travelled south from what is now the Scottish Lowlands is unknown. But there is a record that some of the British aristocracy of Strathclyde migrated to Wales when Cináed mac Ailpín's Scottish dynasty were pressurising their territory in the late 9th century, albeit there are doubts about the accuracy of the late source which contains this detail.

The 'Tale of Cano'

There is a window into the 7th century world we can enter to look at how these tales were told in Dál Riata and elsewhere. The Cruithin hero Mongán mac Fíachnai, as we have seen, died fighting in Scottish Dál Riata in the early 7th century. The tale of this golden hero was related by the poet Forgaill every winter night from Samhain to Beltane (1 November to 1 May). One tale which involves Áedán mac Gabráin possibly has its beginning in the 7th century is *Scéla Cano meic Gartnáin*, the 'Tale of Cano son of Gartnáin'.

This earliest known legend to feature Áedán mac Gabráin is a fascinating blend of pseudo-history and fiction in a narrative woven through with elements and themes common to Irish tales, and perhaps from elsewhere. Its setting is in the late 7th century, on the Island of Skye, although the composition in its current written form was from the late 9th century. In the parallel dimension of Irish legend, abounding with anachronisms, Áedán is very much alive and a central figure in the first part of this story. While the story has been extensively studied for its literary value, since there are motifs woven in it from other Irish and Welsh stories, there has been no recent serious academic dissection of its historical worth. A few of the relevant links to history will be highlighted below, but the main interest here is for showing the developed state of Áedán's character at an early date.

On the face of it, the story has its roots in actual conflict between a Pictish or Picto-Scottish kindred in Skye and other Irish factions who may have been trying to make inroads into Skye and other lands in the area. Even this simple analysis causes difficulties however. In Áedán's time, Dál Riata probably stretched no further north than the Ardnamurchan peninsula in Argyll, some distance from Skye. The northern part of Dál Riata was the territory of the Cenél Loairn, so it is difficult to envisage the Kintyre based Cenél nGabráin spearheading any settlement towards the north of the Hebrides. The kindred in the tale are identified as being related to Cano son of Gartnait, though there is confusion about the father of the latter. (Cano's name, cognate with Welsh Ceneu, means 'cub'.) As we have seen, Áedán himself had a son of that name, possibly a king of the Picts. But, half a century after the death of that ruler, another Gartnait appears in the records, associated with conflict. Around 644, there is the notice of 'The burning of Iarnbodb, Gartnait's son.' Five years later the *Annals of Ulster* inform us there was, 'War between the descendants of Áedán and the descendants of Gartnait, son of Accidan.'

A series of following entries in the annals track the conflict between inhabitants of Skye and possibly one or more segments of the main Irish population in Scotland. The events, as we have them in a skeletal form, are by no means easy to disentangle. We have notice of an exodus in the year 668 recorded by the *Annals of Tigernach*: 'the voyage of the sons of Gartnait to Ireland, with the populace of Skye'. But the family returned from Ireland two years later. Around 673 we have a record of the capture of Conamail (whose name means 'Wolf-like'), Cano's son, and the *Annals of Tigernach* record, under the year 687, 'The killing of Cano, Gartnait's son' which follow after a notice for the year 683 (in the *Annals of Clonmacnoise*) which states that Cano entered into religion. Coblaith, Cano's daughter, died two years after him. Conamail himself died around 705, several years after a battle recorded on Skye.[6] The complicated strands of history and invention have not been fully disentangled in the 'Tale of Cano son of Gartnáin', though there have been several studies which shed light on the elements involved.[7]

At the beginning of the 'Tale of Cano' we are told that there was rivalry in Scotland between Áedán and his own nephew Gartnait (Gartnán), who was apparently the son of Áedán's fictitious 'brother' Áed. So intense was their conflict that half the men of Scotland died in battle. While Garnait lived in luxury on the Isle of Skye, he sent his son away from the island to be fostered. One winter's day Áedán and an army of 2,000 men attacked the island and Gartnait and all his following were massacred. Cano escaped death and fled to Ireland with fifty warriors and their wives, plus fifty servants. He found refuge in Ulster with Diarmait and Blathmác, sons of Aed Sláine (an Uí Néill king who died in 604). Áedán discovered his sanctuary and offered a fortune in gold and silver looted from Skye to the two kings if they would kill Cano.

Diarmait's daughter had loved Cano, for the sake of his great fame, even before she met him. She overheard the messengers from Scotland and gave Cano a cryptic warning which made him go before the two kings. Diarmait stated he would not betray him, even if his house was filled with gold, and Blathmác advised him to pursue Áedán's messengers and slay them. Cano went after them, but let them go unmolested and they said he would be rewarded for his restraint. They advised that he would be king of Scotland after Áedán for twenty-four years. The tale then details the evolution of the love story between Cano and Créd. Cano journeyed to the court of Guaire in Connacht, whose daughter was Créd. When Cano's stay there began to be resented there was a plot to scatter his followers. Créd put a sleeping spell on everyone in the court apart from herself and Cano. She declared her love for him, but he said he would not be her lover wile he was a soldier of fortune, but promised to send for her when he became king of Scotland. Then Cano moved to the court of Illann son of Scannlán and stayed there for three years until messengers came and told him that he was now king of Scotland. (Presumably Áedán had now died.)

Cano returned to Scotland, leaving Créd with a stone which represented his life. Two fairy women had given his mother it when she was pregnant and now Cano gifted it to Créd as a token that he would return for her. The pair arranged a regular meeting, but on the last occasion Cano was attacked by the soldiers of Colcu son of Marcán and he was wounded. When Créd saw him covered with blood she fell, so that the stone containing Cano's life split and he died three days later as he went east back to Scotland.

We can see from this tale, which may have been in circularion orally in the 8th century, that Áedán was already endowed with a ferocious, albeit negative reputation. His portrayal may have been different in tales such as *Echtra Aedán meic Gabráin*, which would have featured him as the hero or at least central character. From the Welsh side, the story about his warband in Triad 29 and his 'complete disappearance', must also have painted him in a different light to the Cano story. If we credit that earlier tradition lies behind the 15th century *Peiryan Vaban* poem too, we can see a picture of Áedán doubtlessly fierce and relentless in warfare, but certainly not viewed as an enemy from the narrator's point of view, but rather an avenging ally of one section of the British against another. The rich mixture of romantic elements which are woven through the sections of the Cano tale which are set in Ireland are in sharp contrast to the start of the story, which seems to be a straight and stark inheritance from a rather partisan folk tale which existed among one part of the Gaelic speaking population resident in Scotland. This kin group is probably a real sept which we can see represented by the following preserved genealogy: 'Congus m. Consamla m. Conai Gairb m. Gartnait m. Ædáin m. Gabráin'.[8] This family was still distinct in the 12th century when the *cland Canan* gave a grant to the monastery of Deer in Aberdeenshire.[9] It was not a kindred which seems to have remembered Áedán fondly.

The birth tales of Áedán connecting him with Leinster give us the warning that there is no guarantee that a legend is necessarily created within living memory of its subject, nor that only truth is preserved in traditional tales. As we have seen, despite it being repeated as fact in several sources, there was no specific historical connection between Leinster and the Cenél nGabráin dynasty of Dál Riata. The birth stories themselves may be seen within the context of *Banshenchas*, 'Womenlore', circulating in Ireland in the 12th century.[10]

Acknowledgments

I would like to thank John K. Bollard for permission to reprint his translation of the poem *Peiryan Vaban* which first appeared in *The Romance of Merlin*, ed. Peter Goodrich (London, 1990), and for his generously provided comments on its context. Thanks also to Jonathan Jarrett, who kindly supplied me with a copy of his unpublished paper on Áedán mac Gabráin before it became widely available on the internet.

A Word about Names and Places

Attempting to impose standard or correct names for peoples and places in a largely non-literate society is difficult and subject to the vagaries of current academic fashion. I have chosen to favour forms such as Colum Cille rather than Columba and use personal names which reflect Gaelic and other native forms. For countries I have tended to use (Northern) Britain rather than Scotland or England as these national identities were far in the future during Áedán's time. Similarly, the name for the Northern British realm is identified by its main stronghold, Dumbarton, or the geographical area, Clydeside. Strathclyde (Ystrad Glud or Arecluta) did not come into usage for the kingdom until the 9th century. The name for Áedán's lineage, Cenél nGabráin, may not have been in use during his lifetime and likewise the kingdom's name, Dál Riata (later Dal Riada), is used in preference to the more correct Corcu Réti, as they reflect more common forms used by most historians.

Confusingly, there are several unrelated rulers named Báetán, Fíachnae, Gartnait, etc. peppered through the pages of this book. However, there was only one Áedán mac Gabráin.

Chronology

c. 501. Death of Fergus Mór, first king of Dál Riata to rule in Britain.

c. 521. Birth of Colum Cille (St Columba) in Ireland.

532. Cairell mac Muiredaig Muinderg, king of the Dál Fiatach dynasty of Ulaid (Ulster) dies on the island of Arran, in Dál Riatan territory.

c. 534. Birth of Áedán mac Gabráin.

c. 537. Death of king Comgal son of Domangart.

c. 547. Beginning of the reign of Ida in Bernicia, Northumbria.

c. 555. Bridei son of Maelchon becomes king of the Picts.

c. 559. Death of king Gabráin son of Domangart. Flight of the men of Dál Riata before the Picts.

? 560 x 590. Battle of Catraeth. Warband of the British Gododdin kingdom, based on Din Eidyn (Edinburgh), defeated.

563. Colum Cille arrives with his companions in Britain. The battle of Móin Daire Lóchair in Ireland where the Cruithin defeated by the Northern Uí Néill.

c. 568. Joint expedition against Iardoman (Inner Hebrides) by king Colmán Bec of the Uí Néill and king Conall son of Comgall of Dál Riata.

573. Battle of Arfderydd (Arthuret) between the Northern Britons.

574. Death of king Conall son of Comgall. The battle of Delgu (or Teloch) in Kintyre among the Dál Riata. Beginning of the reign of Áedán son of Gabrain.

c. 574. Submission of Áedán to king Báetáin mac Cáirill at Ros na Ríg in Semne. *c.* 580. A campaign in Orkney by Áedán.

580. Death of Pictish king Galam Cennalath.

581. Death of Báetáin mac Cáirill, Dál Fiatach king of Ulaid.

c. 583. A battle in Manau, where Áedán was the conquerer.

c. 584. Death of Bridei son of Maelchon, king of the Picts. Áedán's victorious battle of Manau.

c. 589. King Áed Dub, Cruithin king of Dál nAraide killed in Ireland.

*c.*590? British coalition of kings, including Urien of Rheged and Rhydderch Hael, besiege English rulers of Bernicia on Lindisfarne.

590. The Cruithin ruler Fíachnae Lurgan becomes king of Ulster

c. 591. Battle of *Leithrig* fought by Áedán.

c. 592. Æthelfrith becomes king of Bernicia.

c. 590 x 594. Convention of Druim Cett in Ireland between Áedán and Colum Cille and king Áed mac Muirderach.

c. 595. Death of Eoganán, Áedán's brother.

597. Death of Colum Cille on Iona. Augustine arrives as apostle to the English in Kent.

c. 609. Death of Áedán.

c. 614. Death of St Kentigern of Glasgow. Death of Rhydderch Hael, king of the Britons of Dumbarton.

c. 622. Drowning of Conaing, son of Áedán.

c. 625. Cruithin leader Mongán mac Fíachnai dies on Islay, in Dál Riata, slain by a Briton.

c. 627. Battle of Ard Corann in Ireland. Connad Cerr, king of Dál Riata, defeats and kills Cruithin king Fíachnae mac Báetáin.

c. 628. Birth of Adomnán, 9th Abbot of Iona, biographer of Colum Cille.

629. Battle of Fid Eóin in Ireland. Connad Cerr, along with grandsons of Áedán, slaughter in a factional conflict between Cruithin leaders in the north of Ireland.

c. 629. Battle of Dún Ceithirn in Ireland. Dál Riata allied with the victorious Northern Uí Néill against the Cruithin. Death of king Eochaid Buide, son of Áedán.

c. 635. Battle of Calathros (possibly in Islay). Domnall Brecc defeated.

637. Battle of Mag Rath in Ireland. King of Dál Riata, Domnall Brecc, on the losing side.

c. 638. *Din Eidyn* besieged and captured by Northumbrians.

c. 640. Battle of Glend-Mairison in Northern Britain. Domnall Brecc defeated.

c. 642. Battle of Strathcarron in central Scotland. Domnall Brecc slain by Clydeside Britons.

Notes

All works notes by page number except Adomnán's *Life of Columba* (*Vita Columbae*) and Bede's *Ecclesiastical History of the English People* (*Historia ecclesiastica gentis Anglorum*), which are cited by author, book and chapter, except where material is referenced from the editors of different editions. Annal entries are generally from Anderson (1990) unless otherwise stated.

Introduction
1. Duncan (1978), 43.
2. Sharpe (1995), 270.
3. O'Brien (1952), 169–70.
4. Jackson, (1957), 129,131.
5. Hudson (1996), 83.
6. Koch (2003), 193.
7. Morris (1980), 85–86.
8. Anderson (1973), 134.
9. Bruford (2000), 54. Watson (1986), 120–1.
10. Anderson (1990), I, 1.
11. The tract known as *Senchus fer nAlban* or *Míniugud Senchesa fher nAlban*. Bannerman (1974), 49.
12. Mac Cana (1980), 49, 60.
13. Campbell (2001), 291.
14. Woolf (2012).
15. Richmond (1958), 136.
16. Lane and Campbell (2000), 32.
17. MacNeill, (1939), 32, defines the tribal name as 'Little Horse/Pony People'.
18. Thomas (1961), 40.
19. Watson (1986), 121
20. Fraser (2009), 148.
21. Bede, I, 1.
22. Bannerman (1974), 122–4.
23. Watson (1986), 214–15.
24. Fraser (2009), 121.
25. Watson (1986), 24. The name is still present in Argyll, see Duncan (1978), 35.
26. Chadwick (1949), 35, 121.
27. Bannerman (1974), 50. Chadwick (1949), 122.
28. Anderson (1973), 164.
29. Bannerman (1974), 146–8.
30. Bannerman (1974), 140.

31. Anderson (1990), I, 162, 219, 229. Anderson and Anderson (1961), 58.
32. Charles-Edwards (2004), 54.
33. Byrne (2001), 108.
34. Byrne (1964), 61, 76.
35. Byrne (2001), 108.
36. Mac Niocaill (1972), 78.
37. O' Rahilly (1946), 347, states that, out of the sixty-two Ulster kings enumerated in the *Book of Leinster*, only ten of them were Cruithin. Different figures are given by Byrne (1964).
38. See also Bannerman (1974), 2.

Chapter 1

1. O'Brien (1952), 167.
2. Bannerman (1974), 89–90. Prose version text and translation in Best (1927).
3. O'Brien (1952), 157–171. Modern translation in Clancy (1998), 178–82.
4. Meyer (1899), 134, 136.
5. The grain of gold appears also in the 'Feast of Dún na nGéd' in a North British setting. Dillon (1946), 41.
6. O'Brien (1952), 158.
7. O'Brien (1952), 157.
8. Bannerman (1974), 90.
9. Tyndale (1995), 44.
10. Hudson (1996), 90.
11. Hudson (1994), 110.
12. Plummer (1922), I, 34–35, II, 32–34.
13. Plummer (1922), II, 34.
14. Watson (1986), 275.
15. Plummer (1922), II, 328.
16. Stewart and Main (1999).
17. Butter (2007), 104.
18. Coira (2012), 302.
19. McNiven (2011), 46–47.
20. Watson (1986), 392–3.
21. Wyatt (2009)69.
22. Koch (1997), xlvii, lxii, 3, 9, 41.
23. Bartrum (1966), 15. Wade-Evans (1944), 315.
24. Bartrum (1966), 18. Wade-Evans (1944), 317.
25. Wade-Evans (1944), 318–19.
26. *Chronicles of the Kings of Scotland* in Anderson (1990), I, 512.
27. Watson (1986), 112–113.
28. Charles-Edwards (2008), 182.
29. Bartrum (1993), 73.
30. See Gardner (1996), 240–59.
31. Translations in Clancy (1998), 91--92. G Lewis and Williams (2019), 27–29.
32. Bromwich (2006), 354. Haycock (2013), 9.
33. Bromwich and Evans (1992), 9, 90.
34. Hudson (1996), 83.
35. Hudson (1996), 41, 83–84.

36. Bartrum (1966), 72–74. Bromwich (2006), 256–7.
37. Baring-Gould and Fisher (1911), 42.
38. Bromwich (2006), xv.
39. Miller, (1977), 256.
40. Forbes (1874), 88.
41. Rees (1836), 29.
42. Macquarrie (2012), 5.
43. Skene (1872), 108.
44. *Acta S. Lasriana*, in Heist (1965), 340.
45. Miller (1977), 270.
46. Stokes (1905), 53, 116, 117.
47. Bannerman (1974), 89, 106. O' Rahilly (1946), 362. Watson (1986), 392.
48. Skene (1890), II, 402.
49. Macquarrie (2012), 182–3.
50. Watson (1986), 164–5.
51. Charles-Edwards (2013), 8. Clancy (2004), 138. Watson (1986), 209.
52. Fraser (2003), 113.
53. Hewison (1893), I, 154–6.

Chapter 2
1. Anderson (1990), I, 72.
2. Reeves (1874), 249.
3. Macquarrie (1994), 194.
4. O'Donnell (1918), 242–5. Modern translation in Lacey (1998), 129.
5. O'Donnell (1918), 244–7. Lacey (1998), 129–30.
6. Stokes (1899), 284–5.
7. Bannerman (1974), 82–83.
8. Stokes (1899), 284–5.
9. Stokes (1899), 165.
10. Stokes (1899), 401.
11. Adomnán, I, 37, II, 33, 34, 35, 42.

Chapter 3
1. Byrne (2001), 21.
2. Anderson (1990), I, 76. Hudson (1996), 83, 197. Although Hudson thinks that these verses describe king Caustantín mac Fergus (d.820), there is a compelling argument in favour of the reference being to Áedán.
3. Anderson (1990), I, 78.
4. Anderson (1990), I, 78. Bannerman (1974), p. 82. For Báetán's possible military involvement in Argyll, see Anderson and Anderson (1961), 40. Meckler (1990), 146. Miller (1980a), 320.
5. Anderson (1990), I, 21.
6. Anderson (1990), I, 72.
7. Skene (1890), I, 229. II, 204.
8. Lane and Campbell (2000), 98.
9. Adomnán, I, 28.
10. Lane and Campbell (2000), 150.
11. Lane and Campbell (2000), 18–23.

12. Anderson (1990), I, 191, 233.
13. Anderson (1973), 132 cites possible example at Dunino in Fife and Drymen, Stirlingshire. See also Westwood (1985), 419.
14. Duncan (2002), 127.
15. Fitzpatrick (2005), 230. See Hamilton (1912).
16. Duncan (2002), 128.
17. The earliest account of the Finlaggan ceremony is the 'History of the Macdonalds', by Hugh Macdonald in 1628 (1914), I, 23–34. Martin Martin used this source in his *Description of the Western Islands of Scotland* (1703).
18. According to the *Annals of Tigernach*, there was a battle at this important place in the year 728. Anderson (1990), I, 224.
19. Duncan (1978), 115.
20. Duncan (1978), 115–16.
21. Bannerman (1989), 130. The goddess of the sovereignty of Tara was Medb. Byrne (2001).
22. *Topographia Hibernaie*, Giraldus Cambrensis (1185–88). See Simms (2000), 22.
23. Adomnán, III, 5.
24. Adomnán, II, 33, 34, 35.
25. A.P. Smyth (1989), 114.
26. Enright (1985), 8–10, doubts that a ceremony took place. Meckler (1990), 139–50, believes that Adomnán's account represents a genuine event.
27. Translations of 'The Destruction of Dá Derga's Hostel'. in Gantz (1981), 65. Koch (2003),168. For *tarbfeis*, see O' Rahilly (194), 324. The bull feast features in the Ulster saga 'The Sick-bed of Cú Chulainn'. *Serglige Con Culainn*, see Byrne (2001), 62. Sacrificing bulls continued in the north-west Highlands into the early modern period. Dixon (1984), 150–55, 410–11.
28. Adomnán, I, 9.
29. A fragment of Cumméne's work, *Liber de virtutibus sancti Columbae*, was inserted by a later scribe into the chapter of Adomnán's work describing the glass book, angel and Áedán's inauguration, Adomnán, III, 5.
30. Smyth (1989), 95.
31. Woods, (2002), 66, suggests that Adomnán innocently believed a glass book was being referred to. Byrne (2001), 255, suggested the enamel cover. See also Nagy (1997), 138–9.
32. Anderson (1990), I, 87–88. The *Book of Lecan* says Báetain ruled in both Ireland and Britain and compelled Áedán to do homage to him at Ros na Ríg in Ireland.
33. Duncan (1978), 45–46.
34. Stevenson (1927), 1–12.
35. For a suggestion that there was a unique succession procedure in 6th century Dál Riata, see Whitaker (1976), 353–4. Also, Warntjes (2004), 17–18.
36. A Lane and Campbell (2000), 255, 256. Dark (2000a), 224.
37. Bannerman (1989), 128 discusses whether Áedán's immediate ancestors shifted the inauguration site from Antrim to Argyll.
38. Adomnán, I, 28. Campbell (2003), 43–59.

Chapter 4

1. Anderson (1990), I, p. 88. Dobbs (1921), 322–3.
2. These statements are in prose sections of *Senchus Sil hÍr*. Anderson (1990), I, 88. Dobbs (1921), 324–5, 328–9.

3. Dobbs (1921), 322–3.
4. Anderson (1990), I, 87, gives a translation of stanzas 23–26, linking the description to Báetán. Text and translation in Hudson (1996), 25–26, 74. Hudson discusses whether the first verses refer to Fíachnae mac Báetán, the Dál nAraide king (d. 626), and that the following stanzas 27–30 refer to Báetán. But he argues the verses describe two 9th century Viking rulers, Óláfr and Ívarr (1996), 138–43.
5. Byrne (1964), 63, 76.
6. Dobbs (1945), 71. Dobbs (1921), 325. Meyer (1912), 327.
7. Fraser (2009), 160.
8. Miller (1977), 269, (1975), 107. Watson (1986), 305.
9. Mac Niocaill (1972), 77.
10. Byrne (2001), 109.
11. Woolf (2012), 8.
12. Bemmer (2016), 2. Bannerman discusses *cairde* in the context of Druim Cett (1974), 165–70.
13. Anderson (1990), I, 88. Dobbs (1921), 322–3, 325. Áedán's submission is also noted in one Dál Fiatach genealogy, Meyer (1912), 327.
14. Dobbs (1945), 71 disagrees and thinks the northern Manau is intended.
15. Miller (1980a), 306.
16. Byrne (1964), 63, 76.
17. Byrne (1964), 63, 76.
18. Byrne (1964), 64, 77.
19. *Annals of Ulster* refs.
20. For discussion of Áedán's possible military activity in the Isle of Man, see Bannerman (1974), 83–84. F. J. Byrne (2001), 110. O' Rahilly (1946), 504.
21. Dobbs (1921), 338. Dobbs (1945), 72.
22. Bede, II, 5.
23. Anderson (1990), I, 89. Jones (1990), 42.
24. Chadwick and Dillon (1967), 114–15. Charles-Edwards (2013), 151, 468. Jones (1990), 43. Kermode (1897), Kermode (1907), 75, 122–3. Rhys (1897).
25. Chadwick and Dillon (1967), 113.
26. Chadwick and Dillon (1967), 70. Jackson (1953), 173. Thomas (1994), 46. For epigraphic evidence supporting bilingual population on Man, see Charles-Edwards (2013), 111.
27. *Historiarum Adversum Paganos Libri*, quoted by Ó Corráin (2017), 122. See also. Jones (1990), 34. O'Rahilly (1946), 504. Ó Corráin's suggestion that Osorius was a Briton would make his information even more pertinent, though most historians make him an Iberian.
28. 28. Bede, II, 9.
29. The stone, at Ballaqueeney, commemorates BIVAIDONAS MAQI MUCOI CUNAVA, 'Bivaidu [Béoáed] of the Conaillne [the royal lineage of Conall]'. Kermode (1892), 59. Kermode (1907), 98–99. Ó Corráin (2017), 122.
30. Ó Cróinín (1995), 50.
31. Recorded by Trotter (1901), 182. See Chadwick (1949), 156. MacQueen (1954), 83–85, (1990), 45–47. Watson (1924), 132, (1986), 178–9. Irish settlement in west Galloway need not necessarily have been as late as the 6th century as Thomas thinks, (1994) 45. See also MacQueen (1954), 82. Recent research on place-names and archaeology casts doubt on Irish settlement.

32. There was a reputed regional capital (Rerigonium or Penrhyn Rhionydd) on Loch Ryan, near present day Stranraer, which would have allowed a local British elite to control the area and safeguard sea traffic in the North Channel between Galloway and northern Ireland. The Irish of Ulaid and the Cruthin directly faced this territory across the sea. See Bromwich (2006) 4. Brooke (2001), 2–5. Watson (1986), 34.

33. Toop (2011), 95.

34. Charles-Edwards (2013), 150.

35. *Compert Mongáin*, the 'Birth of Mongán', trans. Koch (2003), 218.

36. O'Donovan (1868), 114.

37. Spaan, 'The place of Manannan Mac Lir'. 177.

38. Trans. Koch (2003), 217–18. Text and trans. Meyer and Nutt (1895), I, 42–45.

39. A 15th century version of this legend from the *Book of Fermoy* is summarised by Dillon (1946), 49–55. Trans. Meyer and Nutt (1895), I, 58–84. There is no mention of Áedán in this version of the tale, as his fame in Irish legend had evidently begun to wane by this date. Instead, Fíachnae goes to assist the king of Lochlann in war. Mongán's otherworldly upbringing is also outlined and the tale elaborates his later slaying of his earthly father's killer.

40. *Scél asa mBerar Combad hé Find Mac Cumhaill Mongán aní día fil Aided Fothaid Airgdig a Scél so sís*, trans. Anne Lea, in Koch (2003), 218–220. Meyer and Nutt (1895), I, 49–52.

41. Mac Cana (1972), 138.

42. *Miuiugad sencliusa Ulad*, in Dobbs (1921), 354–5. Mac Cana (1972), 138. MacNeill (1912), 418.

43. Dobbs (1945), 72. Meyer (1912), 329. The suggestion that Demmán was fostered by Domangart, king of Dál Riata, is anachronistic since the latter died around 507.

44. Mac Cana (1972), 139.

45. Mac Cana (1972), 138.

46. Clancy (1998), 237.

47. Chadwick and Dillon (1967), 78, Mac Niocaill (1972), p. 78, supports the sequence of events which would see Áedán battling in the Isle of Man.

48. Anderson (1973), 149.

49. Peniarth 50. ed. Jarman (1952), 104ff. Trans. Bollard (1990). My thanks to John K. Bollard for his thoughts on the poem.

50. Jones (2013), 24. Bollard favours the title Lordly rather than Commanding Youth. See Bollard (2019), 41–42.

51. Ross (1992), 464. Tolstoy (1985), 212–3.

52. Bollard (1990).

53. John Bannerman's statement (1974), 89, that the poem foretells Áedán rising from the dead to succour the Welsh is not supported by the text.

54. Jarman (2003), 104. Bolland, pers. comm., had advised on the difficulty of determining whether the language of *Peiryan Vaban* may be older. Another poem, *Gwasgargerdd Fyrddin yn y Bedd* , 'The Diffused Song of Myrddin in the Grave', shares with *Peiryan Vaban* the concept of the prophet speaking from the grave.

55. Skene (1872), 105.

56. Clancy (2013), 161. Evans (2000), 12, 130.

57. O'Grady, 'The Battle of Magh Mucramha,' (1892), II, 352

58. Lewis and Williams (2019), 105–6.

59. O'Rahilly (1946), 504.
60. Bromwich (2006), 62.
61. Bromwich (1969), 305.
62. Mac Cana (1980), 45. O' Curry (1878), 589. See also Bannerman (1974), 90.
63. Dumville (1976), Hillers (1993).
64. Duignan (2010), 1, 5.
65. Mac Cana (1980), 76.
66. Mac Cana (1980), 45.
67. Máel Umai may feature in the Welsh medieval tale of *Culhwch and Olwen* as Maylwys mab Baedan. Bromwich and Evans (1992), 7, 69.
68. Adomnán, I, 36. The Irish tale *Aided Diarmada* relates how Áed was exiled to Scotland by his royal foster-father, Diarmait mac Cearbaill. O'Grady (1892), I, 72–82, II, 76–82. This may represent the tradition of an earlier visit to Dál Riata, but is possibly a literary construction.
69. Woolf (2012), 9. Mac Niocaill (1972), 88, suggests that Áedán may have assisted Fíachnae's rise, though another factor was the relative dearth of candidates for the Ulster kingship from the Dál Fiatach. Áedán's possible aspirations as an Irish Cruithin overlord have been considered recently by Fraser (2009), 139.

Chapter 5
 1. Adomnán, II, 6.
 2. Anderson (1990) I, 70.
 3. Fraser (2007), 315.
 4. Anderson (1990), I, 79.
 5. Bannerman (1974), 162–8.
 6. Fraser (2007), 319–20 details the changing attitude of historians from long term acceptance of historians to current scepticism.
 7. Fraser (2007), 319–322.
 8. Fraser (2007), 330.
 9. Colum Cille's meeting with the princes occurs in Adomnán, I, 10, 11. The post conference incident with St Comgall occurs in I, 49. His healing is mentioned in II, 6.
10. Byrne (2001), 111. Evans (2010), p. 166. Fraser (2009), 138. Meckler (1997), 44–45. Sharpe (1995), 271, 313. Macquarrie (1997), 212, suggests 594 as the conference date. The problem with dating and Áed was noted by Ryan (1946), 51. Jaski (1998), 340–50, defends the possibility of the earlier date.
11. Sharpe (1995), 312. Fraser (2007), 318 points out that, although this locality was traditional, it can't be proven to be the site of the convention.
12. Bernard and Atkinson (1898), I, 162–83, II, 55–80. Latter reprinted by Anderson (1990), I, 81–85. Modern translation of poem only, Clancy and Márkus (1995), 104–15. Trans. of poem only, Clancy (1998), 102–7. The *Amra* preface's several manuscripts go back no earlier than the early 11th century.
13. Adomnán, I, 10. Fraser (2007), 328 urges caution about accepting the presence of Domnall or Scandlán at the conference.
14. The one leg/one eye stance not only resembles the stance of the crane but also echoes the malevolent beings known as the Formorians in Irish myth. In the sense of good luck, the act was ascribed in literature to the god Lug, but also in a divinatory sense to a female character. Borsje and Kelly (2003), 22–26. Nagy (1997), 183.

15. A crane or heron features as a storm blown refugee from Ireland which arrives on Iona in a vignette in Adomnán, I, 48. There is a suggestion that Colum Cille's mother Eithne came from a tribe in Donegal called the Cortraige, meaning 'Crane or Heron Race'. Sharpe (1995) 312, casts doubt on the connection.

16. Ross (1992), 361.

17. See the preface to the *Amra*, Bernard and Atkinson (1898), I, 162, II, 53. Anderson (1990), I, 83.

18. Irish legal tracts recognised that satire could inflict physical harm as well as loss of dignity and status. McLaughlin (2008), 4–5.

19. Bernard and Atkinson (1898), I, 162, II, 53. Bannerman (1974), 160, points out the poets' status as a subject of debate at the conference only occurs in later literature.

20. Nagy (1990), 370. Nagy (1997), 170.

21. Fíachnae invites a chief poet, Eochaid Rígeíces, to live in his stronghold, Knott (1916). Byrne (2001), 106.

22. Adomnán, I, 11. Some versions confuse Scandlán's parentage and state that he was the son of Cenn Fáelad, his father's successor. Scandlán may have been a forfeited hostage, *gíall díthma*, suffering the consequences of bondage when his father failed to uphold his terms of clientship. See Charles-Edwards (2004), 488.

23. Bernard and Atkinson (1898), I, 153, II , 54. Sharpe (1995), 273. The different versions are summarised by Bannermen (1974), 158.

24. Anderson (1990), I, 83.

25. Nagy (1997), 178–9. Bernard and Atkinson (1898), I, 187, II, 85.

26. *Betha Colaim Chille*, O'Donnell (1918), 341.

27. Lacey (1998), 172–90.

28. Lacey (1998), 56–57.

29. O'Donnell (1918), 367.

30. *Coire Brecain* may originally have been a different place, *Slugnamorra*, between Rathlin and Ballycastle. See Charles-Edwards (2004), 588. The saint's encounter with Brecain is related in the *Dindsenchas*, see Reeves (1874), 252. Brecain and his followers were sucked down into the whirlpool when they were fleeing from his father.

31. Keating (1906), III, 79–97.

32. Bannerman (1974), 170, argued that the only function of the convention was to decide the position of Irish Dál Riata in relation to the king of the Uí Néill. Fraser (2009), 139, cautions against trusting later sources which suggest this.

33. Herbert (1989), 69–71.

34. Anderson (1973), 147.

35. MacNeill (1920), 197–8.

36. Fraser (2009), 139. This Cruithin district was called Mag nEilni and was the northern section of the Uí Chóelbad kingdom.

37. Bannerman (1974), 166.

38. Adomnán, I, 36.

39. Macquarrie (1997), 113, notes that the date of 575 for the convention would be very soon after Áedán's inauguration and difficult to reconcile with another journey to the north of Ireland when he was compelled to submit to Báetán.

40. The *Annals of Ulster* state the meeting was between Columcille and Áed. The *Annals of Clonmacnoise* says it was between Áed and Áedán. Anderson (1990), I, p. 79. Bannerman (1974), p. 19. O' Keefe (1913), p. xxi expressed doubt that Áedán was at the conference.

41. Some sources state the conference lasted four months and others that it continued for one year and three months. Bernard and Atkinson (1898), I, 187, II, 85. Adomnán, II, 6, quoted at the beginning of the chapter may imply a short duration by the saint at the meeting.
42. Bernard and Atkinson (1898), I, 163, II, 56.
43. Anderson (1990), I, 83.
44. Anderson (1973), 147.
45. Adomnán, I, 49.
46. Fraser (2007), 316–17.
47. Adomnán, I, 50.
48. Reeves (1874), 264.
49. Fraser (2009), 160.
50. Marstrander (1911).

Chapter 6
1. Anderson, (1973), 14
2. Stokes (1887), I, 162–3.
3. Stokes (1887), I, 108–9. Given the tribal association of the ruling family with horses, is this perhaps a remembered ember of a folk tale?
4. Bede, III, 4.
5. The *Annals of Tigernach*. Anderson (1990), I, 75.
6. Anderson (1990), I, 22. A similar notice is in the *Annals of Ulster*.
7. Adomnán, II, 33, 42.
8. Anderson (1990), I, 86.
9. Adomnán, II, 42.
10. Anderson (1990), I, 86.
11. Anderson (1973), 91. Chadwick offered the meaning of 'head wound' or 'speckled head' for the epithet and speculated that he had been dethroned by Bridei. Chadwick (1949), 14.
12. Original entries summarised in Macquarrie (1997), 103.
13. Macquarrie (1997), 107.
14. Adomnán, I, 8.
15. Jackson (1969), 25.
16. Adomnán, I, 9.
17. Maxwell (1987), 43.
18. Maxwell (1987), 31.
19. Watson (1986), 58, believed the tribe may have been located by Hadrian's Wall and later migrated northward. Wainwright (1980), 53, envisaged movement from the Stirling area into Circenn.
20. Morris (1980), 37, 79.
21. Sharpe (1995), 269.
22. Sharpe (1995), 269.
23. Bannerman (1974), 85.
24. Bruford (2000), 62.
25. Chadwick (1949), 44.
26. Jarrett (2008), 17–19.
27. Henderson (1967), 48. O' Rahilly (1946), 508.
28. Anderson (1990), I, 241
29. Anderson (1990), I, 91.

30. Anderson (1990), I, 236.
31. Watson (1986), 228–9.
32. Bruford (2000), 47. Fraser (2009), 102.
33. Anderson (1990), I, 121.
34. Mac Neill (1939), 16.
35. Anderson (1990), I, 122. Macquarrie (1997), 178, believes the Abernethy founder may have been another Gartnait, a son of Áedán's son Domnall Brecc.
36. Bannerman (1974), 41, 48. Gartnait's name may mean 'noble champion', see MacNeill (1939), 16.
37. Anderson (1973), 154.
38. Anderson (1990), I, cxxiii, 122. Anderson (1973), 248, 262, 266, 272, 280, 287. Bannerman (1974), 93–94.
39. Fraser (2009), 204–5.
40. Anderson (1973), 151. Bannerman (1974), 93, 95.
41. Anderson (1973), 142, 151. Watson (1986), 113, 225. The genealogies from the *Book of Ballymote* name Eochaid's son Conall Cerr as ancestor of the men of Fife. Anderson (1990), I, p. cliv. His brother, Fergus, in the same text may be designated as founder of a sept who inhabited Gowrie. Anderson and Anderson (1961), cliv. Anderson (1973), 151.
42. Bannerman (1974), 97. Other territorial divisions ruled by this father and son are considered by Anderson (1990), I, 152. See also Fraser (2009), 156.
43. *Annals of Tigernach*, Anderson (1990), I, 152, Hudson (1994), 7.
44. Smyth (1989), 70.
45. Henderson (1967), 44, who regards it as plausible.
46. Jarrett (2008), 23.
47. Hudson (1996), 40, 83–84.

Chapter 7
1. O'Neill (2005), 132.
2. Dark (2000a), 226.
3. Mac Niocaill (1972), 75.
4. N.K. Chadwick introduction to H.M. Chadwick (1949), xxi.
5. O'Rahilly (1946), 213. Watson (1926), 192.
6. Miller, (1975), 115.
7. Bromwich (2006), 217.
8. Bartrum (1993), 3. Bromwich (2006), 221.
9. Morris (1878), 8.
10. Chadwick and Dillon (1967), 81.
11. Bromwich (2006), 221–2.
12. Clarkson (2010), 95. Watson (1986), 368.
13. Adomnán, I, 15.
14. Bromwich (2006), 153.
15. Morris (1980), 38, 79.
16. Bromwich (2006), 272.
17. Chadwick (1949), 152.
18. The name occurs in a variant of Triad 10, Bromwich (2006), 18.
19. R.G. Gruffydd, cited by Rachel Bromwich (2006), 339. Alex Woolf has given the tantalising suggestion that the epithet may represent British *Weredawc*, 'of the Forth', cited by Jarrett, (2008), 29.

20. Anderson (1990), 301–3.
21. Smyth (1989), 215.
22. Anderson (1990), I, 304.
23. Fraser (2009)133.
24. The alternative meaning of *drud* in the triad title is 'costly' rather than 'violent'. Bromwich (2006), 154.
25. Clarkson (2010), 81, favours the Viking raid being the inspiration. Macquarrie notes that similar tales in Ireland favour earlier dates (1994), 200, (1997), 108.
26. Hudson (1994), 42. Mac Cana (1980), 107, 142–6.
27. Bromwich (2006), 62.
28. Miller (1975), 97. Bromwich (2006), 273.

Chapter 8
1. Bede, I, 34.
2. Discussion of dates in Charles-Edwards (2013), 345. Evans (2010), 187.
3. Bannerman (1974), 88. Blair (1959), 157.
4. By the antiquarian Edmund Gibson. Cited by Blair, (1959), 157.
5. Clarkson (2010), 114.
6. Skene (1890), I, 162.
7. Rhys (1882), 156.
8. Aliaga-Kelly (1986), 245.
9. Skene (1872), 30.
10. Anderson (1990), I, 118–19. Bannerman (1974), 84.
11. Adomnán, I, 9.
12. Adomnán, I, 8.
13. Version E, Whitelock (1961), 15.
14. Blair (1959), 156.
15. Chapter 63, Morris (1980), 37, 79.
16. Koch (1997), xlvii, lxii, 3, 9, 41.
17. Alcock (2003), 140.
18. Anderson (1990), I, 123.
19. Blair (1959), 156.
20. Bannerman (1974), 88. Meyer (1910), xiii. Watson (1986), 130.
21. Mac Cana (1980), 45.
22. Mac Cana (1980), 48. Meyer (1910), xiii. Watson (1986), 132.
23. Morris (1980), 36, 76.
24. Byrne (2001), 112. Jackson (1963), 27–28.
25. Hudson (1996), 139
26. Evans (2000), 34–35.
27. Bede, I, 34.
28. Evans (2000), 58–9.
29. Macquarrie (1997), 104.
30. Bede, II, 2.

Chapter 9
1. Anderson (1990), I, 76. Hudson (1996), 84.
2. Hudson's belief (1996), 84, that the verses relate to Causantín son of Fergus, king of the Picts (d. 820), can be queried on several points. Dauvit Broun's argument that

Causantín ruled in Pictland only would counter the verse's statement that he died in Kintyre (1998), 80. The Berchán verses refer to aggression against the Picts, but Causantín appears to have ruled peacefully in the east following a battle among Picts. A passive death in retirement for this ruler in Kintyre may also be questioned because of Viking activity in this area. There is also a possibility that there were other Scottish kings reigning in west Scotland during his reign, A. O. Anderson (1990), I, 255. These may have included Causantín's son Domnall. But there is a tradition of a saint called Constantine dying at Kilchousland, in Kintyre, which is just north of Campbelltown, see Anderson (1990), I, 93.

3. Anderson (1990), I, 125.
4. In Taliesin's poem 'Plea [or Petition] for Reconciliation', translated by Clancy (1990), 88–89 the poet asks forgiveness from Urien for joining in mockery of him as an old man. Also trans. Lewis and Williams (2019), 22–24. Urien and Áedán's age also discussed by Evans (2000), 51.
5. Miller (1980b), 207.
6. Anderson (1973), 137–8. The designation 'Domangart of Kintyre' is given at his death in religion by the *Annals of Innisfallen*. Anderson (1990), I, 5. Anderson and Anderson (1961), 36.
7. Hughes (1966), 265.
8. Anderson (1990), I, 126. Kelly (1857), 1. Anderson and Anderson (1961), 45 and Fraser (2009), 141, deduce from this that Áedán died on Thursday 17 April 609. Bannerman (1974), 80, argues that most annals indicate the year 608.
9. Skene (1872), 109. Bannerman (1974), 81, doubts the tradition. The cave had sporadic occupation into the modern age which would have obliterated earlier occupation. Tolan-Smith (2001), 168–9. There is another dedication to Ciarán of Clonmacnoise at Cikerran, on the island of Bute, which would also have been in Dál Riatan territory, Mackinlay (1914), 86. Ciarán's Scottish dedications in Scotland are detailed by Watson (1986), 278.
10. White (1872), 86.
11. Nieke (1984), II, 32.
12. *Acta S. Lasriana*, in Heist (1965), 340.
13. Westwood and Kingshill (2009), 39–40.
14. Hewison (1893), I, 165.
15. Anderson (1990), I, 152, reporting his death *c.* 630. The reign length may have been slightly less.
16. Mac Niocaill (1972), 56.
17. Anderson (1973), 151. Bannerman (1974), 93, 95.
18. *Annals of Tigernach*, s. a. 619, Anderson (1990), I, 146. The year may have been 622, as recorded by the *Chronicum Scotorum*. The *Annals of Ulster* gives only the first stanza (under the year 621). The poem is not included in the *Annals of Inisfallen* or the *Annals of the Four Masters*. The verse is unlikely to be contemporary with the events it records in its current form. See also Bannerman (1974), 94. Translation also in Clancy (1998), 113.
19. Chadwick and Chadwick (1986), I, 56.
20. Triad 29, Bromwich (2006), 57.
21. Anderson (1973), 13. There is a Dondchad son of Conaing in the *Míniugud Senchesa fher nAlban* who may be confused with a similarly named relative in some sources. John Bannerman (1974), p. 103. It is suggested that the Dubhán ('Little Black

One') in the Scottish king lists may be a nickname for Conaing himself. Williams, Smyth, Kirby (1991), 107.

22. Gwynn (1924), 241–6. See also Muhr (1999), 194–5.
23. Chadwick (1949), 73. Byrne (2001), xvii. The son of a king of Brega in Ireland, who died in 662, also had this name, Byrne (2001), 111.
24. Moisl (1983), 115.
25. Bannerman (1974), 41, 48.
26. Bromwich (2006), 221, 272. This royal name was also borne by a son of Urien of Rheged, see Bromwich (2006), 487. Further details on early forms of the name in Jackson (1953), 393.
27. Anderson (1990), I, 152.
28. Chadwick (1949), 72–73. O' Rahilly (1946), 362. One of these British Morgans possibly features as a tyrant of Strathclyde in the *Life* of St Kentigern.
29. Anderson (1990), I, cli.
30. Bannerman (1974), 91, believes that Artúr was Áedán's grandson, a son of Conaing. This follows the descent stated by *Míniugud Senchesa fher nAlban*, although Adomnán, I, 9, states that Artúr was Áedán's son.
31. Recent popular books which explore the possibility of Arthur of Dál Riata being *the* Arthur include Ardrey (2012), Gardner (1996) and Stirling (2012). More reasoned speculation is found in Moffat (2012). A useful rebalancing of facts was made by Halsall (2013), 152–3. Nora Chadwick suggested a link between an actual northern Arthur, perhaps active in Dál Riata, the Welsh St Illtud and elements of the medieval tale *Culhwch and Olwen*, (1953), 158–9. Her discussion of Áedán's son and the legendary Arthur is in the same article, 179–80.
32. Dark (2000b), 81, and Ziegler (1999) (following Rachel Bromwich) point out the possibility that there were two Arthurs in the royal lineage, a son and grandson of Áedán.
33. Green (2007), 49.
34. Morris (1980), 35, 76.
35. A case for the battles being in the north is made by Breeze (2015). Even if the battles were in Scotland, the date of the list and identity of Arthur is still open to question.
36. The hero's name was Gwawrddur (Gorddur or Guaurdur). Jackson (1969), 112. Koch (1997), 22–23.
37. *Annals of Tigernach.* Anderson (1990), I, 147–8.
38. This prince's father Áedán would surely have been incorporated into Arthurian legend if his offspring was the central figure in that material. Ziegler (1999). Richard Lathe's contention that Comgall son of Domangart (Áedán's uncle, d. 537/8), was Arthur has no basis in any historical or legendary source. Lathe (2004).
39. Barber (1961), 6. This seems to have been prompted by Jackson (1959), 3.
40. Bannerman (1974), 106. For the possibility that the foreign names were honorific and implied cultural exchange between neighbouring peoples, see Charles-Edwards (2004), 6.
41. Morris (1980), 36, 77.
42. Adomnán, I, 47.
43. Adomnán, I, 9.
44. Adomnán, I, 10, 11.
45. Adomnán, I, 15.

46. Woods (2002), 47–51.
47. Picard (1989). An earlier version of the tale may have involved Guaire suffering a threefold death.

Chapter 10
  1. Koch (1997), 27.
  2. Anderson (1990), I, 147–8.
  3. Meyer (1910), 43.
  4. Meyer and Nutt (1895), I, 28–29.
  5. Mac Cana (1972), 130.
  6. O' Donovan (1848), 44–65.
  7. Bannerman (1974), 101. Marstrander (1911), 236–7.
  8. Mac Cana (1972), 105–6.
  9. Marstrander (1911), 242–3.
 10. Adomnán, III, 5.
 11. Anderson (1990), I, 145, 158, 163.

Appendix
  1. Miller (1980a), 325.
  2. Bromwich (2006), lx.
  3. Mac Cana (1980), 41. Murphy (1955), 13.
  4. Mac Cana (1980), 60.
  5. Anderson (1990), I. 142–3.
  6. Anderson (1990), I, pp. 168, 169, 179, 181, 182, 198, 207, 211. Binchy (1975), xix.
  7. Ó Coileáin (1981).
  8. Binchy(1975), xix.
  9. Anderson (1990), II, 179.
 10. Dooley (2004), 16.

Bibliography

Alcock, Leslie (2003), *Kings and Warriors, Craftsmen and Priests* (Edinburgh, 2003).

Aliaga-Kelly, Christopher John (1986), *The Anglo-Saxon Occupation of South-East Scotland*, unpublished PhD thesis (Glasgow, 1986).

Adomnán (1961), *Adomnan's Life of Columba*, ed. Alan O. Anderson and Margaret O. Anderson (London and Edinburgh, 1961).

Anderson, Alan O. (ed.) (1990), *Early Sources of Scottish History* (2 vols., 1922, rep. Stamford, 1990).

Anderson, Alan O. and Anderson, Margaret O. (ed.) (1961), *Adomnan's Life of Columba* (London and Edinburgh, 1961).

Anderson, Margaret O. (1973), *Kings and Kingship in Early Scotland* (Edinburgh, 1973).

Ardrey, Adam (2013), *Finding Arthur, The True Origins of the Once and Future King* (London, 2013).

Bannerman, John (1974), *Studies in the History of Dalriada* (Edinburgh, 1974).

Bannerman, John (1989), 'The King's Poet and the Inauguration of Alexander III'. *Scottish Historical Review* 68 (1989), 120–49.

Barber, R.W. (1961), *Arthur of Albion* (London, 1961).

Baring-Gould, S. and Fisher, John (1911), *The Lives of the British Saints* (volume 3, London, 1911).

Bartrum, Peter C. (ed.) (1966), *Early Welsh Genealogical Tracts* (Cardiff, 1966).

Bartrum, Peter C. (1993), *A Welsh Classical Dictionary, People in History and Legend up to About AD 1000* (Aberystwyth, 1993).

Bede (1969), *Ecclesiastical History of the English People*, ed. Bertram Colgrave and R. A. B. Mynors (Oxford, 1969).

Bemmer, Jaqueline (2016), 'The early Irish hostage surety and inter-territorial alliances', *Historical Research* 89: 244 (May, 2016), 191–207.

Bernard, J. H. and Atkinson., R. (ed. and trans.) (1898), *The Irish Liber Hymnorum*, (London, 1898).

Best, R.I (1927), 'The birth of Brandub son of Eochaid and of Aedan son of Gabran', in R. S. Loomis (ed.), *Medieval Studies in Memory of Gertrude Schoepperle Loomis* (Columbia, 1927), 381–90.

Binchy, D.A. (ed.) (1975), *Scéla Cano Meic Gartnáin* (Dublin, 1963, rep. 1975).

Blair, Peter Hunter, (1959), 'The Bernicians and their northern frontier,' in *Studies in Early British History*. ed. Nora Chadwick (Cambridge, 1959), 137–72.

Bollard, John K., (1990) 'Commanding Youth,' in Peter Goodrich (ed.), *The Romance of Merlin: An Anthology* (New York, 1990), 50–52.

Bollard, John K., (2019), 'The earliest Myrddin Poems', in Ceridwen Lloyd-Morgan and Erich Poppe (ed.), *Arthur in the Celtic Languages* (Cardiff, 2019), 35–50.

Borsje, Jacqueline, and Fergus Kelly, (2003), '"The evil eye" in early Irish literature and law', *Celtica* 24 (2003) 1–39.

Breeze, Andrew J., (2015), 'The historical Arthur and sixth-century Scotland'. *Northern History*, 52: 2 (2015), 158–181.

Bromwich, Rachel, (1969), 'Trioedd Ynys Prydain: the Myvyrian "Third Series"', *The Transactions of the Honourable Cymmrodorion*, Session 1968, Part II (1969), 299–338.

Bromwich, Rachel (ed.) (2006), *Trioedd Ynys Prydein, The Welsh Triads* (3rd. edn., Cardiff, 2006).

Bromwich, Rachel and Evans, Simon (ed.), (1992), *Culhwch and Olwen, An Edition and Study of the Oldest Arthurian Tale* (Cardiff, 1992).

Brooke, Daphne, (2001), *Wild Men and Holy Places, St Ninian, Whithorn and the Medieval Realm of Galloway* (Edinburgh, 2001).

Broun, Dauvit (1998), 'Pictish kings, 761–839', in Sally M. Foster (ed.), *The St Andrews Sarcophagus, a Pictish Masterpiece and its International Connections* (Dublin, 1998).

Broun, Dauvit (2000), 'The Seven Kingdoms in *De situ Albanie*: A Record of Pictish Political Geography or Imaginary Map of Ancient Alba?' in Edward J. Cowan and R. Andrew McDonald (ed.), *Alba, Celtic Scotland in the Middle Ages* (East Linton, 2000), 24–42.

Bruford, Alan (2000), 'What happened to the Caledonians?' in Edward J. Cowan and R. Andrew McDonald (ed.), *Alba, Celtic Scotland in the Middle Ages* (East Linton, 2000), 43–68.

Butter, Rachel, (2007), *Cill-names and saints in Argyll: a way towards understanding the early church in Dál Riata?* unpublished PhD. thesis (Glasgow, 2007).

Byrne, Francis John (1964), 'Clann Ollaman uaisle Emma'. *Studia Hibernica* 34 (1964), 54–94.

Byrne, Francis John (2001), *Irish Kings and High-kings* (2nd edn., Dublin, 2001).

Campbell, Ewen (2003), 'Royal Inauguration in Dál Riata and the Stone of Destiny', in Wellander, R., Breeze, D. and Clancy, T. (ed.) *The Stone of Destiny, Artefact and Icon*. Society of Antiquaries of Scotland (Edinburgh, 2003), 43–59.

Campbell, Ewen (2001), 'Were the Scots Irish?' *Antiquity* 75 (2001), 285–292.

Chadwick, H.M. (1949), *Early Scotland, The Picts, The Scots and The Welsh of Southern Scotland* (Cambridge, 1949).

Chadwick, H M., and Chadwick, N. K. (1986), *The Growth of Literature* (vol. I, 1932, rep. Cambridge, 1986).

Chadwick, N.K. (1953), 'The lost literature of Celtic Scotland,' *Scottish Gaelic Studies* 7 (1953), 115–83.

Chadwick, N.K. and Dillon, Myles (1967), *The Celtic Heroic Age* (London, 1967).

Charles-Edwards, T.M. (2004), *Early Christian Ireland* (Cambridge, 2004).

Charles-Edwards, T.M. (2008), 'Picts and Scots, A review of Alex Woolf, *From Pictland to Alba 789–1070*,' *The Innes Review* 59 no. 2 (Autumn 2008), 168–188.

Charles-Edwards (2013), *Wales and the Britons, 350–1064* (Oxford, 2013).

Clancy, Thomas Owen (2004), 'Philosopher-king: Nechtan mac Der-Ilei'. *Scottish Historical Review* 83 (2004), 125–49.

Clancy, Thomas Owen (2013), 'The kingdoms of the North: poetry, places, politics', in Alex Woolf (ed.), *Beyond the Gododdin, Dark Age Scotland in Medieval Wales* (St Andrews, 2013), 153–76.

Clancy, Thomas Owen (ed.) (1998), *The Triumph Tree, Scotland's Earliest Poetry AD 550–1350* (Edinburgh, 1998).

Clancy, Thomas Owen and Márkus, Gilbert (1995), *Iona, The Earliest Poetry of a Celtic Monastery* (Edinburgh, 1995).

Clarkson, Tim (2010), *The Men of the North, The Britons of Southern Scotland* (Edinburgh, 2010).

Coira, M. Pía (2012), *By Poetic Authority, The Rhetoric of Panegyric in Gaelic Poetry of Scotland to c. 1700* (Edinburgh, 2012).

Dark, Ken (2000a), *Britain and the End of the Roman Empire* (Stroud, 2000).

Dark, Ken (2000b), 'A Famous Arthur in the Sixth Century? Reconsidering the Origins of the Arthurian Legend'. *Reading Medieval Studies* 26 (2000), 77–95.

Dillon, Myles (1946), *The Cycles of The Kings* (Oxford, 1946).

Dillon, Myles and Chadwick, Nora K. (1967), *The Celtic Realms* (London, 1967).

Dixon, J.H. (1984), *Gairloch and Guide to Loch Maree* (1886, rep. Gairloch, 1984).

Dobbs, Margaret E. (1945), 'The Dál Fiatach'. *Ulster Journal of Archaeology* 8 (1945), 66–79.

Dobbs, Margaret E. (1921), 'The History of the descendants of Ir,' in *Zeitschrift für celtische Philologie* 13 (1921), 308–59.

Dooley, Ann (2004), 'Arthur of the Irish: a viable concept?' in Ceridwen Lloyd-Morgan (ed.), *Arthurian Studies XXI* (Cambridge, 2004), 9–28.

Duffy, Seán (ed.) (2005), *Medieval Ireland, An Encyclopedia* (London, 2005).
Duignan, Leonie (2010), *The Echtrae as an Early Irish Literary Genre*, Unpublished Phd thesis (Maynooth, 2010).
Dumville, David (1976), 'Echtrae and Immram: some problems of definition,' *Ériu* 27 (1976), 73–94.
Duncan, A.A.M. (2002), *The Kingdom of the Scots, 842–1292* (Edinburgh, 2002).
Duncan, A.A.M. (1978), *Scotland, The Making of the Kingdom* (Edinburgh, 1975, rep. 1978).
Enright, Michael (1985), *Iona, Tara, Soissons: Origin of the Anointing Ritual* (Berlin, 1985).
Evans, Nicholas (2010), *The Present and the Past in Medieval Irish Chronicles* (Woodbridge, 2010).
Evans, Stephen S. (2000), *Lords of Battle: Image and Reality of the Comitatus in Dark-Age Britain* (1997, rep. Woodbridge, 2000).
Fitzpatrick, Elizabeth (2005), 'Inauguration sites', in Seán Duffy (ed.), *Medieval Ireland, An Encyclopedia* (London, 2005), 230.
Forbes, Alexander P., *Lives of S. Ninian and S. Kentigern* (Edinburgh, 1974).
Fraser, James E. (2007), 'St Columba and the convention at Druim Cete: peace and politics at seventh-century Iona'. *Early Medieval Europe* 15 (3) (2007), 315–344.
Fraser, James E (2009), *From Caledonia to Pictland, Scotland to 795* (Edinburgh, 2009).
Fraser, James E. (2003), 'Strangers on the Clyde, Cenél Comgaill, Clyde Rock and the bishops of Kingarth'. *The Innes Review* 56 (2003), 102–20. '.
Gantz, Jeffrey (ed. and trans.) (1981), *Early Irish Myths and Sagas* (London, 1981).
Gardner, Laurence (1996), *Bloodline of the Holy Grail, The Hidden Lineage of Jesus Revealed* (Shaftesbury, 1996).
Gough-Cooper, Henry W. (ed.) (2015a), 'Annales Cambriae, the A text'. The Welsh Chronicles Research Group, http://croniclau.bangor.ac.uk (2015).
Gough-Cooper, Henry W. (ed.) (2015b), 'Annales Cambriae, the B text'. The Welsh Chronicles Research Group, http://croniclau.bangor.ac.uk (2015).
Green, Thomas (2009), *Arthuriana: Early Arthurian Tradition and the Origins of the Legend* (Louth, 2009).
Green, Thomas (2007), *Concepts of Arthur* (Stroud, 2007).
Gwynn, Edward (ed.) (1924), *The Metrical Dindenchas* (Part IV, Dublin, 1924).
Halsall, Guy (2013), *Worlds of Arthur, Facts and Fictions of the Dark Ages* (Oxford, 2013).
Hamilton, Gustavus (1912), 'Two Ulster inauguration places'. *The Journal of the Royal Society of Antiquaries of Ireland* 2, No. 1 (Mar. 31, 1912).
Haycock, Marged (2013), 'Early Welsh poets look north', in Alex Woolf (ed.), *Beyond the Gododdin, Dark Age Scotland in Medieval Wales* (St Andrews, 2013).
Heist, W.W. (ed.) (1965), *Vitae sanctorum Hiberniae: ex codice olim Salmanticensi, nunc Bruxellensi. Lives of the saints of Ireland, from the Salamanca manuscript now of Brussels*, (Brussels, 1965).
Henderson, Isabel (1967), *The Picts* (London, 1967).
Herbert, Máire (1989), 'The preface to *Amra Coluim Cille*', in Donnchadh Ó Corráin, Liam Breatnach, and Kim R. McCone (ed.), *Sages, Saints and Storytellers: Celtic Studies in Honour of Professor James Carney* (Maynooth, 1989), 67–75.
Hewison, James King (1893), *Bute in the Olden Time* (2 vols., Edinburgh, 1893).
Hillers, Barbara (1993), 'Voyages between heaven and hell, navigating the Early Irish Immram tales'. *Proceedings of the Harvard Celtic Colloquium* 13 (1993), 73–94.
Hudson, Benjamin T. (1996), *Prophecy of Berchán, Irish and Scottish High-Kings of the Early Middle Ages* (Westport, 1996).
Hudson, Benjamin T. (1994), *Kings of Celtic Scotland* (Westport, 1994).
Hughes, Kathleen (1966), *The Church in Early Irish Society* (London, 1966).
Jackson, K.H. (1953), *Language and History in Early Britain, A Chronological Survey of the Brittonic Languages 1st to 12th c. ad* (Edinburgh, 1953).
Jackson, K.H. (1963), 'On the Northern British section in Nennius', in N. K. Chadwick (ed.), *Studies in Early British History* (Cambridge, 1963), 20–62.
Jackson, K.H. (1959), 'The Arthur of history,' in Roger Sherman Loomis (ed.), *Arthurian Literature in the Middle Ages, A Collaborative History* (Oxford, 1959), 1–11.

Jackson, K.H. (1957), 'The Duan Albanach,' *The Scottish Historical Review* 36, No. 122, Part 2 (Oct., 1957), 125–137.

Jackson, K.H. (1969), *The Gododdin, The Oldest Scottish Poem* (Edinburgh, 1969).

Jarman, A.O.H. (2003), 'The Merlin legend and the Welsh tradition of prophecy'. in Peter H. Goodrich and Raymond H. Thompson (ed.), *Merlin, A Casebook* (London, 2003), 103–128.

Jarman, A.O.H. (1952), 'Peiryan Vaban'. *Bulletin of the Board of Celtic Studies* 14 (1950–52), 104–8.

Jarrett, Jonathan (2008), 'The political range of Áedán mac Gabráin King of Dál Riata,' Full unpublished paper available at https://www.academia.edu/304966/The_Political_Range_of_%C3%81ed%C3%A1n_mac_Gabr%C3%A1in_King_of_D%C3%A1l_Riata. Short version in *Pictish Arts Society Journal*, 17 (2008), 3–24.

Jaski, Bart (1998), 'Druim Cett revisited,' *Peritia* 12 (1998), 340–50.

Jones, Aled Llion (2013), *Darogan, Prophecy, Lament and Absent Heroes in Medieval Welsh Literature* (Cardiff, 2013).

Jones, Bedwyr R. (1990), 'Gwriad's heritage: links between Wales and the Isle of Man in the Early Middle Ages,' *Transactions of the Honourable Society of Cymmrodorion* (1990), 29–44.

Keating, Geoffrey (1906), *Foras Feasa ar Éirinn, The History of Ireland*, ed. Rev. Patrick S. Dineen (4 volumes, London, 1902–1913).

Kelly, Rev. Matthew (ed.) (1857), *Calendar of Irish Saints, the Martyrology of Tallagh* (Dublin, 1857).

Kermode, P.M.C. (1892), *Catalogue of Manx Crosses* (2nd edn., Ramsey, 1892).

Kermode, P.M.C. (1907), *Manx Crosses* (London, 1907).

Kermode, P.M.C. (1897), 'A Welsh inscription in the Isle of Man'. *Zeitschrift für celtische Philologie* 1 (1897), 48–51.

Knott, Eleanor (1916), 'Why Mongán was deprived of noble issue'. *Ériu* 8 (1916), 155–60.

Koch, J.T. (1997), *The Gododdin of Aneirin: Texts and Context from Dark-Age North Britain* (Cardiff, 1997).

Koch, John T. (2003), (ed.), with John Carey, *The Celtic Heroic Age, Literary Sources for Ancient Celtic Europe and Early Ireland and Wales* (4th edition, Aberystwyth, 2003).

Lacey, Brian (trans.) (1998), Manus O' Donnell, *The Life of Colum Cille* (Dublin, 1998).

Lane, Alan and Campbell, Ewan (2000), *Dunadd, An Early Dalriadic Capital* (Oxford, 2000).

Lathe, Richard (2004), 'Arthur of Dalriada revisited'. *The Heroic Age* 7 (Spring 2004), https://www.heroicage.org/issues/7/forum.html

Lewis, Gwyneth and Williams, Rowan (trans.) (2019), *The Book of Taliesin, Poems of Warfare and Praise in an Enchanted Britain* (London, 2019).

Mac Cana, Proinsias (1995), 'Aspects of the theme of king and goddess in Irish literature,' *Études Celtiques* 7 (1955), 76–114.

Mac Cana, Proinsias (1980), *The Learned Tales of Medieval Ireland* (Dublin, 1980).

Mac Cana, Proinsias (1972), 'Mongán Mac Fiachna and Immram Brain'. *Ériu* 23 (March 1972), 102–142.

Mackinlay, James Murray (1914), *Ancient Church Dedications in Scotland, Non Scriptural Dedications* (Edinburgh, 1914).

McLaughlin, Roisin (2008), *Early Irish Satire* (Dublin, 2008).

MacNeill, Eoin (1939), 'The language of the Picts'. *Yorkshire Celtic Studies* 2 (1938–39), 3–45.

MacNeill, Eoin (1920), *Phases of Irish History* (Dublin, 1920).

MacNeill, John (1912), 'Notes on the Laud Genealogies'. *Zeitschrift für celtische Philologie* 8 (1912), 411–20.

Mac Niocaill, Gearóid (1972), *Ireland Before the Vikings* (Dublin, 1972).

McNiven, Peter Edward (2011), *Gaelic Place-Names and the Social History of Gaelic Speakers in Medieval Menteith*, unpublished PhD thesis (Glasgow, 2011).

Macphail, J.R.N. (1914), *Highland Papers* (3 vols., Edinburgh, 1914–20).

Macquarrie, Alan (2012), *Legends of Scottish Saints, Readings, Hymns and Prayers for the Commemoration of Saints in the Aberdeen Breviary* (Dublin, 2012).

Macquarrie, Alan (1994), 'St Columba and his lay contemporaries in Scotland and Ireland'. *Records of the Scottish Church History Society* 25 (1994), 188–203.

Macquarrie, Alan (1997), *The Saints of Scotland, Essays in Scottish Church History, AD 450–1093* (Edinburgh, 1997).

MacQueen, John (1991), *St Nynia* (2nd edn., Edinburgh, 1991).

MacQueen, John (1954), 'Welsh and Gaelic in Galloway'. *Transactions of the Dumfriesshire and Galloway Natural History and Antiquarian Society* 32 (1953–54), 77–92.

Marstrander, C. (1911), 'A new version of the battle of Mag Rath'. *Ériu* 5 (1911), 226–247.

Marstrander, C., (ed. and trans.) (1911), 'How Fiachna mac Baedáin Obtained the Kingdom of Scotland', *Ériu* 5 (1911), 113–119.

Maxwell, Gordon S. (1987), 'Settlement in southern Pictland: a new overview', in A. Small (ed.), *The Picts, A New Look at Old Problems* (Dundee, 1987), 31–44.

Meckler, Michael (1997), 'The Annals of Ulster and the date of the meeting at Druim Cett'. *Peritia* 11 (1997), 44–52.

Meckler, Michael (2000), 'Carnal love and priestly ordination on sixth-century Tiree'. *The Innes Review* 51, No. 2 (2000), 95–108.

Meckler, Michael (1990), 'Colum Cille's Ordination of Aedán Mac Gabráin'. *The Innes Review* 41, No. 2 (1990), 139–50.

Meyer, Kuno (1910), *Fianaigecht* (Dublin, 1910).

Meyer, Kuno (ed. and trans.) (1899), 'Gein Brandub maic Echach ocus Aedáin maic Gabráin.' *Zeitschrift für celtische Philologie* 2 (1899), 134–7.

Meyer, Kuno (ed.) (1912), 'The Laud genealogies and tribal histories', *Zeitschrift für celtische Philologie* 8 (1912), 291–338.

Meyer, Kuno and Nutt, Alfred (ed. and trans.) (1895), *The Voyage of Bran son of Febal to the Land of the Living* (2 vols., London, 1895).

Miller, Molly (1975), 'The commanders at Arthuret'. *Transactions of the Cumberland and Westmorland Archaeological and Antiquarian Society*, New Series, 75 (1975), 96–118.

Miller, Molly (1980a), 'Hiberni reversuri', *Proceedings of the Society of Antiquaries of Scotland* 110 (1978–80), 305–27.

Miller, Molly (1977), 'Historicity and the pedigrees of the northcountrymen'. *Bulletin of the Board of Celtic Studies* 26 (1974–7), 255–80.

Miller, Molly (1980b), 'Royal pedigrees of the insular Dark Ages: a progress report,' *History in Africa* 7 (1980), 201–24.

Moffat, Alastair (2012), *Arthur and the Lost Kingdoms* (Edinburgh, 2012).

Moisl, Herman (1983), 'The Bernician royal dynasty and the Irish in the seventh century,' *Peritia* 2 (1983), 103–26.

Morris, John (ed.) (1980), *Nennius, British History and the Welsh Annals* (London and Chichester, 1980).

Morris, Lewis (1878), *Celtic Remains* (London, 1878).

Muhr, Kay (1999), 'Water imagery in Early Irish'. *Celtica* 23 (1999), 193–210.

Murphy, Gerald (1955), *Saga and Myth in Ancient Ireland* (Dublin, 1955).

Nagy, Joseph Falaky (1997), *Conversing with Angels and Ancients, Literary Myths of Medieval Ireland* (Ithaca, 1997).

Nagy, Joseph Falaky (1990), 'The herons of Druim Ceat revisiting, and revisited'. *Celtica* 21 (1990), 368–376.

Nieke, Margaret (1984), *Settlement Patterns in the Atlantic Province of Scotland in the 1st Millennium AD: a study of Argyll*, unpublished PhD thesis (3 vols., Glasgow, 1984).

O'Brien, M.A. (1952), 'A Middle-Irish Poem of the Birth of Áedán mac Gabráin and Brandub Mac Echach', *Ériu* 16 (1952), 157–171.

Ó Coileáin, Seán (1981), 'Some problems of story and history'. *Ériu* 32 (1981), 115–136.

Ó Corráin, Donnchadh (2017), 'Osorius, Ireland, and Christianity'. *Peritia* 28 (2017), 113–34.

Ó Cróinín, Dáibhí (1995), *Early Medieval Ireland, 400–1200* (London, 1995).

Ó Cuív, Brian (1986), 'The two herons of Druim Ceat,' *Ériu* 37 (1986), 194–196.

O'Curry, Eugene (1878), *Lectures of the Manuscript Materials of Ancient Irish History* (Dublin, 1878).

O'Donnell, Manus (1918), *Betha Colaim Chille, Life of Columcille, Compiled by Manus O' Donnell in 1532*, ed. and trans from Rawlinson B. 514, A.O. Kelleher and G. Shoepperle (Urbana, 1918).

O'Donovan, John (1848), *The Banquet of Dún na nGédh and the Battle of Magh Rath* (Dublin, 1848).

O'Donovan, John (trans.) (1868), *Sanas Chormaic*, Cormac's Glossary (Calcutta, 1868).

O' Grady, Standish (ed.) (1892), *Silva Gadelica, A Collection of Tales in Irish* (2 vols., London, 1892).

O'Keefe, James G. (ed.) (1913), *Buile Suibne* (London, 1913).

O'Neill, Pamela (2005), 'The political and ecclesiastical extent of Scottish Dalriada'. *Journal of the Australian Early Medieval Association* 1 (2005), 119–132.

O'Rahilly, Thomas F. (1946), *Early Irish History and Mythology* (Dublin, 1946).

Phillimore, Egerton (1888), 'The Annales Cambriæ and Old Welsh genealogies from Harleian MS 3859'. *Y Cymmrodor* 9 (1888), 141–83.

Picard, Jean-Michel (1989), 'The strange death of Guaire mac Áedáin', in Donnchadh Ó Corráin, Liam Breatnach, Kim McCone (ed.), *Sages, Saints and Storytellers, Celtic Studies in Honour of Professor James Carney* (Maynooth, 1989), 367–375.

Plummer, Charles (ed.) (1922), *Bethada Náem nÉrenn, Lives of Irish Saints* (2 vols., Oxford, 1922).

Rees, Rev. Rice (1836), *An Essay On the Welsh Saints* (London, 1836).

Reeves, William (1874), *Life of St Columba* (Edinburgh, 1874).

Rhys, John (1882), *Celtic Britain* (London, 1882).

Rhys, John (1897), 'Note on Guriat'. *Zeitschrift für celtische Philologie* 1 (1897), 52–53.

Richmond, I.A. (1958), 'Ancient geographical sources for Britain north of Cheviot', in I. A. Richmond (ed.), *Roman and Native in North Britain* (Edinburgh, 1958), 131–56.

Ross, Anne (1992), *Pagan Celtic Britain* (1967, revised edn., London, 1992).

Ryan, John (1946), 'The Convention of Druim Ceat (AU 575)'. *The Journal of the Royal Society of Antiquaries of Ireland* 76, No. 1 (April 1946), 25–55.

Sharpe, Richard (ed.) (1995), *Adomnán of Iona, Life of St Columba* (London, 1995).

Simms, Katherine (2000), *From Kings to Warlords: The Changing Political Structure of Gaelic Ireland in the Later Middle Ages* (Woodbridge, 2000).

Skene, Felix J.H. (trans.), *John of Fordun's Chronicle of the Scottish Nation* (Edinburgh, 1872).

Skene, William F. (1890), *Celtic Scotland, A History of Ancient Alban* (2nd. edn., 3 vols., Edinburgh, 1886–1890).

Skene, William F. (1876), 'Notice of the site of the battle of Ardderyd or Arderyth', *Proceedings of the Society of Antiquaries of Scotland* 6 (1876), 91–98.

Smyth, Alfred P. (1989) *Warlords and Holy Men, Scotland AD 80–1000* (1984, rep. Edinburgh, 1989).

Spaan, David B. (1965), 'The Place of Mannanan mac Lir in Irish Mythology'. *Folklore* 76 (Autumn 1965), 17–195.

Stevenson, J.H. (1927), 'The law of the throne, tanistry and the introduction of the law of primogenture,' *The Scottish Historical Review* 25, No. 97 (Oct., 1927), 1–12.

Stewart, M. and Main, L. (1999), 'Fairy Hill, Dunverig Wood, Aberfoyle, Stirling'. *Discovery and Excavation in Scotland* (1999), 85.

Stirling, Simon Andrew (2012), *The King Arthur Conspiracy, How A Scottish Prince Became A Mythical Hero* (Stroud, 2012).

Stokes, Whitley (ed.) (1905), *Félíre Óengusso Céli Dé, The Martyrology of Oengus the Culdee* (London, 1905).

Stokes, Whitley (ed.) (1899), 'The Bodleian Amra Choluimb Chille'. *Revue Celtique* 20 (1899), 31–55, 132–183, 248–289, 400–437.

Stokes, Whitley (ed.) (1887), *The Tripartite Life of St Patrick* (2 vols., London, 1887).

Thomas, Charles (1994), *And Shall These Mute Stones Speak? Post-Roman Inscriptions in Western Britain* (Cardiff, 1994).

Thomas, Charles (1961), 'The animal art of the Scottish Iron Age and its origins'. *Archaeological Journal* 118 (1961), 14–64.

Tolan-Smith, Christopher (2001), *The Caves of Mid Argyll, An Archaeology of Human Use* (Edinburgh, 2001).

Tolstoy, Nikolai (1985), *The Quest for Merlin* (London, 1985).

Toop, Nicola J (2011), 'Northumbria in the west: considering interaction through monumentality', in David Petts and Sam Turner (ed.), *Early Medieval Northumbria, Kingdoms and Communities, AD 450–1100* (Turnhout, 2011), 85–112.

Trotter, Robert de Bruce (1901), *Galloway Gossip, or the Southern Albanich 80 Years Ago - The Stewartry* (Dumfries, 1901).

Tyndale, Andrea (1995), 'Notes toward a reading of parts of the Glamis stone,' *Pictish Arts Society Journal* 8 (Autumn 1995), 44.

Wade-Evans, A.W. (1944), *Vitae Sanctorum Britanniae et Genealogie* (Cardiff, 1944).

Wainwright, F.T. (1980), 'The Picts and the problem', in F.T. Wainwright (ed.), *The Problem of the Picts* (1955, rep. Perth, 1980), 1–53.

Warntjes, Immo (2004), 'Regnal succession in early medieval Ireland,' Immo Warntjes, *Journal of Medieval History* 30 (2004), 377–410.

Watson, W.J. (1924), 'The Celts (British and Gael) in Dumfriesshire and Galloway', in *Transactions of the Dumfries and Galloway Natural History and Antiquarian Society*, Third Series, 11 (1923–24), 119–48.

Watson, W.J. (1986), *The History of the Celtic Place-names of Scotland* (1926, rep. Edinburgh, 1986).

Westwood, Jennifer (1985), *Albion, A Guide to Legendary Britain* (London, 1985).

Westwood, Jennifer and Kingshill, Sophie (2009), *The Lore of Scotland, A Guide to Scottish Legends* (London, 2009).

Whitaker, Ian (1976), 'Regal succession among the Dálriata'. *Ethnohistory* 23, No. 4 (Autumn 1976), 343–363.

White, T.P. (1872), 'The ecclesiastical antiquities of the district of Kintyre in Argyllshire'. *Proceedings of the Society of Antiquaries of Scotland* 9 (1870–72), 227–30.

Whitelock, Dorothy (ed.) (1961), *The Anglo-Saxon Chronicle, A Revised Translation* (London, 1961).

Williams, Ann, Smyth, Alfred P., and Kirby, D. P. (1991), *A Biographical Dictionary of Dark Age Britain, England Scotland and Wales, c. 500–c. 1050* (London, 1991).

Woods, David (2002), 'Four notes on Adomnán's *Vitae Columbae*'. *Peritia* 16 (2002), 40–67.

Woolf, Alex (2012), 'Ancient Kindred? Dál Riata and the Cruthin' https://www.academia.edu/1502702/Ancient_Kindred_Dal_Riata_and_the_Cruthin

Wyatt, David (2009), *Slaves and Warriors in Britain and Ireland, 800–1200* (Leiden, 2009).

Ziegler, Michelle (1999), 'Artúr mac Aedan of Dalriada', *The Heroic Age* 1 (Spring/Summer 1999), https://www.heroicage.org/issues/1/haaad.htm

Index